BICYCLE MAINTENANCE

PARK TOOL
SILCA

Bicycle Maintenance

Ben Searle

The Crowood Press

First published in 1997 by
The Crowood Press Ltd
Ramsbury, Marlborough
Wiltshire SN8 2HR

British Library Cataloguing in Publication Data

A catalogue record for this book is available from the British Library.

ISBN 1 86126 084 9

All photos were taken and printed by the author, except page 52 (top) which was supplied by W. R. Pashley Ltd.

Dedication
To all cyclists, everywhere, for the part they play in reducing the devastation caused by motor traffic.

Typeface used: New Century Schoolbook (text); Helvetica (labels).

Typeset and designed by
D & N Publishing
Membury Business Park, Lambourn Woodlands
Hungerford, Berkshire.

Printed and bound by The Bath Press.

Contents

Acknowledgements

I am particularly grateful to and wish to thank the following people and organizations for the help they provided:

Raleigh Industries for the loan of M-Trax 300 and Pioneer Chiltern bikes. Trek for the loan of a Trek ZX7000 bike. Madison Cycles for the loan of Park Tools and workstand. Ison Distribution for the loan of other tools. Hope Technology for supplying a hub. Record Tools for supplying a vice. John Quantick for the loan of studio lighting. Shimano, Sturmey Archer and Sachs for permission to use their diagrams. Gavin Boby for patiently modelling for many of the photos. Tony Oliver for suggesting to Crowood that I write this book in the first place. Bristol Bicycle Workshop for digging out worn and knackered examples of bike wear.

Many a pub discussion with Hilary Stone and Russell Gasser, lubricated by Smiles Best, has helped me clarify many points. Not least, I thank my partner, Jade Bashford, for her enduring patience and support throughout the project.

Introduction

This book teaches you how to understand your bike. It offers simple explanations for the complete beginner and tricks and tips for the more advanced. It covers the maintenance of nearly all kinds of bikes. My aim has been to help you become the best possible mechanic, to give you a real feel for the jobs involved, and to encourage you to use your intelligence and senses rather than depend on blindly following instruction.

Any cyclist can make a start to learning how to maintain his bike with the guidance that this book provides, a few inexpensive tools and an active interest in learning.

Learning how to keep your bike running reliably and efficiently will inspire your confidence – you will probably ride a neglected bike much more gingerly and it will require more effort. You will know your bike is safe. Even if you pay someone to overhaul your bike every year, its mechanical state gradually deteriorates until it is next overhauled. Little and often is much better than a yearly purge. If you are patient you can give it the best possible service. In short, if you can do most jobs yourself, or at least know when to seek further advice, your bike will be a greater joy to ride and you will be encouraged to ride more.

Maintaining your bike yourself makes great economic sense. You will need to buy some tools but you will quickly recover the cost when you find you do not need to take your bike to the shop for repair. The parts of your bike will also last longer with regular care.

As you develop your skills as a mechanic, you will begin to pre-empt problems before they occur by recognizing and dealing with the warning signs early on. You will be undertaking preventative maintenance – by far the best form. Many people let things slip to the breakdown stage, a definite sign of lack of maintenance and one that can be almost completely avoided. Left this late, we are talking more about repair than maintenance, and repair is usually a much bigger and more expensive job, and one that you may well leave to a bike shop. Being a good mechanic is not about neglecting your bike until its wheel collapses and then having the skill to rebuild it at the road side.

This book has a wide scope including simple adjustment, complete overhaul, and more specialized forms of repair and renewal such as wheel building. There are a few necessary exceptions. As bicycle technology is constantly evolving, no manual can cover every variation. I have tried to arm you with the knowledge you need for all but uncommon specific components. The book is designed to be as comprehensive as possible, yet concise.

Chapter 1 begins by explaining the main things to be aware of for different types of bikes, and names the parts. It also explains what you will need to do when and explains the summary panels used throughout the book. Chapter 2 explains the tools and techniques used for bicycle maintenance. The remaining chapters focus on given areas of the bike, explaining what you need to be aware of and the techniques and maintenance steps necessary to keep it in perfect condition. Some cross-reference is made to avoid repetition; this is necessary as most parts of the bike connect to each other. The appendices provide useful addresses, suppliers and further reference. A glossary explains unusual or bike-specific terms you may come across, though most of those used in this book are explained at the point where they are first used.

If you are a beginner it will help you to read the complete book, simply checking over and understanding your bike as you go before buying tools and undertaking work; you can then determine your needs and will have some idea where problems occur. Ignore the myths; men are not born better mechanics than women. At my classes I have seen male students confidently lecturing competent women with complete nonsense. The women in turn believe the nonsense they are told, ignoring their own better judgement.

At times you are bound to feel frustrated as problems inevitably arise. Patience is of the essence. Try to think things through before reaching the stage where the only option is to kick the bike (which I must admit I have done myself). Instead, stop and put the job aside if necessary, coming back to it later with a calm mind after thinking about what you can learn from the situation. The process will help enormously in dealing with the next difficult situation, of which I hope there will not be too many. The ability to maintain your bike is certainly satisfying and confidence building – and some call it fun!

1 Basics

To find your way round this book it will first be helpful to familiarize yourself with the parts of your bike. I will also take this opportunity to explain briefly some of the differences between the bike types where this may effect maintenance procedures, component choice and compatibility. Cycle technology has much of its own special terms and nomenclature. I have tried to keep the use of this to a minimum, and explain it as it arises in the book – additional explanations, where relevant, are included in the glossary.

NAMING THE PARTS

All modern bicycles can be divided into four main areas: the frame and forks (often called the frameset), the wheels, the groupset (chiefly the gearing, braking and bearing components), and the finishing kit (the saddle, handlebar and miscellaneous components). The diagram shows the parts of a modern hybrid bike. If you do not recognize the exact parts of your own bike here or in this chapter, refer to the appropriate chapter.

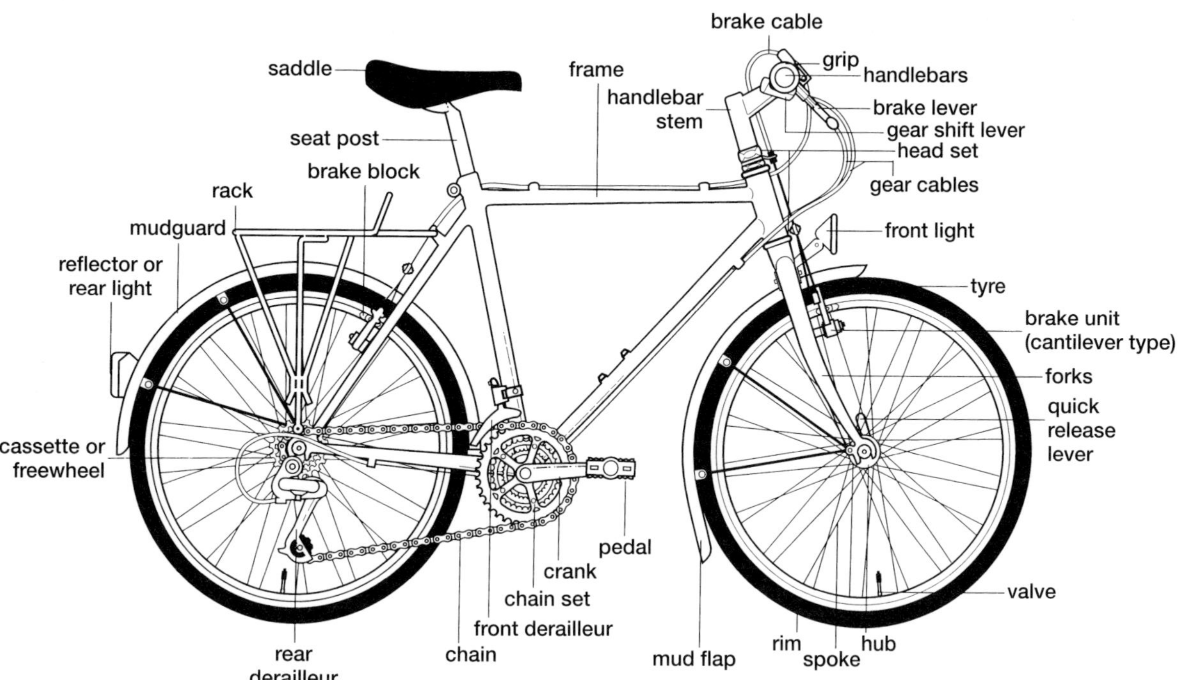

The component parts of a typical hybrid bike.

The Frameset

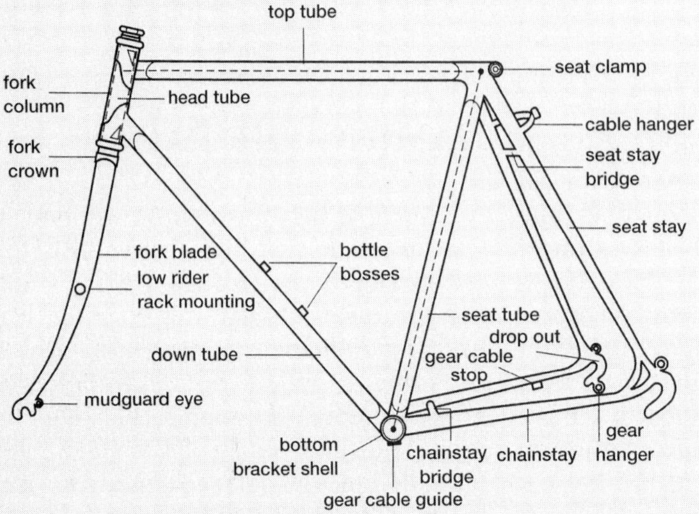

The frameset consists of a number of tubes, elements, fittings and fixings. These will be referred to throughout the book.

(Below) *Racing frames tend to have steeper head tube angles, less fork offset, closer clearances and thinner tubing than touring frames.*

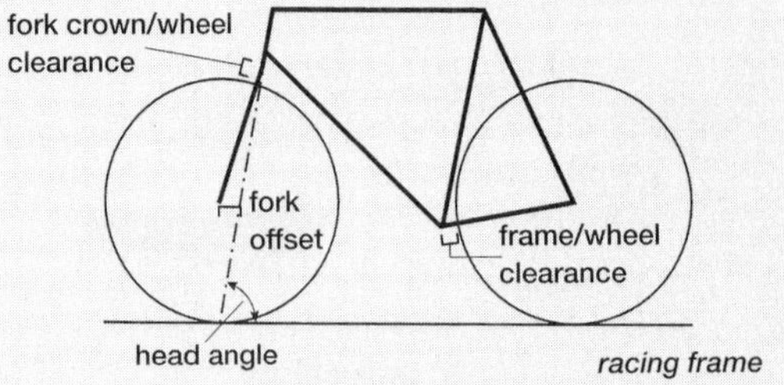

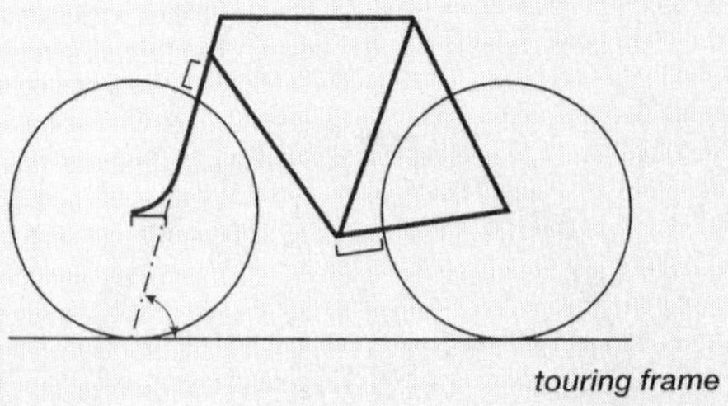

Framesets require minimal maintenance, but note that there are a number of design details that must be taken into account, especially when replacing components; these will be covered in the relevant chapters.

More fundamentally, the geometry and dimensions vary between frames for specific uses, which makes it unreasonable, for example, to 'upgrade' a touring bike into a road racing bike, or a hybrid into an MTB (mountain bike). The differences can go unnoticed by the uninitiated but include clearance for the tyres and mudguards, the steering response (fast to slow) and the effect on the bike's stability. This said, there can be some room to manoeuvre in fine-tuning the use. For example, an ordinary touring bike can sometimes be kitted out to make it more suitable for expedition use (with wider rims and tyres and lower gears), or for fast touring use (with narrower rims and tyres and combined brake/gear levers). Drop bars and less gnarly tyres can be fitted to a hybrid or MTB to make an expedition tourer.

Exact frameset and upgrading recommendations are beyond the scope of this book. The important point is that you need to consider the frame design, the components as a whole, and the use of the bike when making upgrades or changes to components, even if those parts are compatible in fit. Additionally, you do not want to spend a lot of time and money on a frame that is the wrong size or damaged (unless repairable at a cost you can justify), or buying components that are of much higher quality than the frame.

ROADSTER AND UTILITY BIKES

The traditional roadster (and small-wheeled 'shopping bike') typically has straight or upright handlebars and a Sturmey Archer 3-speed hub gear. Typically it was used by many people to ride to work and for errands. Its use is now much less common except in some flatter areas of the UK and continental Europe. From a maintenance point of view, roadsters are quite different from modern bikes, rarely utilizing groupsets or derailleur gears. Some older models used rod-operated brakes, which are not covered in this book.

The roadster has largely been superseded by mountain bikes and hybrids. In the last couple of years, revamped utility bikes are beginning to appear again from most of the major manufacturers, resembling hybrids. These typically use modern hub gear designs with five or seven speeds. The best models have no 'in-between' neutral positions, which cause the dreaded slipping.

Some utility bikes and a few high-performance bikes use small wheels. Many small-wheeled bikes were a disaster – heavy, unpleasant to ride (small fat tyres are highly inefficient), and those that folded were often very awkward and poorly manufactured, making their maintenance a job that even a committed bike shop loathed. The exception has always been the Moulton range, which utilized high-pressure tyres to minimize rolling resistance, with suspension to give a very

The Raleigh Pioneer Chiltern is an updated roadster using Sturmey Archer three-speed gears.

comfortable ride; with these bikes it is highly important that the tyres are fully inflated. Poor small-wheel bikes have now all but gone; instead several much more innovative designs have gained in popularity, especially for the ease with which they may be taken on public transport.

The Mountain Bike (MTB)

The mountain bike phenomena began in the USA in the early eighties and quickly leapfrogged the Atlantic. Early MTBs were heavy and cumbersome, based on 'cruisers' – the American equivalent of a roadster – which are making something of a comeback. These quickly evolved with the vast

The Brompton folding bike. With any folder, take care not to kink the cables and ensure that the clamps are properly fitted and fully tightened.

(Below) *The internal parts of hub gears are not generally user-serviceable. They can be damaged if not correctly adjusted.*

(Right) *The Trek ZX7000 is a typical mid-range MTB featuring front suspension and 'V' brakes, a more powerful variant of the cantilever brake.*

(Below) *Most modern MTBs have what is known as an Aheadset type of headset. To confuse it with a conventional headset could be dangerous.*

(Below right) *A conventional headset. In comparison to an Aheadset it has a 'clean' appearance without outside clamping bolts where it meets the fork.*

amount of interest (and capital) behind them; wide-range derailleur gears, powerful cantilever brakes and fat tyres became *de rigueur*. Over time, the riding position has become more competitive and stretched out, and front suspension at least is standard on all better models. Now the MTB has become what the British public recognize as a 'normal' bike, perhaps by the fact that most of them are rarely ridden off-road. The cheaper models tend to be 'look-a-like' models, which would not fare at all well in rough riding conditions.

Special groupsets of components evolved in conjunction with the MTB and in the course of this, Shimano, the giant Japanese components manufacturer, came to dominate the world bicycle component market. Now 90 per cent of all bikes manufactured are equipped with Shimano groupsets. Sachs are another well-known maker of MTB components.

Many other lesser-known brands are also used, especially at the lower and upper ends of the MTB market, and these are generally Shimano-compatible. The specialized sport of downhill mountain biking is rapidly causing special components to evolve, which this particularly demanding end of the MTB sport market needs.

The Hybrid

The hybrid came into being because mountain bikes can be cumbersome and overbuilt for many applications. The qualities that made the MTB so popular, such as powerful brakes, wide-range, easy-to-use gears, the (former) upright position, and its robustness were combined into a lighter, more efficient bike designed for daily use, smoother trials and touring – an ideal multi-use bike. Most are equipped with mid- to lower-range Shimano MTB groupsets with cantilever brakes, or components specially designed for this type of bike, such as the latest 7-speed hub gears. Most hybrids use larger wheels than MTBs do – 700C as opposed to 26in (these terms are explained in Chapter 9).

The Road-racing Bike

Built entirely for on-road speed and efficiency, road bikes are the greyhounds of cycling; they tend to have a uncluttered looks and a simple elegance. As you pay more, models tend to divide into those suitable for time-trialling and those for massed-start road racing – the main differences being in frame geometry, wheel choice and gear ratios. Compared to a few years ago, the modern 'road' bike requires a minimum of tools to maintain it. Most road bikes now come with combined brake/gear levers for improved ergonomics. Shimano, Campagnolo and Sachs make the majority of racing bike components, although many, mostly upmarket, components are also available from smaller manufacturers. Compatibility

Hybrids, such as this Trek Multi Track 730, are normally easy to equip for everyday use.

The Raleigh M-Trax 300 is an entry-level road bike. Racing calls for a bike in A1 condition if months of training are not to be in vain.

between the gearing components is restricted; use the guidelines in this book to avoid problems.

Sports and Touring Bikes

Sports and touring bikes resemble road bikes but are quite different in detail. Sales of so-called 'sports' bikes that are in fact inexpensive 'racing' bikes have almost disappeared, as these were mostly sold to impressionable teenagers who now go for an MTB. Sports bikes offered a cheap alternative to more upmarket machines for those who wanted more efficiency than a roadster could offer. Current models use some of the cheaper Shimano road groupsets.

Specialist touring bikes sell in relatively small numbers. These are effectively a cross between the hybrid and a road-racing bike. Designed for going long distances with loads, they are also popular for commuting and make good all-round practical bikes. Most will fare surprisingly well in careful off-road use. Touring bikes have benefited greatly from MTB and hybrid groupsets and components, but usually some mix and match with racing components is required. This can sometimes make the selecting of upgrades and replacement parts for touring bikes problematic and limiting, especially for brakes; you may prefer to improve those you have, and this can be done with care. A few components, notably rims and tyres, are specially made for touring use. A few specialist components intended for tandems, such as hubs, can sometimes be useful.

Touring bikes, such as this custom Tony Oliver, are often ridden into the back of beyond, a long way from spares and help. Your ability to cope with any breakdown is a real asset.

BEARING DESIGNS

Two common types of bearing are used on bicycles. Each has its own advantages, although cartridge bearings are increasingly being used, especially for bottom brackets and some upmarket equipment.

Traditional 'Cup and Cone' Bearings

Most bicycle bearing component designs, for example a hub, are based on the principle of a pair of 'cups' and a pair of 'cones', each separated by a set of ball-bearings. The cones and bearings wear most quickly but when the cup part wears the whole component is normally scrapped, the notable exception being Campagnolo hubs. This type of bearing must be kept precisely adjusted. Needle roller bearings, as used for some headsets and bottom brackets, are normally used in a cup and cone design, and often have replaceable insert bearing cups.

Wear life is greatly extended by keeping the bearing full of clean grease, normally by disassembly, cleaning and repacking. The degree of sealing can vary greatly from none to extremely good. When cleaning around these bearings, be careful not to push dirt and grease back into them. If water enters the bearing it can rust, seize, and become irredeemable if neglected.

When you disassemble a cup and cone component you will need to check the bearing size, which can be ⅛, 5⁄32, 3⁄16, 7⁄32 or ¼in; the bearings are always best replaced. Special gauges can be bought for this from bike shops, though it is quite easy to determine the size of a ball-bearing by comparing it to another of known size. Ball bearings vary greatly in quality; do not buy what are simply called 'steel balls'. For anything better than the cheapest components I recommend the use of high quality ball-bearings from a bearing supplier; these can be found in the telephone directory. The best bike shops also stock them. Cones should be exact replacements if possible; if not they must be suited to the same size ball-bearing and generally must have the same width and depth to fit the component properly.

Cartridge Bearings

The standard industrial cartridge bearing is a ubiquitous item used in cars and machinery but less frequently on bicycles.

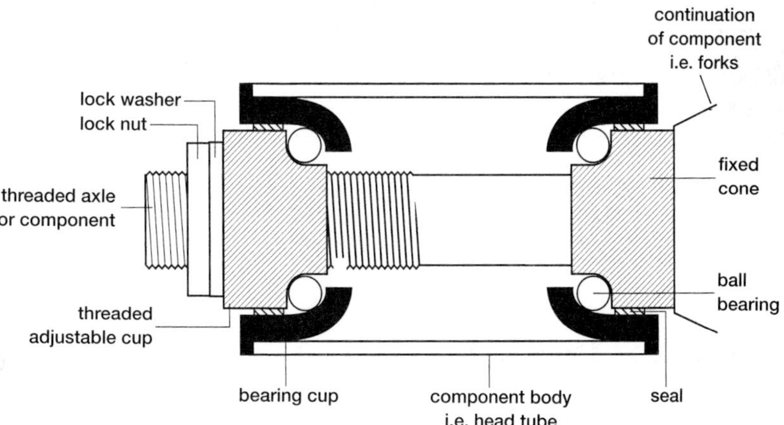

A typical cup and cone bearing component.

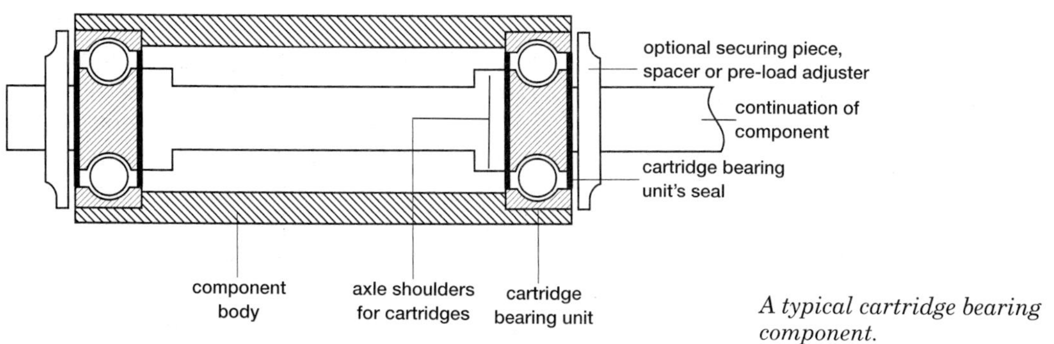

A typical cartridge bearing component.

The bearing surfaces and ball-bearings are combined in a single, sealed, encapsulating unit. It has an interference fit, that is, it is pressed into the component with sufficient tightness so that it will stay in place but not slip. Normally a pair (or more) of units of a commonly available size are used in bicycle components. Cartridge bearing components normally require little maintenance until the cartridges wear out, when they must be replaced. They normally last about two to three seasons of heavy use or sometimes much longer, depending on how well the component has been designed and assembled to ensure that the cartridges are aligned with each other. Cartridge bearings are much less tolerant of misalignment than cup and cone bearings, which can be an issue with some bottom bracket units.

Wear is indicated when the bearing develops play or squeaking that cannot be taken up by any adjustable pre-load (outer adjusting nut). A loose or irregular feeling as the axle is turned also indicates wear; compare to a new bearing. Once a cartridge bearing starts to wear it will normally wear out completely very quickly.

Cartridge bearing components can vary considerably in their overall design, but the cartridges themselves are replaced in the same manner whether used in hubs, bottom brackets (but note that not all 'cartridge' bottom bracket units have replaceable bearings) or pedals. For more information see Chapter 9. Replacement cartridge bearings can be bought from bearing suppliers or the best bike shops; quote the number printed on it, or take the bearing or component with you.

Action	**Use**		
	Occasional	*Regular road*	*Regular off-road*
Check tyres/pressure	before every ride	before every ride	before every ride
Clean bike	monthly	weekly/ fortnightly	weekly or after hard use
Clean chain	twice a year	monthly	weekly or after hard use
Lubricate chain	monthly	weekly	weekly or after hard use
Check and adjust bearings	twice a year	monthly	monthly/fortnightly
Check and adjust brakes	monthly	weekly	weekly or after hard use
Check and adjust gears	monthly	monthly	weekly or after hard use
Check and adjust suspension	monthly	monthly	weekly or after hard use
Complete overhaul	yearly	yearly or twice yearly	2–4 times a year

WHAT YOU NEED TO DO

The attention your bike requires will depend on the type of use it receives. Winter rain, road salt and grime can do a great deal of damage. It pays to defend a bike that sees daily or off-road use by overhauling it just before winter, and then just after. Bikes that are used less frequently should be overhauled once a year. Your bike should, of course, be cleaned and adjusted as appropriate more often. The table on the left gives an indication of what you will need to do when. Use it as a guide in conjunction with the awareness you will build up by reading this book, and your own experience.

Overhaul

An overhaul is taken to mean stripping down all the bike's bearings (headset, both hubs, bottom bracket and pedals), checking for wear, regreasing and precisely adjusting them. The exceptions to this are sealed cartridge bearings, which generally only need to be checked for wear (some adjustment is occasionally necessary to a few components – *see* Chapter 9), and hub gears, which rarely require disassembly but which must always be correctly adjusted.

At overhaul intervals, cables and casings are best replaced. Wheels should be trued. Chains and cassette cogs should be checked for wear and replaced if necessary. All other components should be disassembled, cleaned, checked for wear, parts replaced if necessary, lubricated, reassembled and adjusted. In short, the bike should ride as if mechanically new. Check the summaries throughout the book for details of the chief jobs.

The Summary Panels

Throughout the book, each main job has a summary panel. This grades the job with spanner icons according to the depth and difficulty involved. Here is what they mean:

🔧 Simple and quick, requiring common tools
🔧🔧 Straightforward, often requiring bicycle tools
🔧🔧🔧 Requires some care/skill and appropriate tools
🔧🔧🔧🔧 Requires greater care/skill and specialist tools
🔧🔧🔧🔧🔧 Specialist job for the more experienced mechanic

The panel also explains when you will need to do the job, and lists specialist tools, materials and possible spares required beyond the basic kit described in Chapter 2.

Approximate times for a beginner armed with the correct tools have been given. Until you build up some experience you should allow as much time as possible. Always allow time to buy additional parts (you do not always know what you will need until you are under way), particularly if you need your bike to be roadworthy by a certain time. It is unwise to hurry jobs, as you may damage a part or slip and hurt yourself.

Additional text and panels also provide the information you need to know when buying common replacement parts or upgrading. This information will help you avoid the frustration of incompatibility problems.

Cleaning Your Bike

If you want an efficient and long-wearing bike, cleaning is an essential maintenance task, be it messy and laborious. All maintenance jobs are much more pleasant on a clean bike; not only do you save mess, but you can also see what you are working on, and it is easier to spot problems. It is tempting to use a car jet wash or hose pipe, but I recommend against this unless you are about to undertake a complete overhaul, as under the heat and pressure it is only too easy for water to enter the bearings (including 'sealed' cartridge ones), which will quickly ruin them.

Instead, I recommend the following procedure once a week (less often in summer) or after particularly dirty rides. Cleaning a bike is a good time to look out for problems such as damage to the tyres, loose spokes, and all kinds of detail that you will glean from this book.

Collect together a number of different brushes – tooth, bottle, floor, dustpan and so on (try hardware and home brew shops) – and a couple of sponges. If possible, put the bike in a workstand and remove the wheels. If the bike has a lot of greasy dirt on it, spray these areas with a biodegradable degreaser and leave for about 15 minutes. Fill a bucket with warm water and a generous squirt of dish detergent.

Starting with the handlebars and working down and back, concentrate on loosening all the muck, using the brushes to get into every crevice. The scrubbing brush is good for getting the tyres clean. Keep one of the sponges free of suds for rinsing. Now rinse the bike down and let it dry. You may now wish to polish the frame with a special bike polish such as Finish Line Protectant or with car wax. This will help to protect the frame, and also creates a surface less prone to collecting dirt.

Routine Checks

Maintenance is best applied little and often; for example, you should act as soon as you hear an odd noise, feel a slight knocking, or notice your brake feeling a little spongy. The solution often involves little more than a simple adjustment. Waiting until the problem becomes more dire does not help or save time. For example, a loose bearing will wear out prematurely, one loose spoke may quickly lead to many others and a maladjusted brake block can quickly destroy the tyre. As you read through the book and work on your bike you will begin to build up a wealth of knowledge and gain the experience to recognize potential problems early on.

Hand Care and Personal Safety

Your hands are your most valuable and irreplaceable tools. Look after them and take care to prevent injury. Commonly used lubricants and solvents suck moisture from the skin and can cause dermatitis and eczema. They may be harmful if swallowed or if they come into direct contact with the eyes or skin – check the labels before using and wear eye protection and rubber gloves if necessary.

Prevent oily dirt from engraining itself in your skin by rubbing barrier cream into your hands. When you've finished, use a good hand cleaner such as Finish Line Citrus Gel or Loctite Fast Orange. You can avoid spreading greasy dirt around the house by using just the cleaner, then rags or paper towels before heading for the sink.

A lot of force is sometimes needed to free bicycle components, which may then come free suddenly. Take great care not to slip, especially when you are working near sharp parts of the bike like the chainset. When cutting with a hacksaw or knife, do so away from you with no part of your body immediately behind. If drilling, grinding, or using a hammer always wear eye protection.

If you are not sure about the standard of any work you have done, or the safety of your bike, consult a knowledgeable person before riding it. The author and the publisher cannot accept responsibility for any accidents, injury or loss suffered by readers of this book, however that may be caused.

2 The Home Workshop

Much of the work on your bike may not call for using more than a handful of tools with the bike propped up against a wall, and this is fine up to a point. However, without wanting to put you off with visions of arrays of expensive tools and gadgetry taking over the house, it is worth considering a small investment to make your bike repair easier.

Any successful workshop has two main requirements: sensible organization of a careful selection of tools and materials to do the jobs you intend to undertake, and a suitable space in which to use them. There is nothing worse than hunting for a special tool or part through boxes of junk, while kicking a pot of gungy solvent over the carpet. This chapter first looks at what will help you get started, then looks at the general things you should consider when working on your bike, including good working practice.

Using a purpose-made workstand is the most convenient way to work.

SUPPORTING THE BIKE

A purpose-made workstand keeps the bike stable and enables you to work at a comfortable height, but it is likely to be your biggest expense. Choose carefully: better ones rotate the bike and the best also have adjustable height, and should be of solid construction. Check that the clamping arrangement will fit all the bikes you intend to work on; it should not restrict the movement of the cables. Those from Park, Kestrel, and Wrench Force are recommended. A handlebar support, such as the Cyclo or Park, stops the front of the bike swinging around as you work. If you do not have one, tilting the front of the bike down slightly will keep it pointing forward.

If you have Black & Decker Workmate or similar portable workbench, the well-made Kestrel Workmate stand is a simple solution that clamps to it. Other clamping and support arrangements that fix to a workbench or wall are also available. A cheap alternative that requires you to crouch is a tripod chain-stay uplift that raises the back wheel. Strong plastic-coated hooks from hardware shops can be screwed into a suitable beam; the bike can be hooked on directly or suspended with rope. Although often done, supporting the bike upside down on the bars and saddle can easily damage cables and is never very convenient. As the lightest frames can be very thin, such bikes are best clamped around the seat post to avoid damage.

ORGANIZING THE WORKING SPACE

It helps if you can make a degree of mess and leave kit at hand. Consider how you will support the bike if you do not have a purpose-made workstand. A utility room, a largish shed, an easily accessible cellar, or, perhaps ideally, a garage, are some possibilities, especially as you will only need to use it for perhaps two or three hours a month. Working outdoors is possible but then grit can be a hazard, swirling around in the breeze and contaminating the exposed bearings. Sooner or later most mechanics without a dedicated room gravitate towards the kitchen. It is warm, has a reasonably easy floor to keep clean, a sink to wash hands in and not least, tea-making capability; overall not a bad idea if you can work tidily.

Try to avoid working in some dingy corner. Work near the window or use a desk or inspection lamp to direct light where you need it. A fluorescent light provides lots of bright, even lighting. Painting the walls white will also help. You may need to improvise some heating as holding bare metal in near freezing temperatures is not much fun. However, avoid naked flames as they do not mix well with degreasers and oily rags. The muck that comes off a bike can soon ruin a carpet or table top. It tends to find its way through newspapers so use a piece of vinyl floor covering or tough polythene sheeting going well beyond the work area. Clean up as you go to avoid spreading it around the house.

WORKTOPS AND BENCHES

It is surprising how much gear you can get spread about you, so it is best to have somewhere to put it. A wallpaper-pasting table is cheap and big, and folds down out the way. A covered kitchen table will also suffice. In a permanent workshop you can make a workbench, which needs to be carefully sited.

Depending on the scope you want, make it as solid as possible to allow space to mount a vice with room to put a wheel or frame into it. A wheel-truing stand may also need to be considered if you are keen; you will have a better idea of your likely needs after reading through the book. Do not make your workbench too high for comfortable working – try about 15cm (6in) below your waist. Allow enough space to get to both sides of your bike. If space is at a premium, consider a worktop that folds flat against the wall, possibly with your tools behind it on a tool board.

ORGANIZING AND STORING TOOLS

Your tools need to be easy to see and accessible for you to be able to work efficiently.

There are several ways of organizing and storing them; at the very least store them lightly oiled, clean and dry to prevent seizure and rust. In cases where you only have a handful of tools, a simple tool roll may suffice. Magnetic kitchen racks are also good for smaller tools.

Tool boards work well for regular use: the tools are immediately visible and at hand, you can see if anything is amiss, and placing your hand on a tool becomes a matter of instinct. Metal mirror plates with key hole cutouts (from hardware shops) let you hang it where you need it, then easily remove it. Use 2cm (¾in) plywood, paint it gloss/eggshell white, and lay out your tools with the most used nearest where the bike will be. Screw in hooks or clips to support the tools; you may need to modify them a little. Hang the tools, marking their outlines with an indelible marker.

If you do not have space for a tool board, or must regularly pack your kit away for racing events for example, then consider a purpose-made storage box (from tool shops or DIY centres). Curver make tough and cheap plastic boxes with lift-out compartments. Metal cantilever designs open out to display all the tools; Talco make a good range. It helps to give each compartment a broad theme and label up the outside to help you find hidden items.

THE TOOL KIT

You will need a range of both specialist bike tools bought from bike shops and some more general purpose tools bought from good tool shops The tools suggested below (plus spanners and allen keys – *see* separate panels) are those that are difficult to manage without for a modern bike, but you should double-check your own needs to avoid buying anything unnecessary.

It always pays to buy the best you can afford. Cheap tools, which tend to cost about a third to a half of the best, are not an investment, either in themselves, or for your bike. They are made of softer, inferior metals and tend to round nuts and break with little provocation. In particular, avoid cheap adjustable spanners in the smaller sizes. Cheap pliers, wire cutters and screwdrivers are also a bane; you nearly always end up having to buy something better. High-quality second-hand tools are infinitely preferable to cheap new ones. If you are not sure of some of the terms used, refer to the appropriate chapters and glossary.

General Tools

You may have a number of these tools already or close alternatives. While some of these may not be a first choice they may be adequate and avoid the need to buy something more specialist.

3⁄16in slot head screwdriver For derailleur adjustment. You may need ¼in and 5⁄16in for working on older bikes. A square section shank is useful on the larger sizes for applying extra torque when necessary; this can be applied with a spanner. Small cross-head (Phillips) screwdrivers (Nos 1 and 2) may also be useful.

Stiff wire brush For removing encrusted dirt and rust.

Hammer A ball-pein mechanic's hammer is preferable to the claw type designed for carpentry, though this will suffice. Mostly useful for older bikes.

You will need some general-purpose tools. From left to right: *3/16in slot head screwdriver, wire brush, ball pein hammer, soft-faced hammer, file, vernier callipers, slip-joint pliers, side cutters, vice grip.*

(Below) *Use vernier callipers for accurate measurement.*

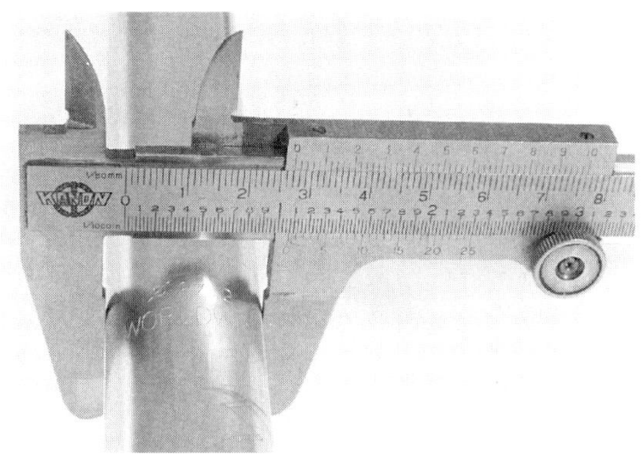

Soft-faced hammer For general freeing and straightening duties with minimal risk of damaging the component.
Files A narrow file to reach the spoke heads may be needed to smooth off any protrusion. For filing cotter pins a 'second cut' ¾in or 1in flat or half-round file is recommended.
Pliers Combination models with a cutting facility are mainly a substitute for the cycle-specific cable tools covered below; only the very best pliers will cut cable housing or inners adequately. Long-nose models in particular are useful for holding fiddly items.
Vernier callipers If you work a lot on bikes, these are very useful for checking the sizes of seat posts, handlebars, bolts and such like, where you may need to know the size to the nearest 0.2mm.
Slip-joint pliers Useful for gaining a grip on awkward and non-standard items but they may leave slight damage.
Side cutters Good ones are great for brake cable casings and not bad for gear cable casings but do tend to squash it. They also cut inner cables and slice through old spokes.
Vice grip (mole grip) Useful for gripping odd or rounded items.

Specific Bicycle Tools

Tyre levers For removing tyres. Metal ones can be easier to use but plastic ones are less likely to damage alloy rims.
Bicycle cable cutters These are designed to cut all types of bicycle cable. They are more expensive than pliers or side cutters but much better.
Cable tensioner This tensions and beds in cables. It pulls brake arms at the same time, while you use your other hand to tighten the pinch bolt.

Cone spanners These are essential for adjusting your hub-bearing cones and sometimes necessary for their lock-nuts. Typically you will need 13 or 14mm for front hubs and 15 or 16mm for rear hubs; you may need two pairs. Note that some spanners economically combine two or four sizes. Make sure they are thin enough to fit your hub.

Spoke key For adjusting spoke nipples. A correctly fitting, single-size type is easiest to use; make sure it is a snug fit.

Chain-link extractor For removing and fitting chains. Get a model with an additional spreading slot for freeing stiff links. Shimano HG and IG compatible models work best on all modern derailleur chains.

Cotterless crank extractor For removing cotterless (all modern) cranks. Extractors come in different designs but basically the outer body is first screwed into the crank and the inner part pushes against the spindle, effectively pulling the crank off. Although cranks now have a universal thread size (22mm × 1mm), you do need to double-check that you have the right extractor for your crank. The main variations are pre-1982 Stronglight (23.35 × 1mm) and TA Professional (23mm × 1mm). Finally, extractors for an axle with nuts (usually cheaper models) rather than bolts require an extractor with a deeper body. Many models combine a socket taking the place of the crank bolt spanner.

These specific bike tools will cover most needs of a modern machine. Clockwise from the bottom left to centre: *tyre levers, cable cutters, cable tensioner, adjustable pin spanner, cotterless crank extractor, cartridge bottom bracket tool, headset spanner, headset/pedal spanner, cassette lock-ring tool, sprocket remover (chain whip), chain-link extractor, spoke key, allen keys, cone spanner.*

General Spanners

Spanners come in several designs for different purposes. Whichever type you choose, you will probably need sizes 8, 9, 10 and 11mm. You may also need 12, 13, 14, 15, 16, and 17mm. On older bikes, 2BA (between 8 and 9 mm), 5⁄16in, and 3⁄8in spanners may also be needed.

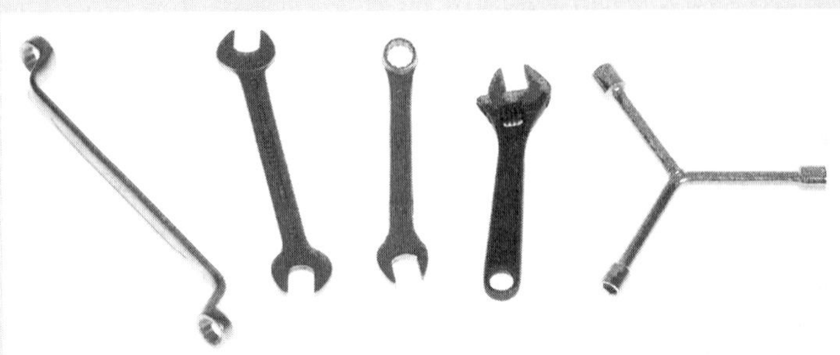

Spanner Types. From left to right: *ring, open-jaw, combination, adjustable and 'Y'.*

Box (tube) spanners reach the parts other spanners cannot. Note the extra addition of leverage.

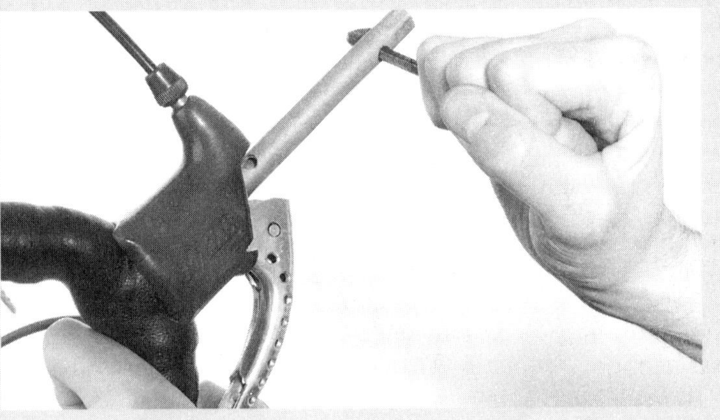

Ring spanners completely encircle the nut for maximum grip on all six sides, avoiding the possibility of slipping and damage to the nut. Deep neck (offset) versions get in behind obstacles allowing the spanner to turn fully.

Open-jaw spanners drive two sides of the nut: the spanner puts the jaw at two different angles of attack to the nut according to which way up it is. In a confined space, you turn the nut a little, then flip the spanner over to continue. These spanners are also the most economical as each one fits two sizes. Combination spanners combine a ring and open spanner and are the most useful.

Y-spanners combining three sockets make cheap and useful alternatives to the above and can be particularly useful for working on small fittings.

Box spanners formed from a tube are ideal for awkward corners. Used with a bar for leverage, they reach right inside the component and grip solidly; they are ideal for older non-allen brake levers and some brake fittings.

Adjustable spanners provide a poor fit compared to fixed spanners but are highly useful for a number of secondary purposes: for example, when you need a size you do not have, when you need two spanners the same size at once, for bending, and applying leverage. A high-quality 15cm (6in) model (such as the Bahco) is recommended. A 30cm (12in) model (where the quality is a little less important) is also useful and can stand in for some cycle tools.

Crank-bolt spanner For tightening the crank bolt. Alternatively, if you have a socket set, use a thin-walled socket to fit your crank bolts (14 or 15mm as appropriate). Allen key bolts are used instead on many modern bikes.

Cassette lock-ring tool For removing and securing the cassette. Freewheel tools can appear to fit cassettes but may damage inner seals as they protrude deeper into the hub.

Freewheel remover Some bikes have a freewheel as opposed to a cassette (*see* Chapter 9). There are about a dozen different freewheel remover types; ask your dealer to sell you the right one.

Bottom bracket cartridge tool For removing and fitting a modern bottom bracket unit. Check model required with your dealer.

Track Pump A floor-standing track pump makes it much easier to inflate bicycle tyres to the high pressures they usually require. Many have a built-in pressure gauge.

Pressure Gauge A highly useful device to ensure your tyres are correctly inflated. If you don't have one, test the pressure by squeezing its side walls with your thumb and for finger – these should barely be able to make an impression.

The following tools can come combined in a number of forms. They are generally about 27cm (11in) long to provide sufficient leverage.

Peg spanner This is needed to adjust some bearings and for some dust caps, or for any component with two small holes. An adjustable one is often most useful.

Lock-ring spanner Used on cup and cone bottom brackets; check the fit as this varies.

Fixed-cup spanner For the right side bottom bracket cup of a traditional unit. Check the size and fit.

Headset spanner/s For adjustment and overhaul of the headset bearings. Check the adjustable race and lock-ring

Allen Keys and Bolts

Allen bolts have become universal fitments on modern bikes. While most of those found on bicycles are metric, imperial fittings are occasionally used. You will need 4, 5 and 6mm; their uses are almost too numerous to mention. You may also need 2, 3, 8 and 10mm; $\frac{7}{32}$in and $\frac{1}{4}$in sizes may be needed for some US and older British-made seat bolts and handlebar clamps. Buying a set of quality long-handled multi-position ones (such as Bondhus) makes the most sense. T-handled models can be very useful for reaching inside confined spaces, such as brake levers.

When using allen keys, inspect the bolt's socket and clean out any crud that would otherwise stop the key from fully entering. Ensure you have the correct size key and insert it fully, then unscrew the bolt; you may need to exert pressure on it to keep it in the socket; not doing so may round it off. If a fitting is a loose fit or already damaged and loose, try the next key size up, which is often an imperial size.

Size	*Next size up*
2mm	$\frac{3}{32}$in (2.38mm)
2.5mm	$\frac{7}{64}$in (2.78mm)
3mm	$\frac{1}{8}$in (3.18mm), 3.5mm
4mm	4.5mm, $\frac{3}{16}$in (4.76mm)
5mm	5.5mm, $\frac{7}{32}$in (5.56mm)
6mm	$\frac{1}{4}$in (6.35mm)
7mm	$\frac{5}{16}$in (7.94mm)

Bolt Types

The cap-head allen bolt is the most common type used on bikes and is universally used in recessed applications. Neat button-head allen bolts are sometimes used to attach accessories and on adjustable pannier racks but these have a shallow socket, making them easier to round off.

Most allen bolts used on bicycles are made from stainless steel. These are a good idea, especially for items that receive frequent use, as they resist corrosion. Chrome-plated bolts tend to go rusty with time and are best protected with an occasional squirt of a water-dispelling agent. High-tensile zinc-plated bolts look dull but are the strongest.

sizes. A large adjustable spanner may suffice on the lock-ring but is not a good idea on softer alloy fittings.

Pedal spanner To remove and fit pedals. Most are 15mm, but a few are 17mm.

Bicycle Threads

A bicycle has numerous threads, ranging from the quite coarse and strong such as a cotterless crank retaining bolt, to fine and surprisingly delicate ones like the freewheel thread of an alloy hub. Special care must be taken to avoid fitting together incompatible threads, cross threading and over-tightening, which can ruin a component.

Threads start better if they are clean and undamaged. Dirty and encrusted threads can be cleaned up well with a stiff wire brush. When starting a threaded component use light even pressure. It can help to turn it backwards half a turn until you feel a slight click or drop, then proceed in the normal direction. This is particularly useful with wider components, such as bottom bracket cups and headset components; it is wise to check them from all sides before proceeding.

Some components have left-handed threads, that is, they tighten anticlockwise – the opposite way to normal. They are usually used to prevent unwanted unscrewing of the component as its parts revolve. Left-side pedal threads and most right-side bottom bracket cups have left threads.

Thread Standards

Most British bikes used to be made with standard British cycle threads known as BSC, these letters sometimes being stamped on components so threaded. This is interchangeable with the ISO modern standard to which almost all new bikes sold in the UK and most of the world are made. The Italian home market generally uses its own thread standard for the frame/frame fitting components and some other components. The French home market also used its own thread standard. The differences are covered in the appropriate chapters.

(Below) *Left threads radiate up to the left, normal right threads radiate up to the right.*

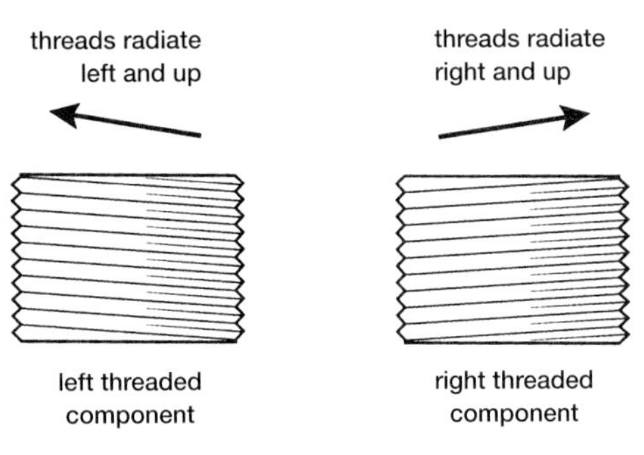

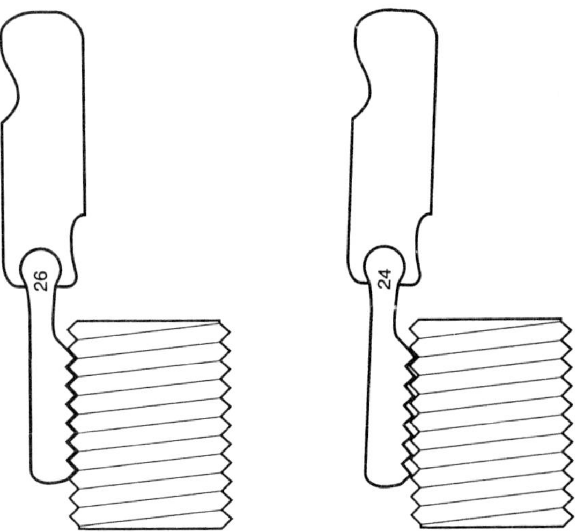

(Right) *Thread sizes can be checked with a set of thread gauges.*

Raleigh and most other brands taken over by them (such as BSA, Triumph, and Rudge) used Raleigh's unique 26TPI (threads per inch) headset and bottom bracket threads until 1985. Spares for these are now hard to find. Good bike shops can retap the frame threads to 24TPI. This will work for all but the heaviest use, enabling you to use standard components. Other thread sizes can also sometimes be converted.

WORKSHOP PRACTICE AND TECHNIQUE

What can take the longest time to develop is what can loosely be called a 'mechanical feel' gained through experience and interest in what you are doing. Mechanical feel ensures that you tighten things sufficiently so that they do not work loose – without stripping the threads. Mechanical feel ensures that you use correctly fitting tools and do not round off all the fittings. Mechanical feel tells you at what point a bearing is correctly adjusted. Of course, you can do jobs without this feel, but the time it takes to do a job and the level of frustration will reduce with it.

It has often been said that a poor worker blames his tools. While you will need the right tools it is equally important that a bicycle mechanic has certain skills and patience. It pays to think things through and isolate problems. Say you have an annoying ticking sound coming from what you think is the bottom bracket. Are you sure it is not coming from the back wheel? Does it only happen under pedalling pressure? Does it only happen while you are freewheeling? It helps to have an analytical mind that does not jump to conclusions.

Once you have identified the problem, do not go at it like a bull in a china shop. An experienced mechanic will know his own limitations and those of his tools, and will stop before causing damage. Some operations require brute strength, but only after you have considered what the end result might be. You might have a handlebar stem corroded into the fork column. Twisting it from side to side will probably get it out, but unless you support and lubricate it correctly you may bend the forks.

Leverage

Always be aware of how much leverage you are exerting on components – too much leverage and you will be surprised by your own strength! It might seem obvious, but holding the end of the spanner helps, and you can of course use longer spanners – or extend their handles (and allen keys) using tubes.

A vice can be very useful to free stuck items. Put the smaller part in the vice and turn the larger for masses of leverage: hold the freewheel (by its removal tool) in the vice and turn the wheel; hold the fixed cup, or seat post, and turn the frame; hold the fork crown and turn the handlebars. Apply a penetrating lubricant to help ease things. The controlled pressure of the vice can also be used (with care) to fit cartridge bearings. Where a vice has been shown in use in this book it has been done to show where it might be useful, but is not usually an essential requirement.

Dealing with Damaged Threads

Threads can often become damaged. For example, a spill can mean the threads at the end of the wheel axle can become burred over. This means that the nut turns the axle around with it instead of undoing. Further tightening the nut on the other side of the axle will help lock the axle and allow the nut to unscrew. Because it has to force its way over this deformed section, the parts may lose some of their thread and need to be inspected and possibly replaced.

If made of steel, damaged threads can often be repaired. Dies and thread chasers are used on externally threaded (male) items such as bolts and the fork column. Taps are used on internally threaded (female) items such as nuts and the inside of the bottom bracket shell. Dies are usually adjustable to get the depth of cut just right. Smaller taps and dies are relatively inexpensive and easy to use compared to larger ones. A 5mm tap for cleaning accessory mountings is useful. Imperial 2BA threads are used on many older bikes for accessory fitting. These are slightly smaller than 5mm, but with care can be enlarged to 5mm. Use 'cutting oil' (Park and Ison supply small quantities) on the tap, die, or thread chaser and turn it back half a turn periodically.

If you do not have the die or tap you need and cannot justify the cost of buying one, bike shops can often do the job for you quite cheaply. Alternatively, for small corrections a file such as one for sharpening the teeth of a saw can be used to clean up the grooves, typically of a fork column or axle thread. Try not to take too much metal off.

You may be able to clean up the thread by starting the component from the other side. This is particularly useful when dealing with damaged crank pedal threads and the derailleur hanger.

If you need to cut a threaded component such as a bolt or fork column, it helps considerably to put a nut or threaded part on first. Cut, then smooth any burrs with a file, then unscrew the threaded item, leaving a good clean thread.

When working on a tight nut or bolt, use a ring spanner in the first instance if possible, ensuring that it is not seized and applying penetrating fluid if necessary. A sharp knock with a hammer can also help break the bond. If you damage it, a file

Small taps are best used with a special tap holder.

Top left: *a plain washer.*
Top middle and right: *two forms of hub gear axle lock washers.*
Bottom left to right: *spring, star and lock (tanged) washers.*

can be used to remake the edges, so you can try again, perhaps using a smaller spanner. Once a nut is damaged, Vice grips are also very useful. Adjust them so that they snap onto the nut very tightly.

Keeping Things Tight

A number of bicycle threads have a habit of shaking loose, especially the small bolts holding accessories like mudguards and racks. Plastic-like compounds such as Loctite Thread Locker stop most items working loose. Such a compound is best applied to clean dry components. Use these compounds to avoid over-torquing delicate items such as chainset bolts. Sometimes fitments such as head-set races are plainly loose in the frame, or cartridge bearings in their recess; use Loctite Bearing Fit in these instances. It is a good idea to check such repairs made to highly stressed items.

Greasing larger bolts makes it easier to tighten them and reduces the chance of seizure; it is particularly important to grease stem expander bolts and seat clamp and post bolts.

Keep a selection of washers. Spring washers exert pressure against a nut, helping to prevent it from loosening. Star washers do a similar job and ensure good electrical contact where thread lock would insulate. Larger-head plain brass washers enable mudguard stay fixings to be tightened firmly without opening up the 'eye'. Lock washers exert a force against the nut or bolt, helping to prevent it from shaking free. Nylock-nuts have a Nylon ring built in that grips the bolt; these are commonly used for brake, rack and mudguard mountings.

LUBRICATION

Lubrication is a fundamental aspect of bike maintenance. Its purpose is to put a thin slippery layer of grease or oil between moving parts so that they slide or roll easily without actually making contact. This eliminates or reduces friction, wear and damage. If bearings are to last as long as possible they must be clean, well lubricated and properly adjusted. Lubrication is also necessary to reduce the friction of other sliding parts, such as cables.

Modern lubricating oils are made either from a mineral oil made from refined crude oil, or are 'synthesized' –

these are called synthetic oils. Synthesizing gives greater precision and flexibility over the finished product, allowing the manufacturer to meet exact needs. Additives are frequently mixed in to both types of oil to improve certain properties such as its slipperiness, viscosity (thickness) or performance at extreme temperatures; the last variable is not usually relevant to cyclists unless touring Lapland in winter.

Oils

Oils are mainly used where grease cannot penetrate, or would be very messy – for example on the chain (to reach the bushings and pins) and the numerous pivot points of brake and gear components. Generally the best bike oils are tenacious and of a high viscosity – that is they stick in place and do not get flung off. They should be used in moderation to avoid collecting too much dirt, and the chain will need cleaning more often than it does with most other lubricants. They are best used in the wettest conditions.

An alternative to oils are synthetic 'solid' sprays contained in an aerosol, which are usually based on PTFE (Teflon); examples are Finish Line Bicycle Lubricant and Superspray Lube. These use a solvent that helps the lubricant penetrate but then quickly evaporates away, which is ideal for chains. These sprays may also contain rust and surface tension inhibitors and water repellents. Leave the lubricant to solidify for a few minutes before riding. These feel dry to the touch and are therefore the least messy, so the chain will require less frequent cleaning. The latest chain lubricants such as White Lightning and Finish Line Fortified Paraffin use paraffin wax with special additives and degreasers to help apply it and keep it stuck on.

A special type of synthetic oil is based on petroleum distillate chemicals; WD40 is the best known. These are only modest lubricants but have the special property of displacing water. If sprayed on a wet chain they will form a self-healing layer between the steel and the water, forcing the water to form droplets on the surface of the oil. They are an excellent rust preventative after a long, wet ride and will also improve the electrical contacts of your lights.

Chain Lubrication

Chain lubrication is best achieved with the chain on the middle rear cog; rotate the pedals backwards, and apply the lubricant to the chain over the cassette. It will spread itself out, so try not to over-do it.

'Solid' lubricants such as Linklyfe (from motorbike shops) containing molybdenum disulphide and graphite (*see* below) and Hock's Chainwax containing PTFE are good for winter use but you have to remove the chain to apply them. The whole tin is warmed up to melt the lubricant. The chain is dunked in it and left for several minutes. Remove and let the chain drip back into the tin. The chain may be stiffer at first, resulting in slower shifting. This method ensures that lubricant penetrates the bushing, so is a good idea after the chain has been cleaned several times.

Greases

Grease is oil that contains a thickening agent to make it into a solid. This is almost always a soap that forms a microscopic network of fibrous strands, which trap tiny droplets of oil and keep them distributed evenly around the moving parts. Frequently the soap is lithium based and is therefore called lithium grease. Some greases use zinc oxide as a filler, making it creamy white in colour; this make contamination easier to see. Greases have the function of stopping dirt and water entering the bearings, and this is particularly important with components that are not in themselves well sealed. In general, over a long time greases containing mineral oils will slowly oxidize and go hard, thus failing to lubricate.

Synthetic oils (and hence the greases made from them) are generally much more stable and last much longer, though they do tend to cost more. As bicycle bearings are not usually repacked with new grease all that often, these synthetic greases make a good deal of sense; pack the bearing as fully as you can. Better greases also tend to have solid lubricants added to them, such as graphite, PTFE (Teflon), and molybdenum disulphide, which have special slippery properties. These are ideal for bearings that run slowly but at high pressure, such as the headset. As it receives a high shock loading, and because the ball bearings do not normally rotate more than a few degrees, grease tends to get squashed out from around the bearing surfaces and is not replenished by the rolling action of a fully rotating bearing. If you can inject grease into your bearings a cheaper grease is perfectly adequate as it will be changed long before it breaks down (*see* below).

Sheer strength is a term often used with greases. This is the ability of the grease to resist being pulled away from surfaces. A high sheer strength means reduced risk of metal to metal contact. Some greases tend to have a poor 'memory', being easily squashed out of the way by the rotating ball bearings; it will then no longer do its job and can leave space for water to enter. Greases also help prevent seizure of assembled parts. Special greases containing copper are specially designed for this and are recommended.

Whatever grease you use, try to keep it clean. For this purpose, tubes are better than tubs, and best of all is a grease gun (such as the Dualco or Finish line), which makes application simple and can be used for 'injection maintenance'.

Penetrants and Freeing Agents

Traditional (and cheap) penetrating fluids containing graphite are highly useful for easing the chemical bond that forms between metals that are in close contact – either rust or the chemical weld-like bond that forms between aluminium and steel. One special synthetic freeing agent is Plus Gas (from engineer's suppliers and motor accessory shops). A small squirt is all that is needed, but give it a few minutes to do its work. If something is really stubborn, then leave it overnight and/or reapply as necessary.

Degreasers (Solvents)

Degreasers dissolve oil and grease, and some, in turn, can be dissolved in water. They are most useful for cleaning the chain, but are also useful for removing old grease and crud, and general cleaning. Petrol, while effective, is just too flammable. White spirit or paraffin, which is cheaper, are just as effective. They do evaporate rather slowly so it helps to use a rag to wipe dry the components as much as possible. However, I do not recommend any of these degreasers, as biodegradable ones such as Finish Line EcoTech, Pedros, and Natural Blue are just as effective and are much healthier for you as well as the environment.

You can reuse degreasers. Leave the degreaser to settle and strain it, and it will be as good as new. Keep a good supply of small cotton rags, and have a separate container for clean and semi-soiled ones. To clean small parts take a jam jar, half fill it with foam rubber and cover with degreaser. Put the parts in, replace the lid and shake. The clean parts are left clean and clear of the liquid.

Easy Regreasing

Rather than overhaul cup and cone bearings by stripping them down, it is possible to inject grease into some components (and many others with adaptation), flushing out the crud and any ingress of water and leaving behind a bearing packed in fresh new grease – without any disassembly. You will need a grease gun to do this, and an additional injection nozzle or needle can be helpful. As it is so easy, it can be done after any hard use and the life of the component can be greatly extended.

A few components can be injected without modification, which will be mentioned in the appropriate chapters. Otherwise the component will need adaptation using a kit (*see* Further Information) or the fitting of a conventional grease nipple. This involves some minor metal work – drilling a hole and tapping a thread. You should also fill any holes that you do not want to fill with grease inadvertently – like the bike frame! Epoxy resin (for example Araldite glue) works well for this. Grease nipples can now be hard to find as they really are a bygone from another era, but try old, established car accessory shops.

Sometimes a cartridge bearing will need regreasing before it has worn out, especially if water has entered. If so, the seal can be carefully prised up, enabling you to repack it. Carefully replace the seal, pressing it into place with your thumbs.

(Above) *A grease nipple fitted to a bottom bracket enables quick and easy injection maintenance – simply pump out the crud.*

Cartridge bearing seals can be prised up for lubrication.

3 The Frame and Forks

Your frame and forks, that is the frameset, are the heart and soul of your machine. In function the frameset should hold the bike together, support your weight and transmit your efforts in the most efficient and comfortable manner. Optimum handling depends on correct alignment (amongst other things), which is easily lost in a spill or crash. Frame design is always a compromise, for example between weight, strength, reliability and efficiency – thin tubes are efficient but are easily dented and possibly liable to fatigue wear.

Once a material has been sprung and sprung back so many times it can begin to crack – its fatigue limit has been reached. This springing happens all the time as you push on each pedal, honk (stand on the pedals) up a hill or go over bumps. For a given thickness of material, the fatigue limit is much lower for aluminium alloys than for steel and titanium, but modern frame designs take this into account. Still, it is prudent to check the frame regularly, especially the region around the bottom bracket and forks – once started, a crack can develop very quickly. Look for cracks in the tubes, sometimes pinpointed by signs of rust. Strange creaking noises, most noticeable under effort, are another indication of a crack developing – try flexing the frame slightly by pushing against the bottom bracket with your foot. The seat tube of open 'ladies' frames are particularly prone to cracking at the point where the top tube meets it as this is a stress-concentration point.

If you have bent your forks you should seek professional advice. Normally they will need to be replaced, especially if they are not made from steel, however mild the bend may be. Bending back the fork can seriously weaken it and it could then break without warning. If your forks are a high-quality steel pair it may be worth having them repaired – a new fork column or blade can be brazed in.

Frame problems can fundamentally affect the correct working of your machine and are usually very difficult to solve yourself, let alone in the middle of nowhere on a long tour. Leave them to a reputable frame builder, who on a steel frame can undertake many kinds of salvage operations safely. Minor misalignment, bent tubes, damaged dropouts and small dents can usually be rectified economically. New tubes can be fitted to a particularly valued frame. However, greater awareness on your part will help you avoid having the problems in the first place.

Many MTBs now incorporate a special suspension fork, and sometimes rear suspension. Apart from the checks and maintenance outlined in this chapter you should check the suitability of the front hub and tyre; this is covered in Chapter 9.

Summary – Checking for Frame Damage

🔧🔧🔧🔧 2 hours

When?
- If you suspect something is wrong, through the handling feeling strange
- If you have had a crash or spill
- When buying a second-hand bike

Special Tools
- Long straight edges will help; also useful are fine thread, ruler or vernier calliper and graph paper

Preparation/Notes
- Frame alignment is difficult to check with accuracy without professional tools and experience, so this information is intended to help you spot problems – you should seek further advice if the symptoms described are found.
- Some checks may require additional partial disassembly of the bike.

FRAME AND FORK ALIGNMENT

If all is correct, riding the bike no-handed should be possible with care (unless the wheels are under 24in). Before attempting this ensure that the wheels are correctly dished and centred in the frame (*see* Chapter 9), and the headset is unworn and adjusted correctly (*see* Overhauling the Headset, below), as these can significantly effect the handling.

Checking Frame Alignment

A definite indication of crash damage is bulging of the frame tubes (run your finger tip over likely areas), often made obvious by wrinkled or cracked paint (perhaps with rust lines). In particular, check around the head tube and near the meeting of the top and down tubes. Also check the top of the fork blades and the base of the fork column.

Check that the head and seat tube appear parallel when viewing them from the front, almost head on – one against the other. A straight edge placed alongside the head tube will help.

Check the rear triangle alignment by running some fine thread around the frame from the head tube to the dropouts; check each side lies taut on equal parts of the frame, for example, around the head tube lugs. Measure the distance between the seat tube and thread on both sides. Ideally the distances should be within 2mm of each other but rarely are. If out by more than 5mm, seek further advice.

The frame and fork dropouts should be perfectly parallel to avoid placing strain on the hubs; professional tools are required to check and rectify this. Additionally, the gear hanger should be parallel to the cassette (and thus the wheel rim) in all planes. If not, poor gear-shifting, and the possibility of the derailleur fouling the spokes can result. If the hanger has bent, the derailleur and its mounting thread are also likely to have suffered and may have tell-tale signs of damage. If you suspect the gear hanger to be misaligned, any good dealer should be able to check and correct it very quickly with a specialist alignment tool, without which this task is almost impossible.

Checking Fork Alignment

The fork's alignment can be tricky to check. Unless it has a dead straight design that leaves the crown at an angle

Check the rear triangle alignment.

(Below) *A special tool is essential to align the gear hanger.*

(so-called 'power forks'), its blades must leave the fork crown, continuing the same angle as the head tube, before sweeping forwards. In an accident, they will most often bend back, one side frequently bending more than the other. The dropouts must have equidistant forwards and sideways spread.

Fork alignment can be checked by resting the fork over graph paper. With one eye closed, look down the exact centre of the fork column. Also try placing a straight edge at ninety degrees across the fork crown – the blades should appear to be equally far forward.

As a final check of both the frame and fork alignment, check that the wheels have perfect tracking, that is, the rear wheel should follow the front in the same plane. Check this by putting the bike in a workstand and running some fine thread (or two straight edges) from a point a quarter of the way up the rear wheel, along both sides to the front wheel; each thread should touch both sides of both wheels.

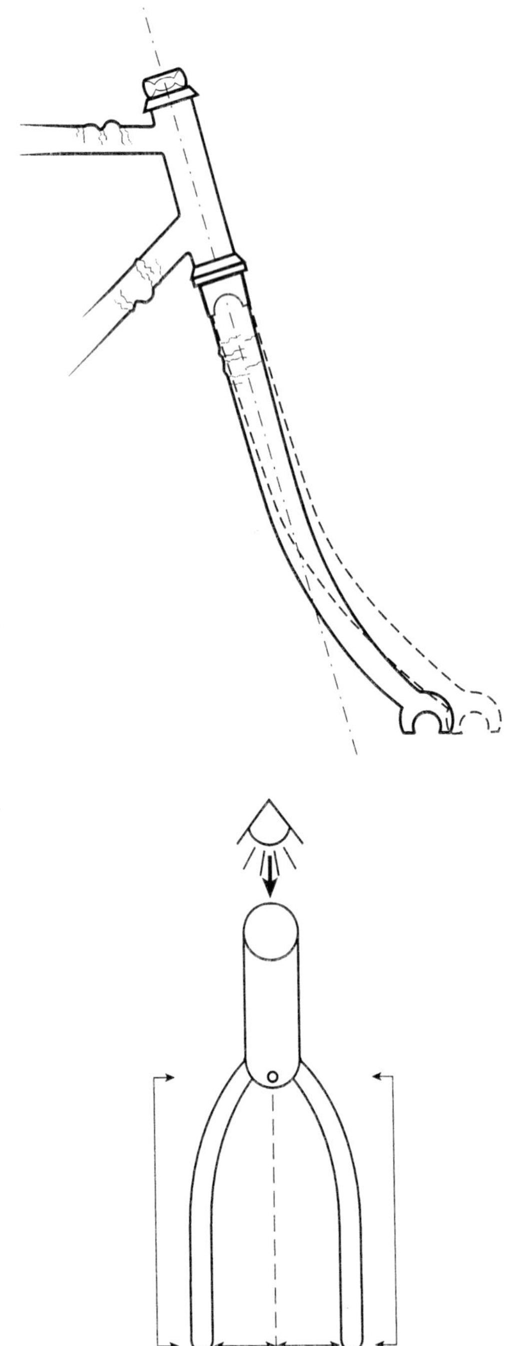

(Left) *The dotted outline shows the fork's former correct alignment. The main outline shows the fork bent back and the likely areas of bulging and wrinkled paint caused by a frontal impact.*

When the forks are viewed from directly above, the blades should appear mirror images of each other in all planes.

Frame Care

Steel frame tubes, even hi-tech alloys such as Reynolds 753 and 853, are just as liable to rust as a nail! Clean and touch up scratches as necessary. Model shops have a wide range of enamel paints in tiny pots, which can be mixed to produce the right colour. T-Cut (from car accessory shops) helps restore jaded finishes. After cleaning, finish the frame with a protectant polish to bring back the gleam – this helps to protect the frame by repelling dirt and water. Repainting a frame is a very difficult task to complete to a high standard, but most good bikes shops can get your frame professionally stove enamelled. Carbon-fibre frames are 'soft', so rubbing cables easily wear into them if they are not correctly routed.

Rust Prevention

Unseen from the inside, rust can destroy your favourite steel frame. Water can drip in and condensation can collect in the tubes. The seat tube just above the bottom bracket shell is very vulnerable if it does not have a drainage hole into the bottom bracket, which in turn should have its own drainage hole.

You can treat the frame to help prevent internal rust. Ensure the frame interior is completely dry by disassembling it as far as possible and leaving it in a warm place for several days, rotating it occasionally. Then apply a rust prevention agent: Waxoil such as Finnigins is the best option. Warm it slightly and pour into the frame tubes, rotating them to fully distribute it. It can be thinned with proprietary thinners to help to produce a thinner, lighter cover. Let it drain before rebuilding the bike!

Petroleum distillate sprays such as WD40 can be sprayed into the frame without drying it first, but their effect will not last as long. Such sprays can, however, be sprayed into inaccessible areas, even through some bottle mounts.

HEADSETS

The headset must keep the forks and frame rigidly attached with no trace of play. Equally it must allow the forks to turn completely freely and smoothly with no hint of sticking or binding. Failure of the headset to do these two jobs can result in rapid wear and impaired or even dangerous handling. It is most vital in the potentially most dangerous situations: on mountain roads, going over ruts, during lapses of concentration. Failure of the headset to do its job properly can mean the difference between a spill and staying aboard. Apply the front brake and rock the front of the bike; there should be no play. Then lift the front end of the bike and turn it from side to side; it should turn freely with no hint of resistance or 'notching'.

Headsets look simple but their replacement can become complex. Routine maintenance is essential and much easier. The lower bearing wears most quickly, being subject to loads along its axis (like a hammer hitting a nail) as you ride over road irregularities. Headset life can therefore be very short, especially with off-road or tandem use.

Unlike other bicycle bearings, the ones in your headset are not revolving, so the ball-bearings can impart indentations into the races – an effect known as brinelling. A temporary solution to such wear is to move the crown race 90 degrees so that a 'fresh' part of the race is receiving the bulk of impact.

Buying a Replacement Headset

Buy the same make and model if at all possible to avoid cup and crown race fitting problems. You may, however, want to upgrade your headset – some models (such as Stronglight and Tecora) have roller bearings. These generally offer very long life as the rollers have a much bigger contact area. They also have replaceable inner race inserts, saving money and the considerable inconvenience of changing the frame cups and crown race. One or two top-end headsets such as the Campagnolo Record have built-in ports for injection maintenance. Aheadsets-type systems use dedicated forks and handlebar stems and cannot be interchanged with conventional headsets.

If buying a different make or model of headset it can be advisable to have a good dealer fit it for you, especially if it is a roller-bearing model; the head tube may need to be specially faced to ensure that the cups are parallel and precisely aligned.

Threads

Italian and English threads are interchangeable. French and Raleigh threaded forks require their own headsets.

Diameter

Headsets are designed for 1, 1⅛ and 1¼in fork columns (metric measurements are not used for this sizing), as measured across the column outside diameter; 1in headsets vary slightly but significantly in their precise fitting diameter. Use a vernier calliper to measure the original crown race inside diameter and the frame race's outside diameter (the narrower section that goes into the frame). So-called 'professional' and Campagnolo models usually use 30.2mm frame cups in place of 30.0mm and a 26.4mm crown race in place of 27mm. Get the closest size you can. A frame can usually be milled by a frame builder to take professional quality headsets, which is a good move if you find the cheaper ones a loose fit.

Stack Height

The stack height is the space taken by the assembled headset between the fork crown and the bottom of the head tube plus the distance between the top of the head tube and the underside of the lock-nut lip. This must also include the thickness of any extra items fitted, such as a brake hanger. The stack height must be the same or less than the original. If it is less, you will probably need an additional spacing piece (packing) or two. Shimano headsets have a very low stack height; Tecora make a readily available alternative with roller bearings.

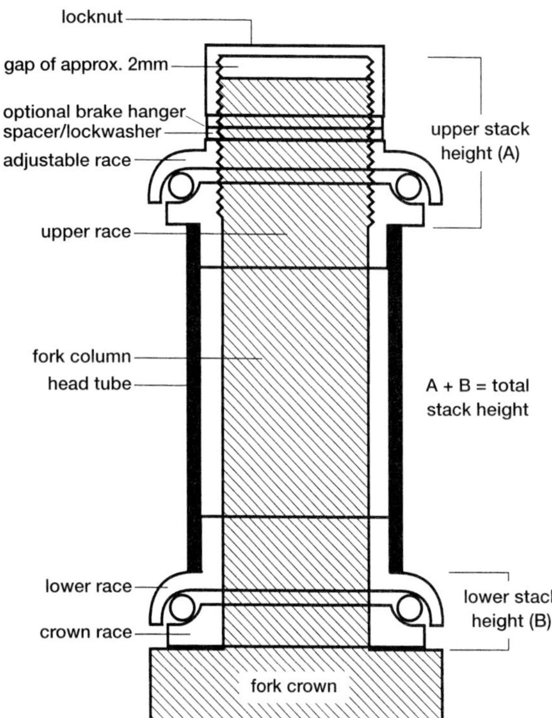

When replacing a headset the stack height should be carefully measured.

HEADSET OVERHAUL

Summary – Headset Overhaul

🔧🔧🔧 1 hour

When?

- Overhaul once a year at minimum, or when correct adjustment becomes difficult
- Always maintain the correct adjustment (check as described above)

Preparation

- Remove conventional handlebar stems (*see* Chapter 4)
- Remove the front wheel (*see* Chapter 9)
- Remove calliper-type brakes (*see* Chapter 8)

Disassembly

Conventional Headset

Using a spanner on the adjusting race, slacken off and remove the top lock-nut. Lift off the cable hanger (if applicable) and spacing piece (lock washer). Holding the forks, unscrew the adjusting race. Noting which way up they go, lift off the ball cages, the steel races if separate from the cups, and any seals, and remove the forks.

Aheadsets

First note the order of the spacing pieces around the stem. These determine your bar height. Remove the top retaining bolt and plastic cover. Loosen the stem clamp bolts and slide the stem off. Once you have removed the stem, slide off the cable hanger (if applicable) and all seals

To remove the forks, hold the headset adjusting race, and unscrew the lock-nut.

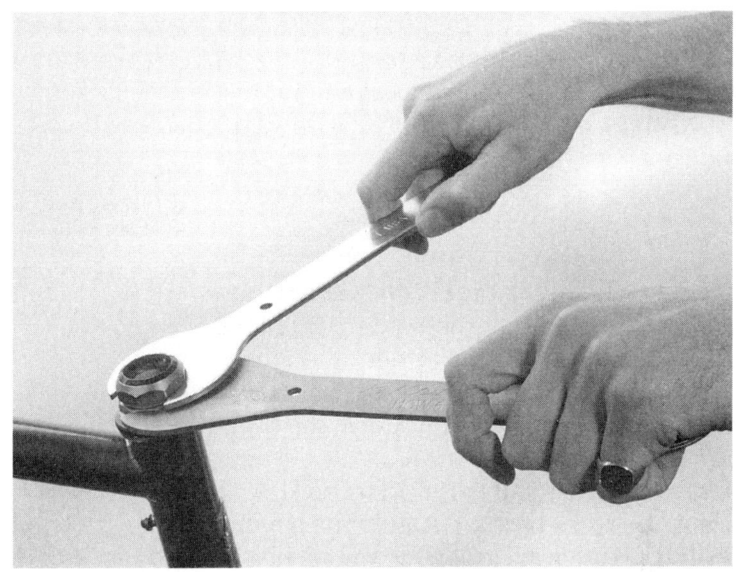

(Below) *Removing an Aheadset pre-load bolt and top cap; next, loosen the stem's two clamping bolts to the left.*

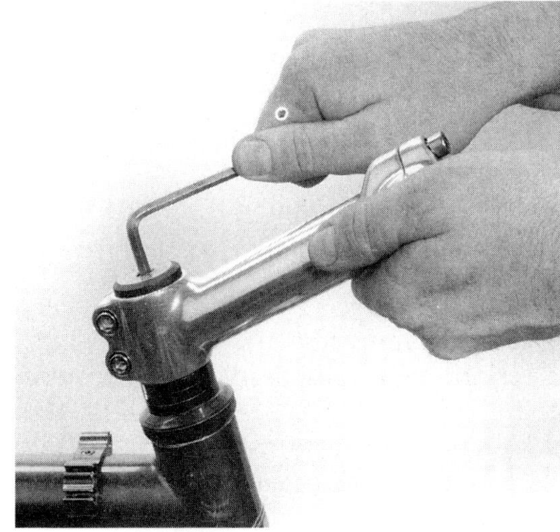

and spacers. Give the top of the forks a sharp knock with a soft-faced hammer to free them. Safeguard the top race and compression ring (the wedge that fits into the sliding adjustable race).

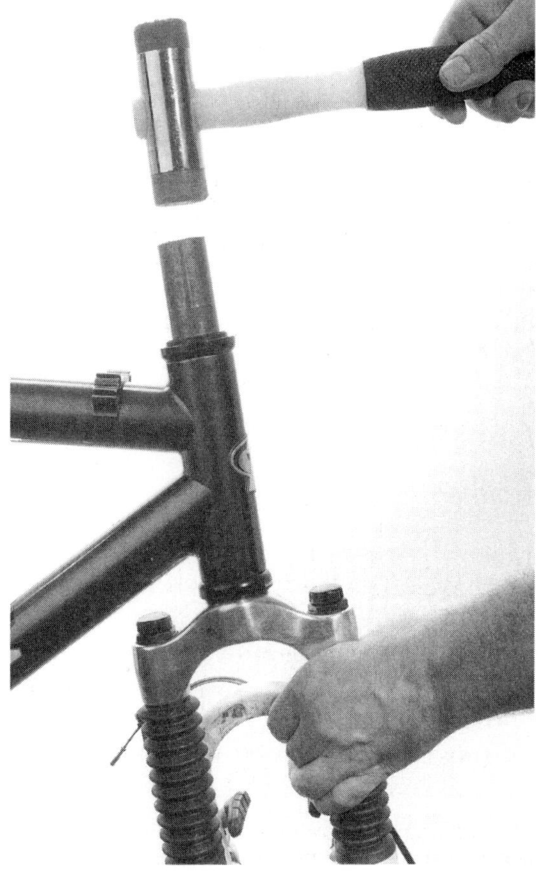

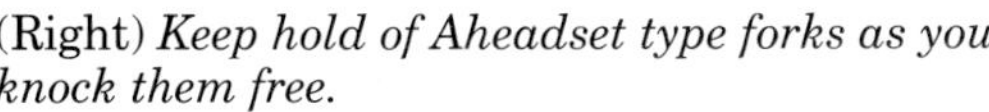

(Right) *Keep hold of Aheadset type forks as you knock them free.*

These two headset races have worn bearing tracks and are starting to show signs of brinelling.

(Below) *Make sure that you replace clipped bearings the correct way up.*

Cleaning and Inspecting the Parts

Use degreaser and an old toothbrush to clean the races and ball cages. You need to look for brinelling, grooving and pitting in all the races; if you find more than very slight traces of wear, it is best to replace the headset. Old ball cages are best replaced by loose ball-bearings of the same size unless you can buy exact replacements. A few headsets do not work well with loose ball-bearings, so do not throw away the clips until after assembly. With care, new ball-bearings can be popped into old cages; be careful not to bend the cage. Note that a few headsets use different size bearings in the upper and lower races.

Assembly

Conventional Headsets

Liberally grease the races and install the ball cages. The lower cage always goes in facing dish down. The top usually faces dish down. If you cannot remember how yours was, test by fitting the top stack without the forks and rotate. If it feels at all rough or strange, try it the other way up and compare. If you are using loose ball-bearings, stick them in shoulder to shoulder on the crown race and in the top

Align the lock washer tang with the groove or slot of the fork column.

cup, leaving a gap of one and a half to two bearings. Replace the forks and finger tighten the adjusting race.

Next, normally one spacing piece is fitted followed by the cable hanger (if applicable) and lock-nut. Align the spacer's tang or flat with the fork's recess or flat. Replace the lock-nut: it must tighten properly against the spacer, not against the top of the forks. If this happens you will need an extra spacer. If there are insufficient threads for the lock-nut, remove the spacing piece, bearing in mind that this may make spanner access to the adjusting race difficult.

The final adjustment is made as follows. Using a headset spanner, hold the adjusting race in position. Then using another spanner, tighten the lock-nut firmly down onto it. Check that the forks turn freely and smoothly with no sign of play when you rock the fork blades back and forth; test them in all positions. You will probably have to repeat the adjustment, experimenting with the adjustable race position to get it just right. Replace the wheel, brake and handlebar stem.

Before you fit an Aheadset top cap, check the gap.

Aheadsets

Liberally grease the races and install the ball cages – the lower cage dish down, the upper cage dish up. Slide over the top race and compression ring, then the seal (if applicable), spacing pieces and cable hanger (if applicable) in the order removed. You can change the bar height by altering their order but do not remove or add spacers. Refit the handlebar stem, and press it down to take up the slack but do not tighten its clamps; its top must sit 3–5mm above the top of the fork column. Position, but don't yet tighten the pre-load bolt and the top cap.

When fitting Aheadset-type forks, take care to position the bearings, adjustable race and thrust ring correctly.

Tighten the pre-load bolt little by little, checking as you go until all play has been taken from the system. The forks must turn freely with no sign of play when you rock the fork blades back and forth – try for play in all positions. Once correct, tighten the handlebar stem clamp bolts. If you over-tightened the pre-load bolt, making the steering stiff, you will need to free the forks again as described under disassembly.

Replacing the Headset Races

Removing the Old Races

Use a hammer and an old screwdriver to knock out both cups from the inside. Work from side to side to ensure that they come out evenly, avoiding the risk of distorting

Summary – Headset Replacement

🔧🔧🔧🔧 1 hour

When?
- When the headset races are worn – do not remove them otherwise

Special Tools
- You will need to improvise some tools unless you want to spend a small fortune

Preparation
- It is assumed you have already removed the forks in the course of overhaul
- If you have had the frame re-enamelled ensure that paint will not interfere with fitting the races; scrape it away with a knife blade if necessary

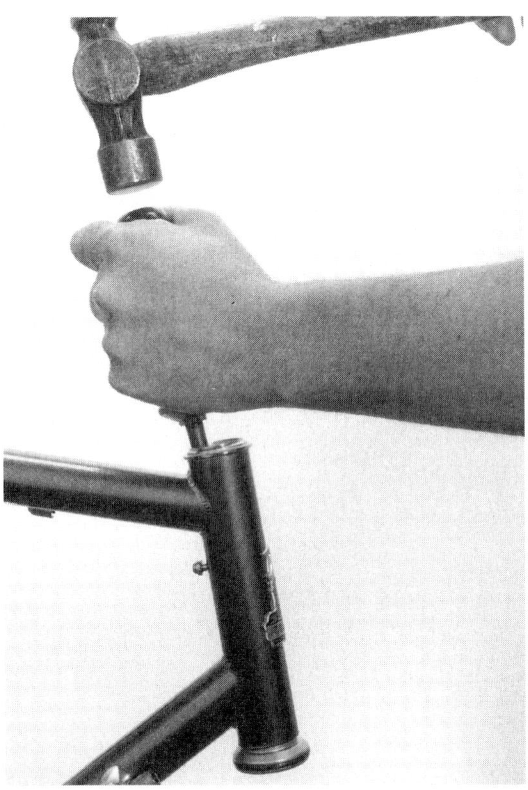

(Above) *Knocking out the frame races.*

(Right) *Tapping the crown race off; note the protection to the fork column threads.*

the head tube. You can also work from the outside, but watch the paintwork.

To remove the crown race, fit the headset lock-nut as protection, then supporting this over a block of wood, use a blunt screwdriver or drift to tap the crown race free. Again work from side to side. Check that the depth of any visible reaming inside the head tube will exceed the depth of the new cups; if it does not you may need to have the head tube rereamed in order for the cups to enter the frame properly.

Fitting New Races

This is the most tricky part of fitting a new headset, so proceed cautiously! You will need a length of ½in threaded studding and two old bottom bracket cups (or better still, improvise some hardwood or resin blocks) to make a simple press. Alternatively use a wide vice (with protection), or as a last resort, a nylon hammer; support the frame or opposite race on a wooden bench edge. If the cups have neoprene seals that just lift off, remove them to avoid damage.

To fit the frame races, position the lower, deeper-bellied cup and top shallower cup and assemble the press. Tighten the nuts against each other to squeeze the cups in. Keep a close eye on them to ensure that they go in straight – alloy cups are easily damaged. Knock them free and start again if necessary. Finally ensure that they are fully seated.

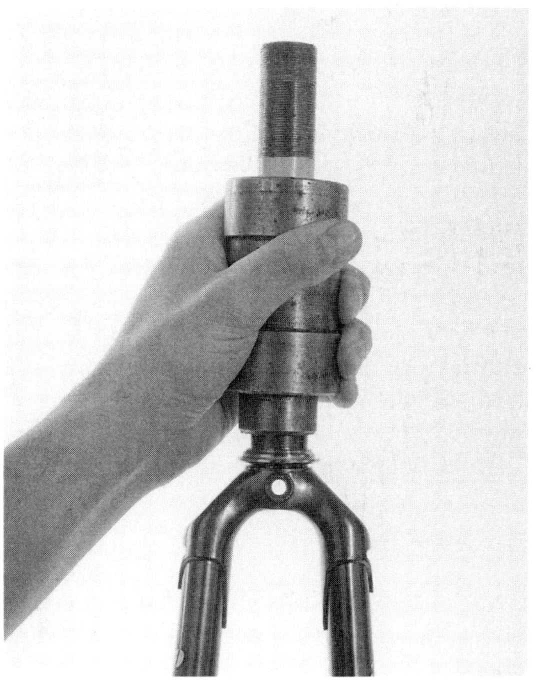

(Top right) *Squeezing in the frame cups with an improvised press.*

(Right) *A purpose-made tool for seating the crown race.*

To fit the crown race, use a piece of tubing (a 28mm down tube from a scrap frame is ideal for 1in fork columns) to ram the race down, ensuring it is fully seated. You can also slide the forks sideways in a carefully opened vice; try to avoid hitting the bearing surfaces. Finally refit any seals and assemble the headset as described above.

If even a 'professional' headset is loose, or you do not want any extra expense you can shim the gap with strips of coke can. Cut strips about 5–10mm wide and pull them tight under a ruler to give them a natural curve. Wrap them around the cup or fork column and use as many pieces as necessary to make a tight fit. This can be a fiddle but is worth the effort.

NEW FORKS

Buying Replacement Forks

Usually the best course is to buy a pair of forks matching the original from the bike's manufacturer; quality, offset (*see* below) and colour should then be matched in the most cost-effective way. Cheap forks often have poor alignment and brazing. High-quality replacements are available for the best frames; these are typically made from Reynolds 531 tubing, but at about four or five times the cost of the cheapest. Unless using a matching pair, you will need to take the factors below into account.

Calliper Brake Reach

This is the distance from the centre of the brake mounting point to the centre of the rim braking surface; brakes come in varying 'depths' to match this. You may also need to check that there is sufficient clearance for the tyre sizes you wish to use and for mudguards.

Fork Offset

Fork offset is the horizontal distance from an imaginary line through the head tube to the centre of the dropout/hub. This should be the same as with your former forks to within 5mm; this can be difficult to measure but good bike shops have tools to measure this accurately. A greater distance than this will noticeably slow the steering, while a shorter distance will quicken it. If the fork offset is wildly different, the handling can become peculiar. On the other hand, with the advice of an expert, it can also be possible to improve the handling of some bikes.

Fork Length

A longer fork than the original (effectively with increased brake reach) will decrease the angle of the head tube; this will make the steering feel slower and may increase stability. This effect is partly negated if the offset is increased by about a quarter of the increase in fork length for a 26in/700C wheel bike.

Fork Column

Forks come with either 1, 1⅛ and 1¼in fork columns (external diameter), and in threadless versions for Aheadsets.

The length of the fork column must be suited to the length of the frame's head tube and the headset stack height (*see* Buying a Headset above). Unless you are changing any of the parts, this can be the same length as your previous forks. You may need to cut the column down to size but check that, once cut, you will have sufficient thread (allow the same as the upper stack height). You may have problems if you shorten a fork to less than 4in (10cm) because its internal diameter usually increases towards the bottom, preventing the stem from entering.

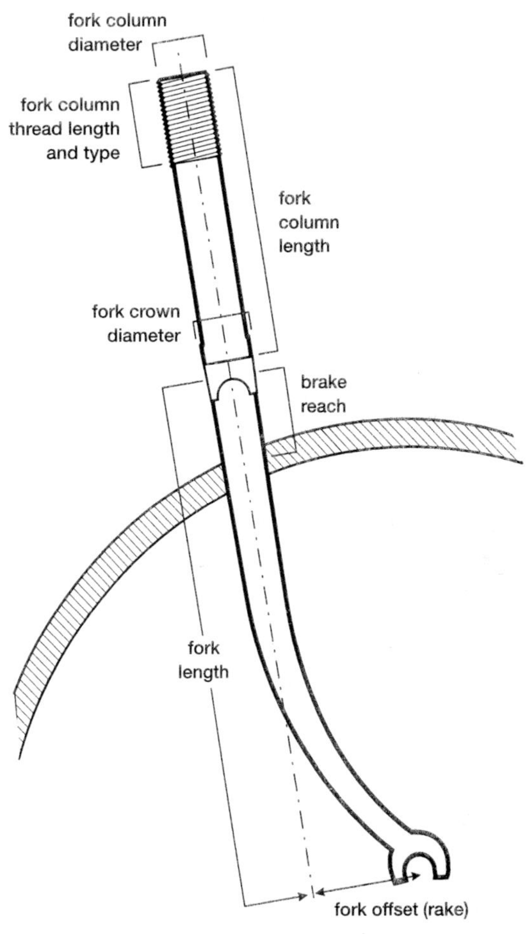

The critical dimensions to consider when choosing replacement forks.

Crown Diameter

It will be helpful to bring your headset crown race for your dealer to fit, or to supply a correctly fitting one. If you do need a new headset, it may have a different stack height and therefore affect how much fork column you need – ask your dealer for advice.

Dropout Width

If your dropouts are less than 5mm thick, your wheel's quick-release will clamp against the axle end and not the dropout. The quick-release will be doing nothing at all to clamp the wheel to the fork. This is highly dangerous and the solution is to shorten the axle, fit an axle with nuts, or use different forks.

Suspension Forks

Suspension forks can be retrofitted to most MTBs, but ask your dealer for advice. Modern MTBs all use very similar steering geometry, but suspension forks may have unsuitable fork offset and length for some cheaper and older bikes that were not specifically designed for them.

If you had a cable hanger, this will not be needed for most suspension forks. If they have one built in, it must be used instead. This may affect the fork column length needed. Suspension forks are normally best fitted by your dealer unless you are absolutely sure of what you are doing.

Be aware that as you will need to cut the fork column to size, you may not be able to transfer the suspension forks to another bike, though separate crown/fork column assemblies are available for some models.

Fitting New Forks

Cutting to Size

Having calculated the column length needed, mark the new fork accordingly. Screw on the two old adjusting races level with the fork end of the mark and tighten them together. Hold the fork in a vice further down the column, using wood or soft jaws to protect it. Saw through the column with the blade against the top race, using it as a guide. Use a file to clean off the swarf, then remove the old races. You may need to file a flat for the spacing pieces/brake hanger to fit over, but first fit an adjustable race to help clean the thread.

Summary – Fitting New Forks

2 hours

When?

- When replacing a damaged fork, or when fitting suspension
- Aheadset (threadless) fork columns are best cut to size by your dealer

Special Tools

- To cut threaded fork columns, you will need a vice, two old headset adjusting races and a hacksaw with a new 32 or 24 teeth per inch blade

Preparation

- Remove the old forks (*see* Headset Overhaul above). Check for frame damage if you had an accident
- Suspension forks (unless of the linkage type) should be used with a special, stiffer 'parallax' suspension hub

Cutting a fork column to size.

Assembly and Final Adjustment

Fit the crown race and the forks as detailed earlier in this chapter. Replace the front wheel, adjusting the quick release to fit the new dropouts if necessary. Brakes will need setting up and checking from scratch – *see* Chapter 9. Most suspension forks will need a new brake cable and casing cut to size for the brake arch of the forks.

Suspension forks must have sufficient clearance between the absolute top of the tyre and the underside of the crown; check the instructions. You need at least 50mm (2in) for Rock Shocks and Pace and 45mm (1¾in) for Manitou. This clearance also has to be borne in mind if you change the tyre. Adjust the damping and pre-load as detailed in the guidelines below and in accordance with the instructions that came with the fork.

SUSPENSION

Suspension is designed to isolate the rider from shocks and improve handling by giving the suspended tyres more continuous grip on the road or trail. This is best achieved if there is as much free movement in the system as possible, but this in turn must be balanced against the excessive rebound, or 'bobbing', that may occur, and wastage of the rider's efforts: a compromise is called for. Some adjustment is therefore nearly always provided both in the pre-load (degree of springiness) and damping (friction used to control the rate of rebound).

Do not be too alarmed if suspension forks feel a little strange at first and not up to your expectations. The ride quality is different from that provided by static forks, and you may need to adapt your riding style subtly to obtain the most from them.

The amount of adjustment and maintenance necessary varies according to the system, its use, the weight of rider and luggage, and the rider's preferences. Some systems need to be regularly tuned, others need and offer little adjustment. Adjustment is best made after any routine cleaning and lubrication recommended by the manufacturer. As suspension systems vary greatly in general design and much in detail I have covered only the basic principals of setting up and adjustment. It is recommend that you consult the manufacturer's literature to ensure the best performance from your system.

Suspension Types

Three main suspension types are found on bikes. Systems using elastomers are the most common. An elastomer is a compressible urethane or rubber-like material. The amount it can be compressed is determined by its exact composition, shape, and the structure it is contained in. In many cases the pre-load can only be altered by changing or adding to the elastomers. Do not be in a hurry to change the elastomers for softer or harder ones until you have fully explored the ones you have got. Damping cannot always be adjusted, but increased pre-load often increases the damping.

Steel springs are typically used for many inexpensive systems but this is not exclusively so, their design and quality of manufacture being just as important as price. Systems without some kind of external linkage do not have reliable damping adjustment.

Air/oil (hydraulic) systems are the most sophisticated. The air is compressed and the pre-load is determined by its pressure. Damping is achieved by oil being forced through small holes and valves; the degree of damping depends on the size and number of these and the viscosity of the oil.

Adjustment

You will probably need to experiment with varying amounts of pre-load and damping to get results that suit you. Bear in mind that the seals may be a little tight until they have been ridden in a bit. Beyond routine adjustment and cleaning, most are fairly trouble free.

The shock absorber, be it a steel spring or elastomer, is partly pre-loaded (compressed or selected) so that a certain force is needed to start it working. Too much pre-load stops the suspension absorbing high-frequency, small, frequent bumps such as cobbles; too little and some travel is already used up just by sitting on the bike – this is the degree of 'sag'. Always adjust each stanchion (arm of the fork) to the same setting.

The pre-load of steel spring systems is increased by compressing the spring. If there is a separate lock-nut, loosen this first, then nip it tight against the adjuster.

Elastomer-type forks often have adjusters at the upper or lower end of the stanchions. Give each the same number of turns, turning clockwise to increase the pre-load. In some cases, the pre-load can only be altered by changing the elastomers.

If you have a pressurized gas/oil system, you will ideally need a specialized pump with an accurate pressure gauge. If not, an ordinary bicycle pump with a football inflater (available from sports shops) will suffice. Unscrew or pop off the protective dust cap and insert the pump needle. In the case of air/oil type Rock Shocks pump each stanchion to 40–42lb or 35–45lb if you want to experiment with the pre-load. If you need to drop the pressure use the bleed button. Check the pressure every two to three months or more often if the bike is used regularly. Rear systems use much higher pressures in a single cylinder, where the exact pressure is less critical.

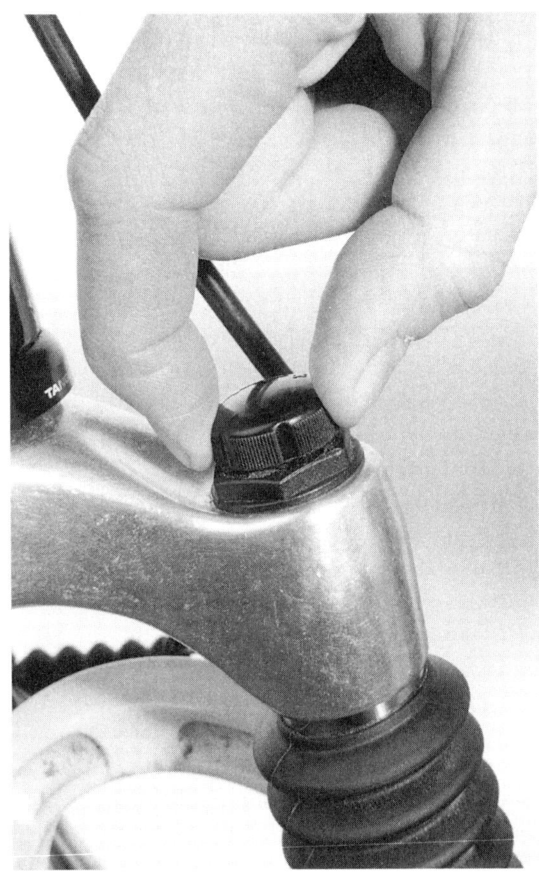

Adjusting the pre-load of a Rockshock Indy fork.

Adjusting a steel spring rear suspension system.

(Below) *The ride qualities of most elastomer systems can be adjusted by changing the elastomer, here held in the lower hand. This is usually a simple job.*

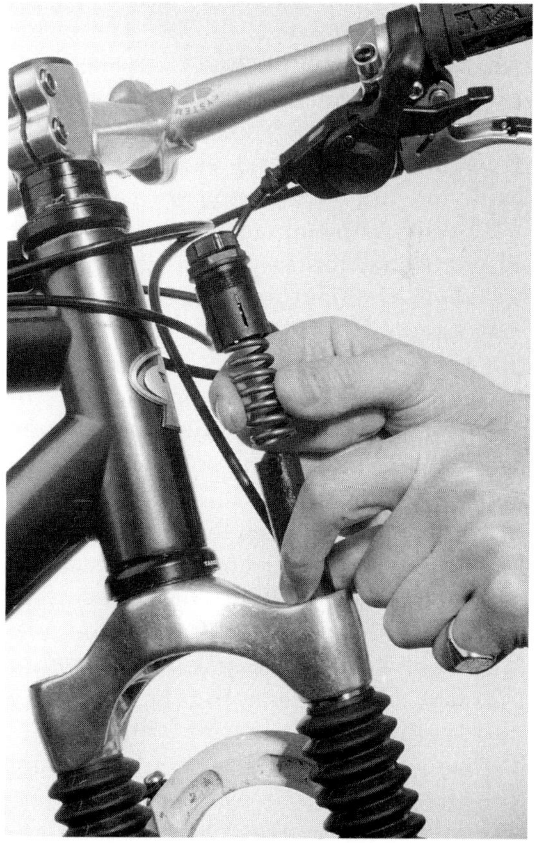

Damping is usually an adjustable form of friction used to control the speed of reaction of the suspension system, rather than the amount of force. It also absorbs some of the blow. Damping controls rebound but decreases sensitivity on high-frequency bumps. Consult the manufacturer's literature or your dealer for instruction on how to adjust the damping of your system if this is not obvious.

Current Moultons use a hidden steel spring within the fork column with a pre-load adjuster just above the fork column. Damping is provided by adjustable friction plates acting against the linkage part of the fork.

General Maintenance

The stanchions and any other sliding parts should be cleaned and lightly lubricated after use to avoid excessive abrasion and unwanted friction. Stanchion seals (wipers) need to be in good condition and cleaned out after approximately

Moulton front suspensions have adjustable friction plates to control damping.

(Below) *Suspension fork maintenance. Lift up the rubber boot, and any tension band around the stanchion wiper, then clean out any trapped debris. Grease the stanchions.*

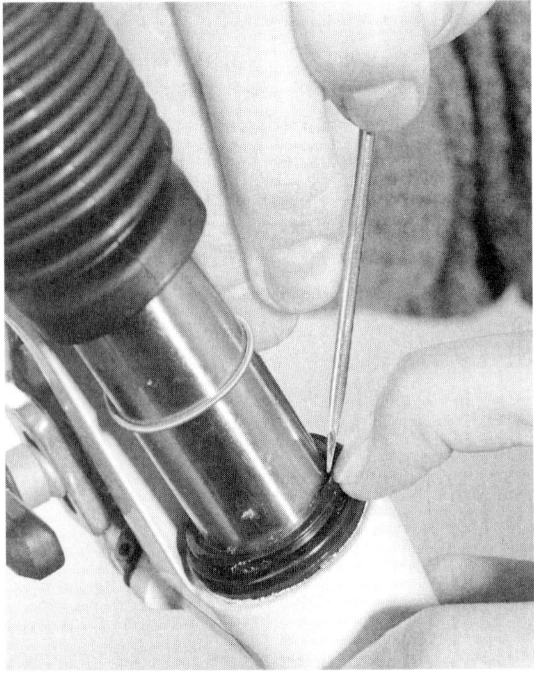

every fifty hours' use. Grease the stanchions with a non-lithium grease: one containing Teflon is ideal. Only ever use the manufacturer's recommended lubricants; some seals and elastomers may swell and jam if the wrong ones are used.

Systems using oil need cleaning and an oil change once a year. This is normally best done by an authorized service centre.

Periodically check any bolts clamping the stanchions to the fork crown – never raise or lower the stanchions.

If you have a linkage system, such as the Moulton or Girvin, occasionally apply a few drops of a Teflon lubricant to the pivot points. Check for wear and play in the system; this can sometimes be taken out by adjustment, or alternatively the bushings may need replacement.

In rear systems, check for any play in the system by grasping the assembly and trying to rock it from side to side. Tighten the bolts to take up all play, but ensure that the assembly still pivots freely. Pivot assemblies should be disassembled and greased to prevent seizing. This normally only needs to be done at major service intervals.

4 *Saddle and Handlebars*

Your saddle and bars must be set up properly or they can creep out of position or, more dangerously, suddenly slip when you hit a bump, as your weight is effectively magnified two or three times. You must ensure that you use correctly fitting components, or they can be a nightmare to remove. Additionally, seat posts and handlebar stems are notorious for seizing into the frame; this is especially true of aluminium alloy parts in a steel frame, as an electrical charge is set up that produces a chemical welding effect between the two metals. This can be avoided by applying copper-based anti-seize grease to the hidden sections of these parts.

Spills and crashes can bend your bars. To check, view from directly above and below and from directly in front to check that the tops are horizontal. Use a straight edge to help. Sometimes the stem can be bent. Always replace bent aluminium alloy components as they can fail unexpectedly.

RIDING POSITION

The saddle, seat post, handlebar stem and handlebars determine your fit on a given frame, both through exact model choices and their adjustment. You should ensure that you have found your optimal riding position as a poor one will seriously affect your riding efficiency and can lead to a variety of aches, pains and possible injuries. Detailed information on riding position is beyond the scope of this book; further reference is included in the Further Information.

As a general guide, with the ball of your foot on the pedal, your leg should have a slight bend. To confirm this, put your heel on the pedal: your leg should now just lock straight. More scientifically, the correct saddle height, as measured from the pedal top to the centre-top of the saddle, has been found to be 105–109 per cent of the inside leg measurement. If you use this method, start at 105 per cent and work up slowly, 3mm (⅛in) at a time. If aches or pains develop, backtrack to the point where they disappear.

The fore-aft adjustment of the saddle determines your position in relation to the handlebars (reach) but this adjustment has several other effects, for example on weight distribution and its effect on the bike's handling. Women often benefit from a forward saddle position as they have wider hips, while a lean man may benefit from the opposite. The further back the saddle, or the more forward the bars, the flatter your back becomes, and the more you need to bend it. While a flat back is aerodynamically more efficient, your riding position should remain comfortable for you for the whole duration of your ride. The arms should not be so stretched that they lock out, but should retain some give. You may need to consider a different handlebar stem length, or at worst, a different frame to obtain your perfect riding position.

Handlebars should be set level with the nose of the saddle, or more often, a little lower. To increase the efficiency of your position, gradually work the bars down to the point where comfort is compromised, bearing in mind that a new position will take time to become accustomed to; backtrack if necessary.

THE SEAT POST

Buying a Seat Post

It is vital that you fit the correct diameter seat post (to the nearest 0.2mm); there are at least ten regularly used sizes, which are not interchangeable. Some frames/seat posts utilize sleeves to obtain the fit, but these may not be sufficiently reliable. Most seat posts are stamped with their size in millimetres. If not, measure the diameter with vernier callipers. If you do not have an existing post or if it is the wrong size, good shops have special sizing tools; you cannot measure the frame opening accurately even with vernier callipers. Most road racing and touring bikes use 27.2 or 27.0mm posts. MTBs commonly use 26.6, 26.8 and 27.0mm posts.

Most seat posts are adjusted with a single 6mm allen key from below, acting on a set-back, serrated rocking cradle. These designs do not always allow precise saddle angle adjustment. Straight-through models with twin bolts on either side of the post position you 15mm further forward than the standard design. These usually have a smooth cradle arrangement that allows precise adjustment without increments. Cheaper bikes use a plain tube with a separate clip that normally comes with the saddle. Do not ride on a loose saddle, as you will wear the clamp serrations, thereafter making the saddle impossible to tighten.

Seat posts have a marked safety limit giving 6.5cm (2½in) minimum insertion into the frame. It is potentially dangerous to exceed this limit and you may damage your frame if you do. Lengths up to 30cm (12in) or more are available in most diameters.

Fitting and Adjusting the Seat Post and Saddle

Summary – Fitting and Adjusting the Seat Post and Saddle

30 minutes

When?
- To improve your riding position
- Every six months to prevent seizure in frame

Preparation/Notes
- A new post is almost inevitably scratched as soon as you insert it, particularly if it is the wrong diameter or your seat tube is poorly finished, making it unreturnable to your dealer
- To prevent visible scratching, establish your exact needs first and do not insert the seat post beyond your correct saddle height.

A poorly finished seat tube can scratch the seat post. You can improve it by having it reamed out by a frame builder, something you may have to do anyway with a correctly sized seat post that will not go down far enough. Alternatively you can check for rough edges, especially around the clamp slot. Use a needle file and fine emery paper to smooth things. This is best done with the bike upside down to prevent filings finding their way into the bottom bracket bearings, if they are the cup and cone type.

Fitting the Saddle

If you are fitting the saddle to an integral seat post, note the order of the pieces, remove them and grease the bolt threads. Reassemble, clamping the saddle's rails between the clamp pieces, checking that each is the correct way up, and the right way round, if relevant. If the saddle rails are wider than the clamp, squeeze them in gently with slip-joint pliers or a vice. With the clamp loose enough to allow the saddle to move, set the rails to your desired fore-aft position and set level, then tighten the clamp bolt firmly.

If the saddle has a twin bolt design, tighten each bolt a few turns at a time. You need to tighten the bolts evenly, as tightening one more than the other will pull the saddle down towards it, so keep noting the saddle position. Tighten until firm.

If you have a plain tube seat post and separate clamp, again note the order of the pieces and grease the threads. Fit the clamp to the saddle so that it sits below the saddle rail. Only fit it the other way up as a last resort to lower the saddle further; if you do this you may find that the saddle top makes contact with the clip as you go over bumps, and that the clamp nuts are harder to reach. Now fit the saddle to the seat post with the clamp bolt behind it and the clamp bottom resting on the shoulder post's shoulder; fit it the other way round if you need a more forward position. Set the saddle level and tighten the bolt. If there are nuts on each side, tighten them evenly so that an equal amount of bolt protrudes on each side.

Fitting the Seat Post

Fitting a seat post is much easier with the saddle fitted; do not worry about the saddle's exact cradle clamp position until after the post is fitted.

When fitting a saddle, ensure separate clamp designs sit properly over the post.

Fully loosen or remove the binder bolt. Liberally apply copper-based anti-seize grease to all sections of the post that will be in the frame and the frame's seat clamp threads. Insert the post, sliding it in firmly to your correct height. Align it with the top tube. Replace and tighten the frame's seat clamp, taking care not to over-tighten and stretch it – with a correctly fitting post, the clamp slot should not pull in towards the top, but be straight. The post should slide without difficulty to any required height, but an oversize post may only enter the frame up to 3 or 4cm (1½in) or so. Seat posts must be fitted with any aero section or fluting above the top of the seat tube in order to prevent water running into it. As long as you have 65mm (2½in) of post in the frame, you can cut off any excess post with a hacksaw.

Freeing a Seized Post

Initially this is easiest when the bike is complete. Remove the frame's seat post binder bolt. Apply penetrant to the frame/post interface. If your bottom bracket allows it, you could also apply penetrant from below. Use the saddle to apply as much leverage as possible to both twist and pull it free. A valued saddle may be better exchanged for a discarded one to avoid damage. Leave for a few hours and repeat.

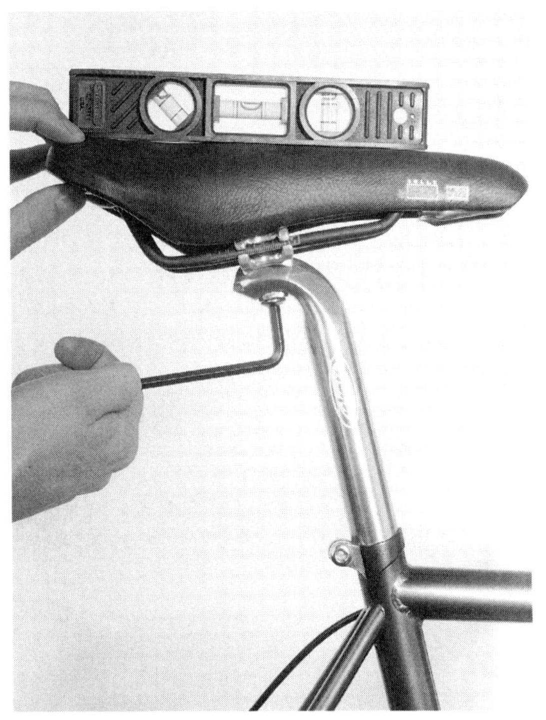

Use a spirit level to set the saddle level, but ensure that you are working with the bike on a flat floor! Then tighten the clamp.

Once correctly positioned, tighten the frame's seat clamp.

If this does not work you will need a vice on a workbench; you may need to remove the wheels and other parts. Grip the post's cradle section firmly in the vice; you may need to fit a bar inside the post to stop it collapsing in. Twist the frame relative to the seat post. The post will begin to come free often with a crack or creaking sound. Stand on the bench if necessary, twisting, pulling and applying penetrant. Finally, you may need to have the seat tube reamed out, as little bits of aluminium can be left stuck to the inside.

THE HANDLEBARS

Buying Handlebars and Stems

You should take the following into account when buying any handlebar or stem: stem choice may determine which bars can be used, which may then determine brake and gear lever choice.

The Fork Column

Conventional stems clamp inside the fork column, while Aheadset stems clamp on the outside of a threadless column and have very limited height adjustment. Both types are designed for either 1, 1⅛ and 1¼in outside diameters.

Clamp and Bar Compatibility

Bar clamps vary, and must be exactly sized. Using the wrong size can lead to cracking of the stem clamp. Same-make combinations are usually best (*see* table).

Stem Length and Rise

These determine your riding position. A change in stem length can affect the weight distribution and handling. A longer stem puts more weight on the front wheel, making steering slower, while a shorter stem can make the steering feel more skittish. Cinelli, 3TTT and DiaCompe make stems that allow you to change bars without removing the levers, grips and so on.

Material

Stems can be made from aluminium alloy (cast, cold-forged or hollow-tubed), steel (usually CrMo tube) or titanium. The material and design will affect the stem's stiffness, which has important implications for hard racing use, heavier riders, and those using tri-bars.

Brake and Gear Controls

These are not normally interchangeable between MTB bars, which are generally

Exact clamp size	*Recommended stems and bars*	*Notes*
26.4mm	Cinelli	Cinelli's own size and copies
26.0mm	3TTT, Mavic, Modolo, most ITM	highest-quality bars and stems
25.4mm	SR, Kalloy, some ITM, all MTB	cheaper drop bars/stems

22.2mm in diameter, and alloy drop and 'all-rounder' roadster-type bars, which are 24mm.

Fitting and Adjusting Handlebars

Summary – Fitting and Adjusting Handlebars

⚒ 15 minutes (to adjust)

When?

- To change the bars or stem
- To prevent seizure of the stem in the forks and creaking. If the bars creak, this is usually caused by a very dry interface between the stem/fork column or the bars/stem. Disassemble, applying a smear of grease around the bar's central area. Also check for cracking!
- To prepare for headset overhaul
- To remove/fit Aheadset-type stems (*see* Chapter 3, Headset Overhaul)

Preparation/Notes

- You may need to release brake and gear cables, or remove the levers (*see* Chapters 6, 7 and 8 as appropriate)
- If removing the bars, remove all fittings, tape, grips and so on from one side

Removing the Handlebars from the Stem

Use a 5 or 6mm allen key as appropriate to remove the stem clamp bolt, so allowing the stem to open to its maximum. Wiggle the bars out of the stem by revolving them and trying different positions to get them past each bend; do not force them. Try levering open the stem a little; do not overdo it, however, or you could induce hairline cracks and also make it more difficult to reinsert the clamp bolt.

Fitting Handlebars to the Stem

Remove the clamp bolt. Slide the bars into the stem with great care – it is very easy to scuff them up. When you reach the central section of the bars keep the clamp facing down so that any scratches will be out of sight; prise the stem opening a little if necessary. Centre the bars, set the angle to suit you and tighten the clamp bolt. The straight part of drop bars normally point down slightly at about 10 degrees to the ground. Check that the bars cannot move in the stem clamp by putting your weight on them and trying to twist them down with some force.

If the bars move in the stem, despite being properly tightened, check component compatibility. Try greasing the clamp bolt threads to make the bolt easier to tighten. You could try a wider section bar, or a special knurling tool that some bike shops have to effectively widen your bar diameter by 0.5mm. Refit the brake and gear levers.

Removing a Stem from the Frame

On conventional stems, undo the expander bolt about 10mm. You may need to use an allen T-wrench on recessed bolts. Give the bolt a sharp but protected knock to free its wedge; the bolt should drop and feel loose. The stem should now lift out with gentle twisting and pulling. If it proves resistant, apply penetrant to the stem/fork interface and try again. If you have already removed the wheel, put a hammer handle or piece of wood through the fork crown to brace the forks while you free the stem.

If you cannot free the stem, remove the headset lock-nut and liberally apply more penetrant, leave for a few hours,

Once you have set the bar's position, tighten the clamp bolt.

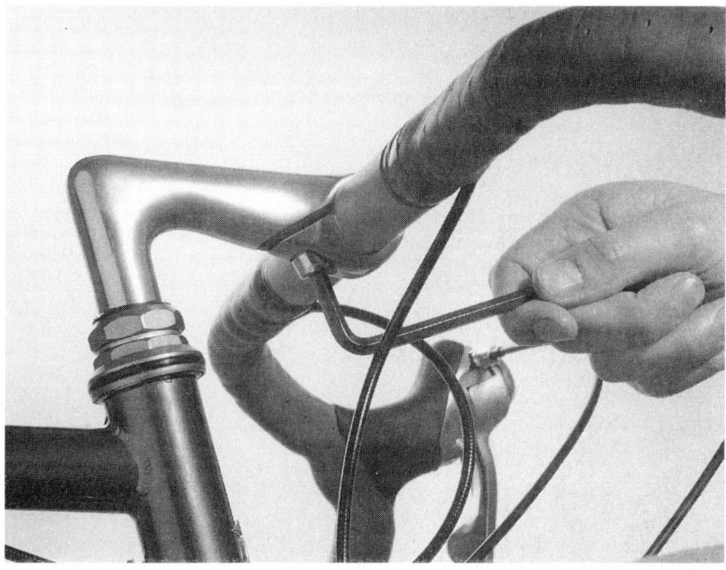

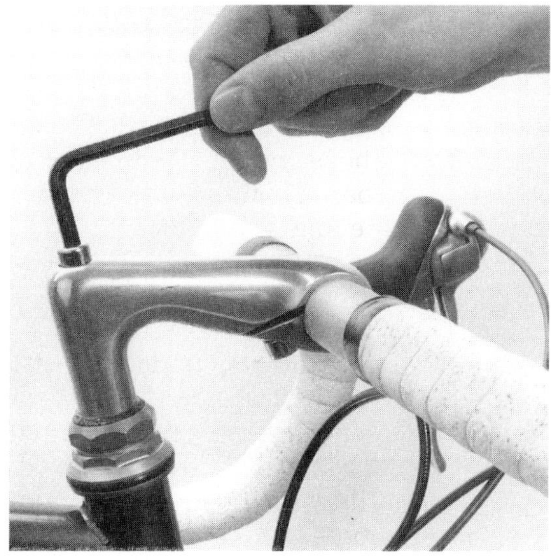

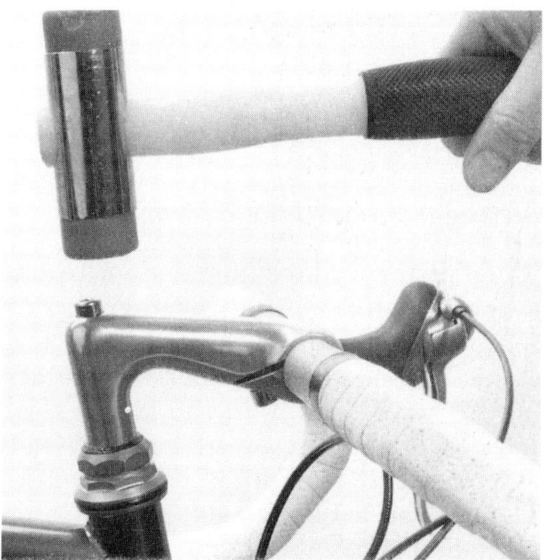

Undo the stem expander bolt about 10mm.

Use a soft-faced hammer or protection when knocking the stem bolt free.

then invert the bike and apply some to the bottom of the stem. Do not twist the bars too severely as you may bend the forks! Instead, remove the front wheel and grip the fork crown between blocks of wood in a vice; you can now exert a full twisting motion to break the stem free, but apply more penetrant as you go.

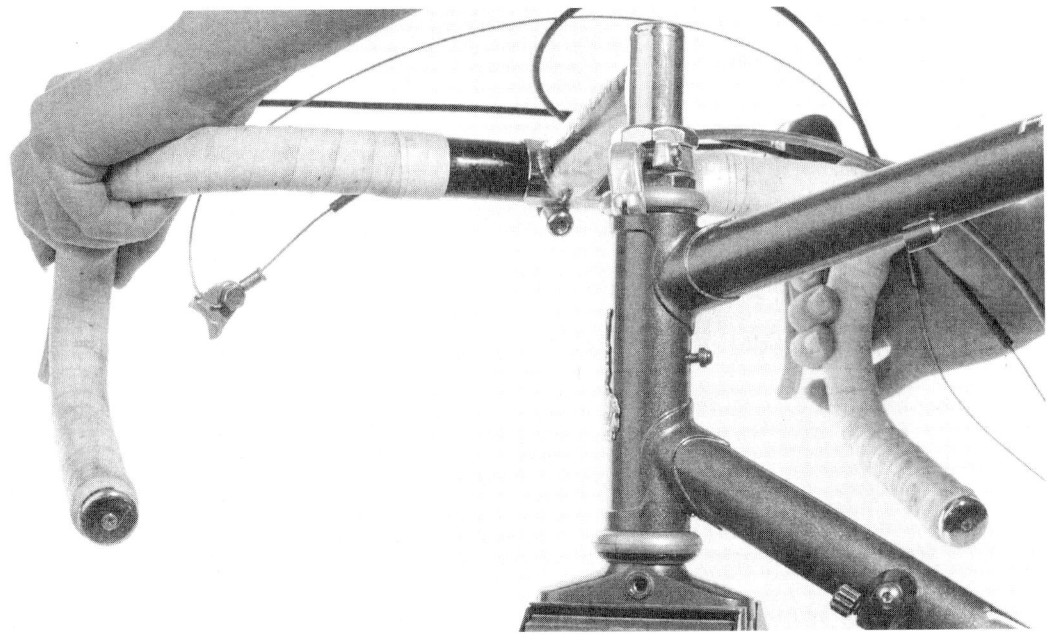

The last resort in stem removal. Secure the fork crown in a vice to avoid bending the forks.

Fitting a Stem to the Frame

When fitting a conventional stem, apply a liberal coating of anti-seize grease to the bolt, wedge and outside face of the stem. Tighten the expander bolt, locating the wedge's tang in the stem's slot. Insert the stem at desired height, not exceeding its maximum height mark. Tighten the expander bolt to nip it in place and check its alignment with the front wheel, then tighten firmly. Without undue force, twist the bars from side to side to make sure that they are secure.

To fit an Aheadset-type stem *see* Chapter 3, Aheadset Adjustment. It cannot be removed without readjusting the headset.

Grease the clamping wedge and hidden part of the stem.

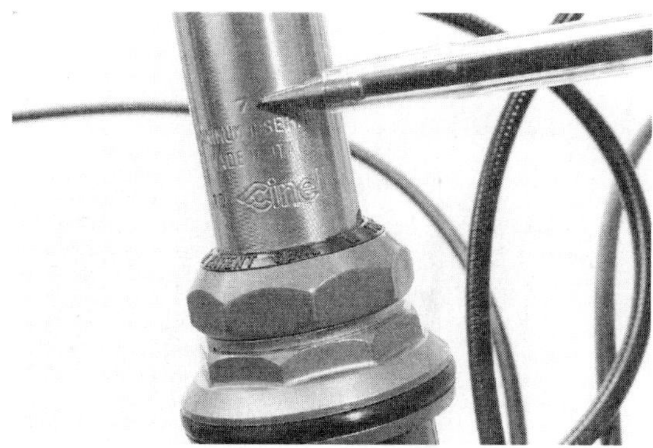

When fitting the stem, ensure that its maximum height mark is below the top of the lock-nut.

Fitting Handlebar Tape

Handlebar tape provides grip, comfort, a small degree of shock absorption, and insulates the rider's hand from the cold metal. Before you start, check that the brake levers are tight and correctly positioned and pull back their rubber hoods. Remove all the old bar tape and end plugs. Any concealed cables should be taped firmly to the bars in the channels provided. If not supplied separately, you will need to cut two 5cm (2in) pieces of bar tape.

Starting at the bottom, overlap the bar end by about 1cm (⅓in) and continue up the bars, overlapping each wind by about one-third of the width of the tape, but more on the inside of curves and less on the outside. Keep the tape taut but take care not to break it.

Just before you reach the brake lever, wrap one of the short pieces around the back of the lever. Secure it with the main length of tape, pulling this snugly against the bottom of the lever, then go round to its top. Avoid leaving uncovered areas – a figure of eight may be necessary. Keep the tape clear of moving parts of Campagnolo Ergopower shifters.

Continue in the same manner up to the bar's central sleeve and finish by trimming the tape to a taper and winding several turns of insulation tape around the end to secure it. Fold the first wind into the bars and secure by hammering in a handlebar plug.

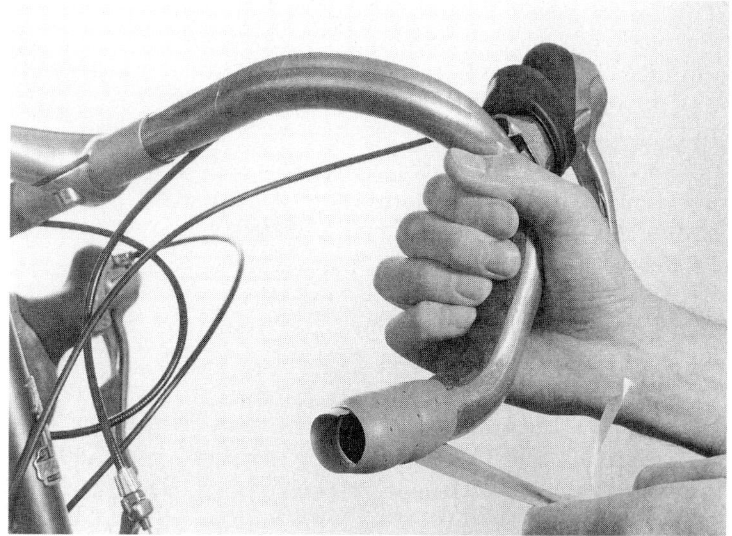

Tape is applied from the bottom up as this helps prevent unwanted lifting of its edges.

Use a 2in (5cm) piece of tape to help cover gaps around the brake lever.

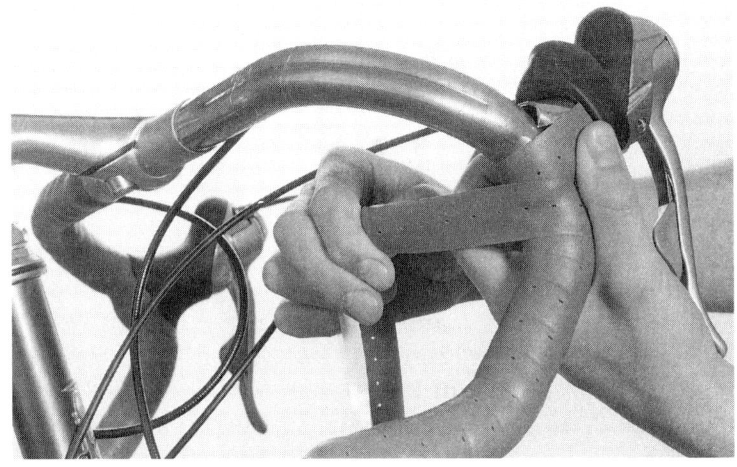

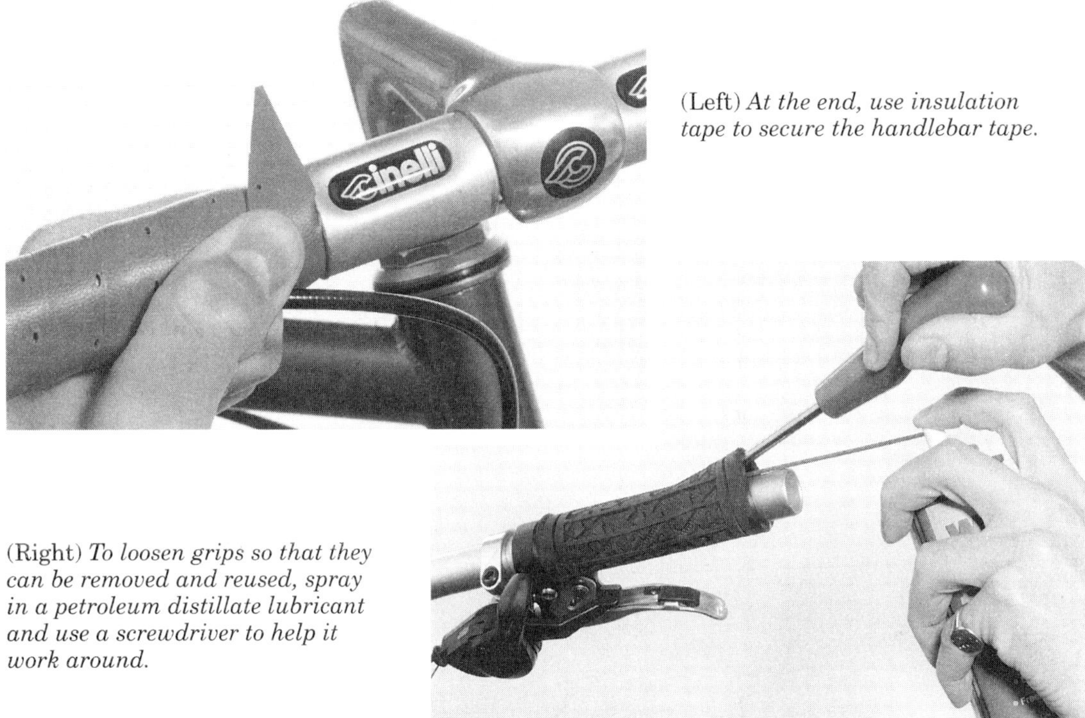

(Left) *At the end, use insulation tape to secure the handlebar tape.*

(Right) *To loosen grips so that they can be removed and reused, spray in a petroleum distillate lubricant and use a screwdriver to help it work around.*

Fitting Handlebar Grips

Check that there is room to fit the complete grips, and reposition the brake levers if necessary. Rubber grips are best fitted by putting them in very hot water for a few minutes, then sliding them on quickly before they cool. Alternatively, and for foam grips, a little saliva helps! Do not use soap, as this will make the grips slide off when it rains.

5 The Bottom Bracket, Chainset and Pedals

The pedals, chainset and bottom bracket take your efforts and convert them into a smooth flow, the chain taking this to the rear wheel. All your strength goes through these components, twisting them from side to side. Any weaknesses such as play, a loose cup or bearing wear will very quickly cause problems. Another more

The Chainset

The chainset is a slightly confusing term for the right crank and the chainrings (sprockets), which in most cases are bolted to its 'spider'. Triple chainsets with three chainrings are used on mountain and modern touring bikes and double chainsets with two chainrings are used on most road-racing bikes.

The very cheapest chainsets and those fitted to most ordinary bikes until the early 1980s were of the cottered type; these are fitted to the bottom bracket axle with cotter pins, in effect a wedge jamming the crank against a flat on the axle. Although rather crude, the cotter pin is actually quite easy to fit, and if fitted properly will be entirely reliable.

Virtually all modern cranks are now of the cotterless type – the crank has a tapered, squared recess bolted tight onto a matching axle. Instead of a tapered square, Shimano XTR and Dura Ace cranks now use a special spline.

(Below) *A section through a cottered bottom bracket crank and axle, seen end on.*

(Right) *A section through a typical cotterless crank and axle, seen from the side.*

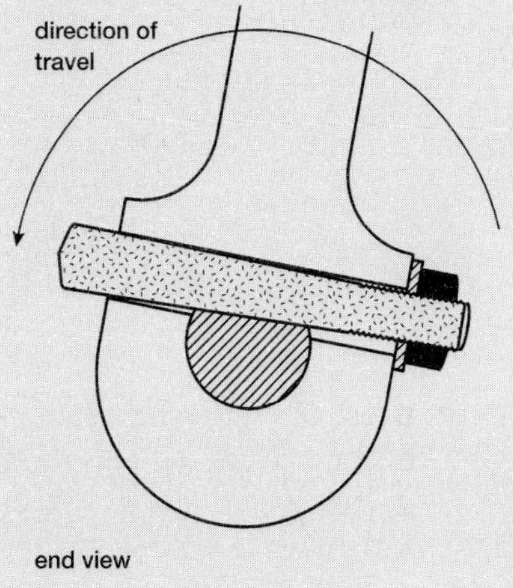

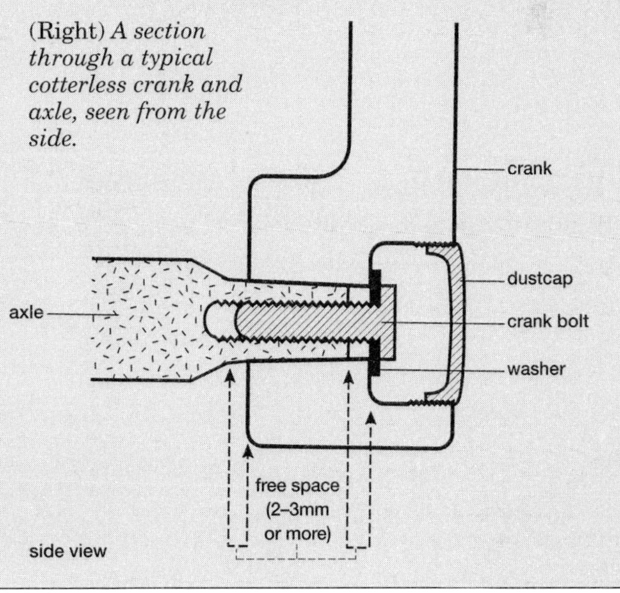

serious consequence is that the pedalling motion can induce the loose bearing cups to rock in the bottom bracket shell, stripping away its internal threads in the process. This can be very expensive to rectify, possibly resulting a trip to a custom frame builder to save a valued frame.

You must watch out for the cranks working loose. Riding on a loose crank will round off its square, meaning it will never tighten onto the spindle properly. If you detect an odd movement as you pedal or hear creaking noises, firmly grasp each crank in turn while you try to rock the other one against it. If you try this with both cranks you should be able to deduce which crank is loose, or whether you have another problem, such as loose bearings. A loose pedal can quickly destroy the threads in the crank.

THE BOTTOM BRACKET

By far the most common type of bottom bracket used for all quality bikes and most others is based on a threaded frame shell. You should check which thread type you have before you can proceed with disassembly and obtain replacements. By far the majority of bikes in the UK use the standard English dimensions given in bold in the table below. Within the standard bottom bracket shell two types of bearing unit can be used: cup and cone units and cartridge types (*see* Chapter 1).

Cup and Cone Units

Cup and cone units are made up of a separate axle, ball-bearings (loose or clipped) and bearing cups. The right cup is called the fixed cup because it screws into a fixed position in the frame. The left one is called the adjustable cup, and this determines the tightness of the bearings and is held in position by the lock-ring. Such units are found on older bikes of all types and on a few others, and are still common. Note, however, that availability is now very limited; French TA and Stronglight, and Taiwanese/Japanese

Thread type and size	*Bottom bracket width (nominal)*	*Cup thread direction*	
		right side	*left side*
English/ISO **(1,37/1.375in × 24tpi)**	**68mm**/73mm°	**left**	**right**
French* (35mm × 1mm)	68mm	right	right
Italian* (36mm × 24tpi)	70mm	right	right
Raleigh** (1⅜in × 26tpi)	71mm	left	right

° Some MTB bottom bracket shells use a special 73mm shell

* French threads are no longer used. Older French frames and Italian ones sold in the UK may have their own or English threads.

** Raleigh bikes (and other brands made by them such as BSA, Triumph and Rudge) manufactured before 1985. A bottom bracket width of 71mm and a fixed cup with 16mm spanner flats are sure indications of this thread size.

Tange brands can still be obtained and a few other unbranded/ old stock models. Replacement by a suitable cartridge unit is normally recommended when the axle or cups are worn.

Cartridge Units

Cartridge units are now standard on new bikes. These have become popular because they are easy to fit and because of the many consumer-end problems of maintaining the cup and cone type unit. Most cartridge units require no adjustment, and can normally be fitted and forgotten for two to three years. Upmarket brands allow you to replace the bearing cartridges alone, which can make them better value in the long term. If you are fitting a high-quality cartridge bottom bracket, the threads must be precision tapped 'in line' and the facing checked – a task for your dealer.

Bottom Bracket Shell Problems

Poor bottom bracket threads make it difficult to screw in the cartridge or cups without cross-threading them. Poor facing (where the cups are not at ninety degrees to the threads) means that as the cups are tightened they can push out of line and be difficult to tighten fully home, which carries the risk of stripping the frame threads.

To check the facing, screw in a pair of greased quality cups taking great care to ensure they are not cross-threaded (remember that most bottom brackets are left-threaded on their right side). The right side's flange (or lock-ring in the case of some cartridge units) and the left side's lock-ring should butt squarely against the full circumference of the bottom bracket shell face. Cups should screw in without free play or undue tightness. If there is paint in the threads remove it with Nitromores paint remover and a tooth brush. Facing is not an issue if using a cartridge/cartridge cup without an external flange. A good bike shop has the special tools to resolve these problems.

Buying a Bottom Bracket Bearing Unit

Do not buy anything until you have removed and checked the original's thread type and axle dimensions. You should aim to preserve the chain-line – the distance from the right side of the bottom bracket shell to the right end of the axle. Use a long straight edge to check this, laying it flat across the central chainring and noting its position relative to the rear cogs.

The chain-line: the chain wheels should be central to the cassette/freewheel or in an exact line with the rear sprocket on single-speed and hub-gear bikes.

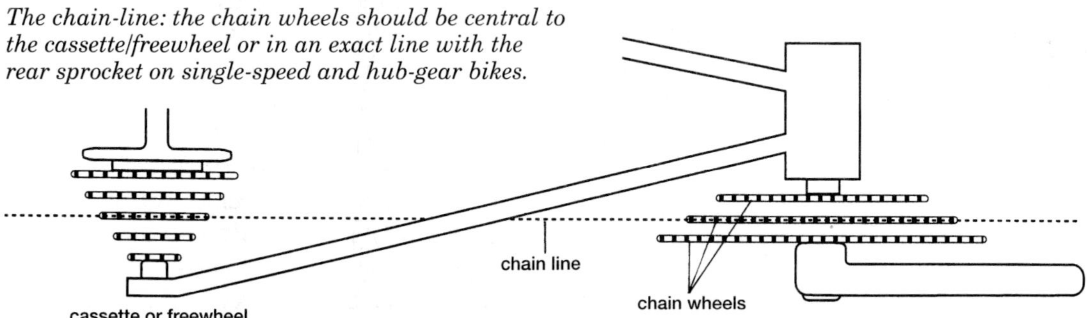

Cup and Cone

Assuming your original axle was correctly sized, your replacement axle must have the same dimensions between the shoulders, and from the shoulder to the longest (right) end of the axle. Equally, the thickness of the fixed cup's outer face must be the same as the original's to maintain the same chain-line and ensure that about four threads of the adjustable cup will protrude for the lock-ring. Thicker cup ends than your original can be compensated for by narrower axle shoulders and vice versa. A spacer can also be used behind the cup; those used for Sturmey Archer hub gear sprockets are ideal.

It is generally best to use the same make of axle and cups; if their dimensions vary, the bearings may not run in the centre of their tracks. This can be checked by loosely assembling the components with a little grease, rotating the axle, and checking the ball track.

Cartridge Units

These generally suit 68mm shells unless otherwise specified. Some units fit 68 and 73mm shells; check with the dealer or the technical information supplied. Most cartridge units are symmetrical, with equal left and right axle protrusion. The quoted size refers to the total axle width, but check like with like to ensure the chain-line will be unaffected. Some models offer a few millimetres of chain-line adjustment.

Axle/Crank Fit

Most modern cotterless axle/crank combinations are compatible, but check as described. Tighten the crank onto the axle, remove the bolt and check that the underside of the crank is not resting on the axle shoulder – you may need to grind the shoulder back a bit if it does. Also check that the axle end is at least 2mm from the bottom of the crank extractor hole. Cottered crank axles have a standard fit.

BOTTOM BRACKET OVERHAUL

Cup and Cone Brackets

Summary – Cup and Cone Overhaul

⏲⏲ 1 hour

When?
- At overhaul intervals
- If knocking or strange sounds occur
- If the cranks wobble when grasped firmly and pushed from side to side
- If adjustment alone (*see* below) does not result in smooth running

Specialist Tools
- The basic tools may not remove the fixed cup – *see* below for alternatives

Preparation
- Remove the cranks (*see* below)
- You will normally need twenty-two ¼in ball-bearings
- You may want to consider fitting a cartridge or injection maintenance unit

Disassembly

Remove the lock-ring by unscrewing it anticlockwise. Tools vary, but whatever tool you choose should fit well. Remove the adjusting cup by unscrewing it anticlockwise. Most cups have two or more holes for

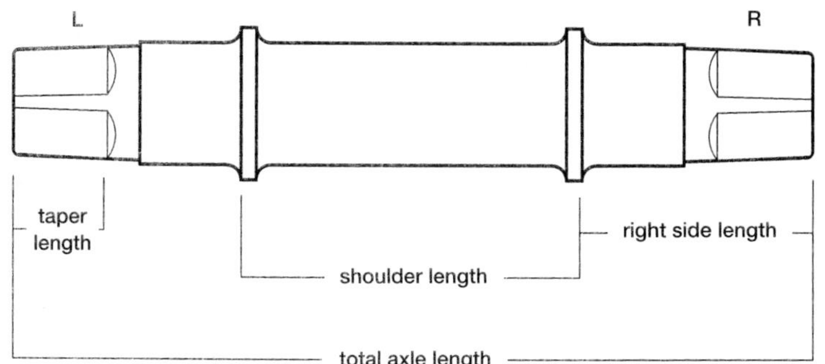

The critical dimensions of a cotterless cup and cone bottom bracket unit.

Ashtabula Chainsets

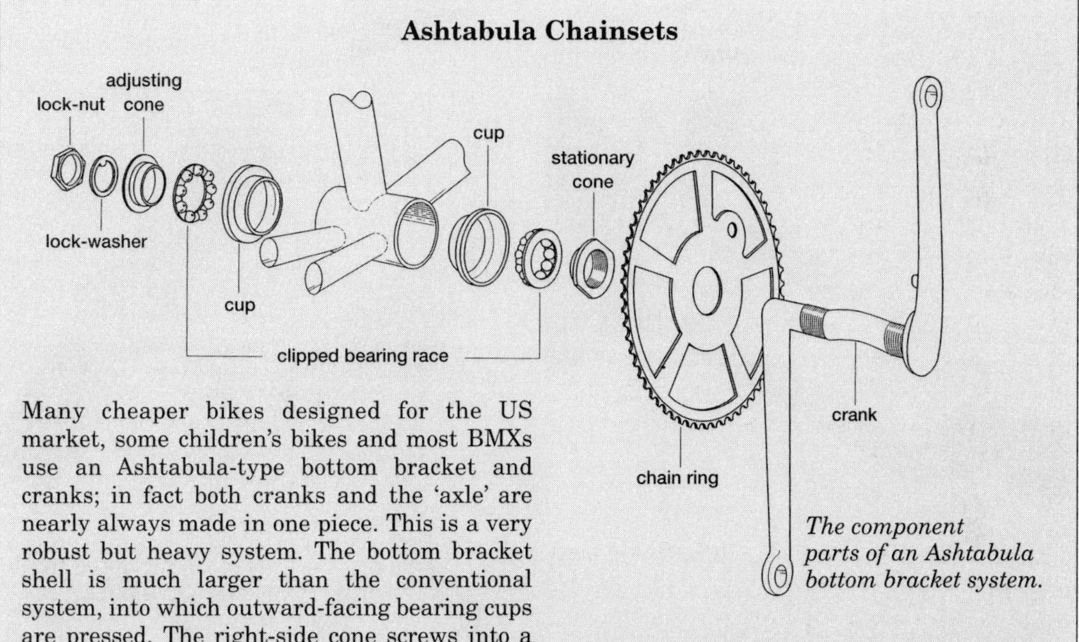

The component parts of an Ashtabula bottom bracket system.

Many cheaper bikes designed for the US market, some children's bikes and most BMXs use an Ashtabula-type bottom bracket and cranks; in fact both cranks and the 'axle' are nearly always made in one piece. This is a very robust but heavy system. The bottom bracket shell is much larger than the conventional system, into which outward-facing bearing cups are pressed. The right-side cone screws into a fixed position on the 'axle' and everything is then threaded through the frame for attachment of the left-side adjusting cone, followed by the lock washer and lock-ring (left-hand threads are used). If the assembly is not one piece, a special cotterless spindle is used, threaded for the cones, and normal cotterless cranks are utilized. (Another design, the Thompson, also exists, which is similar except that the bottom bracket shell is closer in size to a conventional one.)

To adjust an Ashtabula bottom bracket, loosen the lock-ring (clockwise), tighten the cone with a screwdriver or chisel in its slot, then back it off one-eighth of a turn. Retighten the lock-ring. To overhaul, the left pedal must be removed, and the parts unscrewed and slid over the crank.

a peg spanner. If your cup has flats, a large adjustable spanner, kept perfectly level against the cup, works best. Lay the whole bike on the floor and press down on it if needed. If the cup is stiff, apply penetrant. As you take the cup out, keep the bike upright in case loose ball-bearings run down the tubes. The axle will now just pull out. Remove any plastic liner and the bearings from the other side.

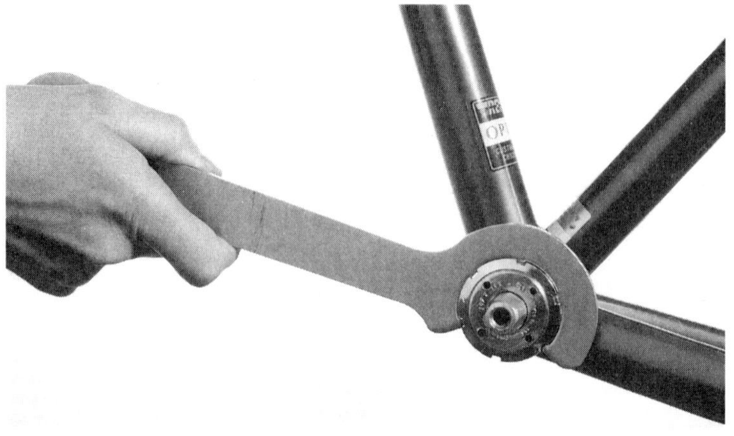

Be careful not to gouge into the frame as you remove the lock-ring.

(Below left) *Keep the peg spanner fully engaged in the cup as you unscrew it.*

(Below right) *The left axle is stained but perfectly usable, but the right one is very worn. The uneven wear and scouring are caused by riding it while too loose, or with the cup askew.*

(Right) *A clipped bearing race, before and after use. These can break up prematurely, destroying the cups and spindle.*

Clean and inspect the axle and cups with the fixed cup still in situ – a torch may help. Look for pitting, scouring and general unevenness of the bearing surfaces, or a deep or wide bearing track; compare with a new one if you are unsure of the wear. Replace the worn items – cups are normally best replaced as a pair.

Removing and Fitting the Fixed Cup

If you need to remove the fixed cup, use one of the following methods according to your resources. In all cases, you should ensure that the fixed cup is tight before proceeding. Remember it normally has a left-hand thread. When refitting, grease the threads and start the cup into the frame by hand, ensuring it is not cross-threaded. It must be tightened firmly, but be careful with high leverage methods, as you do not want to strip the frame threads.

Most better-quality cups take a 35 or 36mm closed-end spanner (the type that normally come as a set of three to fit the bottom bracket and headset). Unless the cup is exceptionally tight, these spanners are quite adequate. You can use a large adjustable, but it must be unworn and a good fit, because if you slip it is quite easy to damage the spanner flats. Keep the spanner flat against the cup and turn right to undo a left-hand thread.

If the cup is exceptionally tight, or offers little material to hold on to, a 16×100mm bolt and two fitting nuts from an engineers' supplier can be used. Screw one nut about 3cm (1½in) down onto the bolt. For standard left-threaded cups put the threaded end through the fixed cup from the left side and screw the other nut onto the threads protruding from the cup. Do it up tight and keep turning – the fixed cup will unscrew.

You could also try gripping the cup flats in the jaws of a vice, while ensuring that the frame is horizontal. You will probably need a friend to help. Turn the frame clockwise to loosen the cup if it has

A special fixed-cup spanner is the usual way to remove and fit fixed cups.

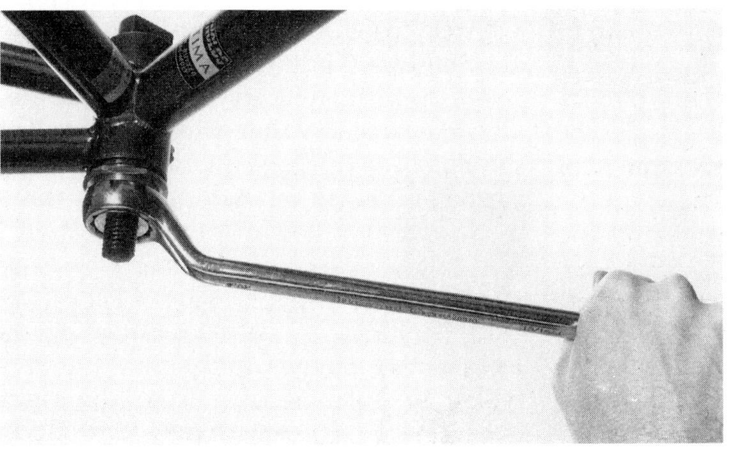

The Jackson Fixed Cup Tool is a refined version of the bolt method of removing a fixed cup – useful for anyone who works regularly on older bikes.

Be careful not to dislodge the bearings as you reassemble the unit.

> **Summary – Replacing a Cartridge Bottom Bracket**
>
> 1 hour
>
> *When?*
> - If play, roughness or squeaking develops
>
> *Special Tools*
> Dedicated tools to fit your cartridge are normally required
>
> *Preparation*
> - Remove the cranks (*see* below)
> - If your cartridge unit design allows it, you may want to fit new bearing cartridges; these are fitted in a similar manner to those used in hubs (*see* Chapter 9). It is advisable to consult the manufacturer or your dealer.

the usual left-hand thread. This method is awkward but can be effective.

Assembly and Adjustment

Wipe out the inside of the cup and bottom bracket shell. Grease the threads, put a layer of grease around both cups, insert eleven ¼in new ball bearings and cover with more grease.

Push the axle into the shell, longest side first. Keep it well pressed in while you push in the bearing sleeve (if there is one, this helps prevent condensation and debris in the seat tube from reaching the bearings) and screw in the adjusting cup until axle play is just taken away. Replace the lock-ring and keeping the fixed cup in position, tighten it till it fits snugly. Check that the axle turns freely without play; it may help to fit the right crank. Loosen the lock-ring and try a different adjustment of the adjustable cup if necessary.

Cartridge Brackets

Removal

For Shimano and similar cartridges, position the spines of the removal tool in the right (chain wheel) side of the cartridge. Use a large adjustable spanner or socket handle to unscrew and remove the cartridge clockwise (unless you have right-hand threads). Repeat for the left-side retaining collar, which has a normal thread, so turn it anticlockwise. Take care not to damage the cartridge or collar as the notched material is often made of resin or soft alloy. Damaging it can make it a costly expert's job to remove.

If you have a cartridge with lock-rings, such as Stronglight or Royce, note that the alloy cups and lock-rings are very easy to gouge up without a correctly fitting or ideally dedicated tool that grips most or all of the notches. Unscrew the lock-rings and cups as directed for cup and cone units (above), taking note of thread directions.

Fitting

Grease the threads and screw the cartridge in anticlockwise from the right side. With Shimano-type cartridges,

Use a dedicated remover to extract first the cartridge from the right side, then the retaining collar.

(Left) *Start the fit of the cartridge by hand to ensure that the threads are not crossed.*

continue until the cup sits tightly against the frame. With lock-ring cartridges continue until about four threads remain visible.

Grease the threads and screw in the retaining collar or cup from the left side until it tightens, either against the cartridge or frame. Fit the lock-ring if applicable. To adjust the chain-line of lock-ring cartridges, screw the cups left or right as appropriate, ensuring that they are snug against the cartridge and that the lock-rings are fully engaged and tight when you have the adjustment you want.

CRANK REMOVAL AND FITTING

Cotterless Cranks

Removal

Many modern crank bolts use an 8mm allen key and include an integral dust cap. If not, you will first need to remove the dust cap. If it has two small holes, use an adjustable peg spanner or the tips

Summary – Refitting Cotterless Cranks

⚒ 30 minutes

When?

- If cranks loose or creaking
- For access to bottom bracket unit
- To replace chainrings
- If all chainrings appear 'bent'
- Do not remove cranks unnecessarily!

Preparation/Notes

- Ensure that your crank extractor is a perfect fit (*see* Chapter 2)
- A few cranks use a special fitment that enables you to remove the crank simply by unscrewing the crank bolt; these models are identified by a central allen bolt surrounded by a collar with two small holes. These fitments can also be retrofitted to most cranks.

of a pair of needle-nose pliers. A folded-over spoke (and pliers or adjustable spanner to hold firmly) will also work. Apply penetrant if it is tight. Be careful not to ruin the dust cap, as it might then prove very difficult to remove. If it does break, try drilling two new holes in it. Slot types can be undone with a wide screwdriver or coin; other types may require a 5mm allen key or may on occasion be prised off.

To remove the crank bolt, use a 14 or 15mm socket (often incorporated into the back of a crank extractor) or a 6 or 8mm allen key, as appropriate. Guard against slipping, as the chain wheel teeth are very sharp; it can help to squeeze the crank arm against the spanner. If using an allen key you may need to apply extra leverage to it with a tube or adjustable spanner. Be sure to remove the washer under the bolt (not usually used with allen bolts).

If you have a separate dust cap, remove it with an appropriate tool.

Guard against slipping as you remove the crank bolt.

Screw in the extractor body, taking care not to damage the threads.

(Below) *Tighten the inner bolt to pull the crank off.*

Grease the extractor and crank threads, and the end that will butt against the axle to avoid excessive friction and galling. Ensure that the bolt section is fully retracted, then screw the extractor body fully into the crank threads; to be sure not to cross-thread it, start it with your fingers. The extractor follows the line of the spindle, not the outer face of the crank, which is not always at 90 degrees to the threads, and so is not a suitable reference point. If you are at all unsure, unscrew the extractor, look closely at the threads to check that they are not damaged, and try again. Use a spanner to ensure it is fully seated.

Now screw the extractor's inner bolt section in while holding the crank firmly. Keep going until the crank is eased off its taper. Remove the extractor from the crank. If the worst happens and you damage the thread, good bike shops have a Bicycle Research tool that can sometimes repair it; if not they can at least remove the crank for you with a special prising tool.

Fitting

Use a degreaser to clean the tapered axle end free from oil and grease. Dirt can stop the crank from fitting snugly. Any lubricant will allow the crank to slide on further than it is designed to, with the risk of cracking the crank. Push the crank over the axle and replace the washer and greased bolt or nut. Tighten firmly, as tightly as you can manage with 15cm (6in) spanner. Replace the dust caps, being careful not to cross-thread them. It is very important to use dust caps, as they keep dirt out of the threads and help stop the retaining bolt underneath from rusting onto the spindle. Recheck the crank bolt tightness after 100 miles (160km).

If you have weight-saving aluminium alloy or titanium bolts, first fit conventional steel bolts, tightening the crank to the spindle. Now remove them and fit the alloy bolts, just nipping them tight. This procedure will often cure creaking if you have allen-type crank bolts. If creaking persists you can try a smear of grease on the axle tapers but keep a note of how far the crank travels on (*see* diagram on page 63).

Cottered Cranks

Refitting Cottered Cranks

🔧🔧/🔧 30 minutes plus

When?
- If the crank is loose
- For access to the bottom bracket unit

Special Tools
- Drift (an old dimpled-end bottom bracket axle is ideal)
- Vice

Preparation/Notes
- You will need new good-quality cotter pins to refit the cranks; 'Reliant' brand are recommended. British pins are 9.5mm but some European cranks require a 9.0mm 'Continental' pin. Cranks can be drilled out to the 9.5mm standard.
- Although this job is normally straightforward it can become problematic, if not infuriating!

Removal

Cotter pins that have become loose and have still been ridden can have a V-shaped nick worn into them. This can catch against the edge of the axle flat, preventing it from coming out. If you suspect this is the case, try twisting the cranks round the spindle a few degrees (normally to bring them back to 180 degrees to each other); you may need to use some force.

Remove the nut and washer. Position the drift over the threaded end. Hit hard and squarely with a heavy hammer. A hard blow is much more effective than lots of faint-hearted ones, so be brave! You may want to hold the drift with pliers or a vice grip. If the pin does not budge easily, repeat the hammer blow with the crank positioned over something to give it more support, such as a vice, and open the jaw just enough to allow the pin to pass through. This will protect the bearings and bottom bracket shell while increasing the force applied to the cotter pin.

If the pin bends, use the drift to bend it back – the threaded section should snap off; alternatively, cut it off with a hacksaw. Apply penetrant and continue with a suitably sized drift or old pedal axle, which works brilliantly. As a last resort you can drill the pin out. Centre-punch it, then drill right through with a 3mm bit, then 5mm. When hit, the pin should now collapse and come free. If it does not, drill it out a little more.

Fitting

Cotter pins are fitted so that on the crank's down stroke, the nut is facing upwards; thus the pins go in opposite directions to each other. Put the crank in the ten o' clock position and, while looking down on it, set the bottom bracket axle's upper flat edge level with the crank's cotter hole; the crank's outer face should be level with the axle end. Fit the pin with its flat side parallel to the axle flat, then give it a couple of sharp knocks with a hammer. The threaded part should protrude about 8mm; the nut must engage by all its threads and must not 'bottom out' on the pin's shoulder. It will probably need to be tapped free and filed to achieve this.

If the pin needs filing, secure it in a vice, flat side up and level. Use a flat file to remove metal evenly from the whole of the flat. Take off a little at a time and then recheck the fit. Once the fit is correct, hit it fully home with some force, using support if possible. Fit the washer and tighten the nut firmly. Check that the cranks are at 180 degrees to each other; additional filing of the pin positions the crank further clockwise. If you continue to have problems with the fit, try a different axle. If the pin was loose to begin with, buy a special 'unmilled' pin.

CHAINSET PROBLEMS

Chainrings wear out at approximately a half to a third of the rate of the cassette; much more rapidly if ridden with a worn chain. Very small rings of around 22 to 26 teeth can wear much more quickly,

(Above) *To remove a cotter pin, support the bottom bracket and use a drift, or old axle, to impart maximum force.*

Remove material from the cotter's flat edge, testing the fit as you go.

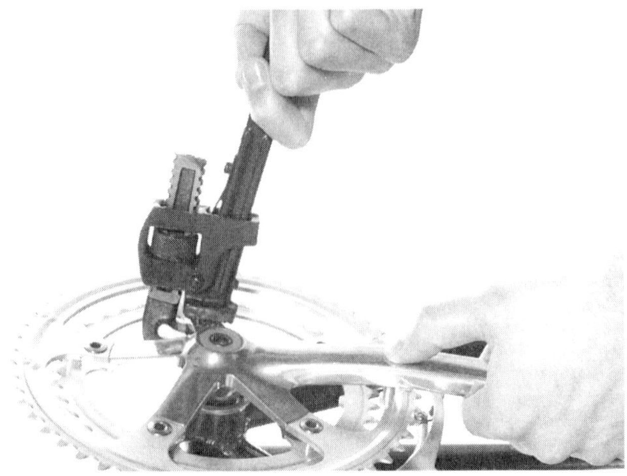

Straightening a chain wheel spider with a monkey wrench.

(Below) *The Bicycle Research chain wheel straightener in use*

especially if made from aluminium alloy; for this reason, harder-wearing stainless steel is commonly used. Chain and chainring wear is covered in more depth in Chapter 6, Transmission Wear and Chain Maintenance.

Chainrings can often appear to be bent or out of true. This will interfere with gear-shifting and can dump the chain, and the chainset will rub irritatingly on your front derailleur. Often the chainset is not square on the axle taper; a likely cause of out of true chainrings if both (or all three) chainrings follow the same line of untruth. Try refitting the chainset, ensuring that the axle tapers are clean, and tighten fully.

Sometimes the same symptoms can be caused by a bent spider; check for this by measuring between a frame tube and the tops of the spiders – they should all be the same distance apart. A monkey wrench can be used to apply leverage and bend the spider back.

If only a single ring is out of true, rotate the cranks and identify the high and low points. Use an appropriate tool to twist the ring back, or hit it carefully, side on, with a soft-faced hammer.

Bent teeth cause the chain to jump or catch. A tooth can become bent from hitting a rock or from a forced gear-shift. Use an adjustable spanner to bend it back. Inner rings may need to be removed and held in a vice to do this.

A spill can bend a crank. Cranks of a straight profile can simply be checked with a straight edge. Modern 'curved'-profiled cranks can be difficult to check. Try fitting a pedal you know to be good, then sighting from above; check that at all points of the crank's rotation, the pedal remains totally in line (at 180 degrees) to the bottom bracket axle. Unless they are made of steel, which can be bent back, damaged cranks are usually best replaced.

Buying Chainrings

Good-quality chainsets allow you to remove the chainrings and replace them. Replacement chainrings should have the same number of teeth as the original, unless you want to change your gear ratios. If changing the number of teeth, you may need to take derailleur capacity into account (*see* Chapter 6).

The BCD (bolt circle diameter) of the spider must be taken into account, as this will determine the range of sizes available. Adapters can be used to fit a third or smaller than standard chainring to a double chainset.

Most modern chainrings have a combination of ramps, pins and gates to help the chain shift more cleanly from one ring to another.

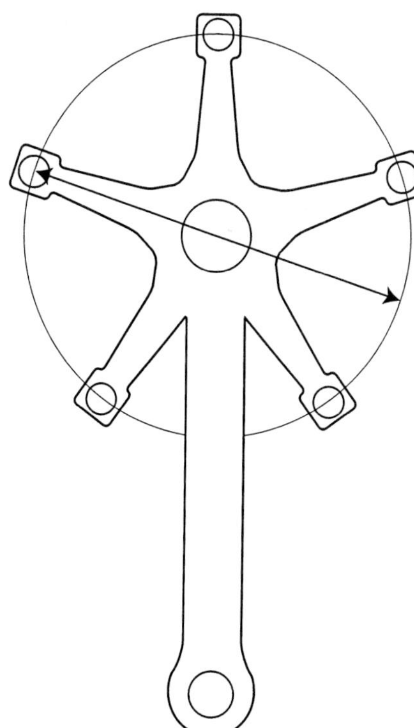

The BCD is the diameter across the circle made by the centres of the chain wheel bolts.

Replacing Chainrings

Summary – Replacing Chainrings

30 minutes

When?
- When worn, damaged or changing gear ratios

Special Tools
- Chainset back-nut spanner (a coin or edge of a cone spanner may substitute)

Preparation
- Remove chainset (*see* above)
- Consider derailleur capacity (*see* Chapter 6)

Use a back nut spanner to help you tighten the chainring bolts.

Check the orientation of the original chainrings. Remove the chainring/s by loosening the attachment bolts; you may need to use a back-nut spanner to prevent the bolt simply rotating. Keep note of where the spacing pieces go. Clean the spider's mounting points and lightly grease them and the outside faces of the mounting bolts. Check the position of the new chainrings and note any recess for the bolt heads. Normally the flatter, more highly finished side faces outwards. The side with the more profiled ramping and small pegs, and the stamping showing the number of teeth usually faces inwards. A few chainrings have a small peg on their outside edge to prevent an over-shifted chain jamming between the crank and chainring.

Loosely assemble all the bolts, applying a little thread lock to each. Tighten the bolts to take up the slack, then little by little until tight; be careful, as it is easy to over-tighten the bolts, breaking them.

REMOVING AND FITTING PEDALS

Summary – Removing and Fitting Pedals

10 minutes

When?

- Pedal overhaul is easier if you remove pedals, but this is not essential
- Go through this routine occasionally as pedals can seize into the cranks, which is not what you need when packing your bike for travel.

Preparation / Notes

- All right pedals have a right-hand thread (usually stamped R or D) and all left pedals have a left-hand thread (usually stamped L or G)
- Many left pedal axles often additionally have a knurled outer
- Most pedals have a 9⁄16in axle, but some children's bikes have a ½in axle

The left pedal being removed; note the anticlockwise thread.

Removal

Undo the right pedal anticlockwise and the left pedal clockwise. Position yourself to gain maximum leverage without the crank moving. Take care, as a lot of effort may be needed to get it started, and try not to gash your hand on the chain wheel.

Fitting

Grease the pedal threads with anti-seize grease. Make sure that you start the correct pedal (*see* summary panel) into each crank and that it is not cross-threaded. The left pedal screws anticlockwise into the left crank. The right pedal clockwise into the right (chain wheel side) crank. To ensure that they will not unscrew, tighten firmly with a pedal spanner.

PEDAL OVERHAUL
Conventional Pedals

Conventional Pedal Overhaul

⚒⚒ 1 hour

When?

- At overhaul intervals, sooner if you hear ticking or clicking sounds or if the pedals do not spin freely or do so with a dry sound
- Adjust if play or stiffness is felt when rocking the pedal with your hand

Preparation/Notes

- It can help to remove the pedals
- Note that some pedals can look serviceable but under the dust cap, the end of the axle is riveted over
- For Shimano 1055 pedals, *see* Clipless Pedal Overhaul section

Most conventional pedals are of mediocre quality. This, combined with their vulnerability to road knocks and water and often poor initial greasing, means their life can be very short. If the pedal has a resin body, it can make more sense to drill a small hole in it and inject grease instead of replacing. Block the hole with a small self-tapping screw.

Disassembly

Remove the dust caps by either prising them off or unscrewing as appropriate. Try to remove them without causing any damage as spares can be hard to come by. Some are made from chromed plastic so may not be as strong as they first appear.

Unscrew the lock-nut and lift off the tanged washer. Use a screwdriver tip on the side of the cone to unscrew it. Lift off the pedal cage, being aware of any seals.

A ring spanner prevents burring of the lock-nut edges. The lock-nut can be hard to reach and surprisingly tight.

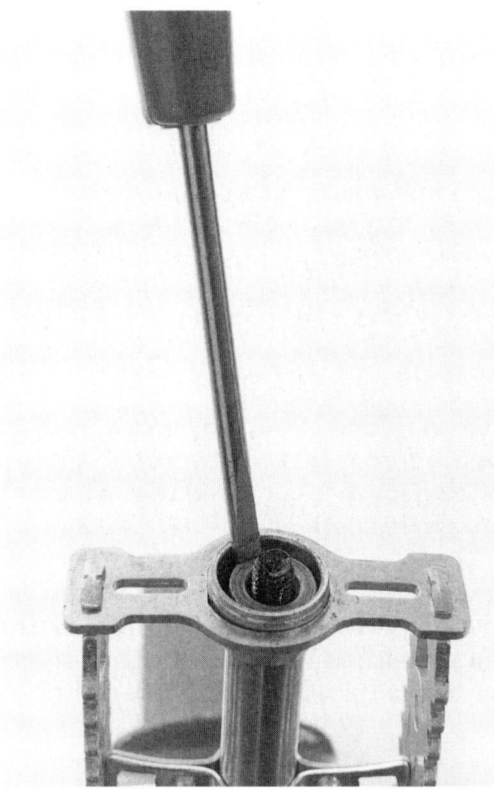

A screwdriver tip reaches in to unscrew the cone.

Check for Wear

Check the bearing size, then discard. Clean the inner races, cone and axle with degreaser, wipe clean and inspect for wear. Roll the axle on a sheet of glass; if it wobbles, it is bent and should be replaced as it could cause injury to your knee. Cones, axle races and the inner races may show scouring or pitting. Replace worn parts if you can; otherwise a small degree of wear can be tolerated.

Assembly and Adjustment

Grease each of the pedal cage's races and insert new ball-bearings of the correct size, shoulder to shoulder in their fully seated position. Leave a gap of one and a half ball-bearings. Replace any seals removed and put the same side axle through the pedal's inner side, press it home and check that it runs well on the bearings. Keeping the axle in place and being careful not to dislodge the bearings, fit the cone and tighten it

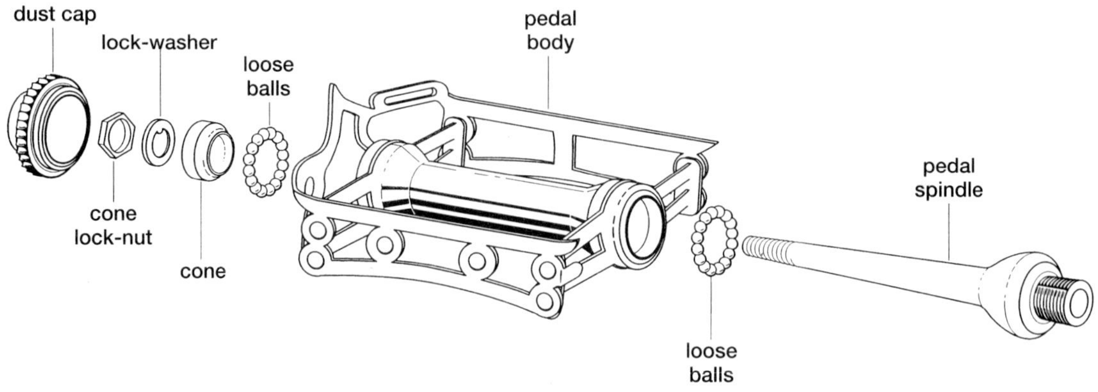

A typical conventional pedal.

Most pedals use 5⁄32 or 1⁄8 in bearings; stick them in shoulder to shoulder with a gap equal to one and a half bearings, then replace the axle.

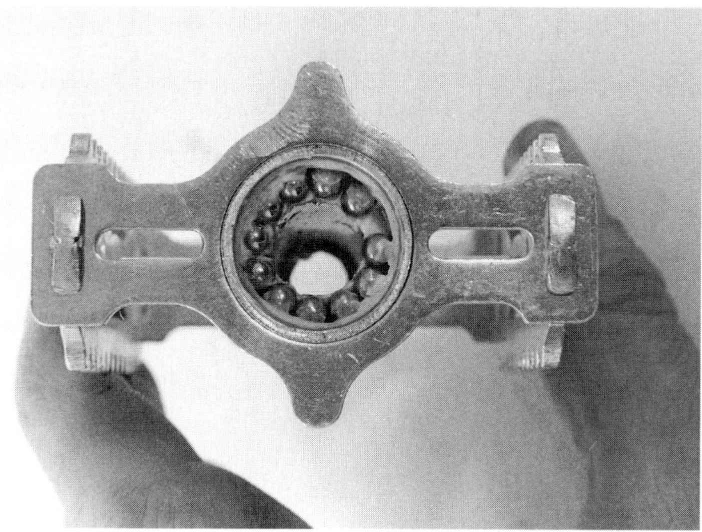

to give a trace of play. Replace the tanged washer and tighten the lock-nut down. The pedal should now spin freely with no play – experiment with the cone adjustment until it is correct. Replace the dust cap.

Fitting Toe-Clips and Straps

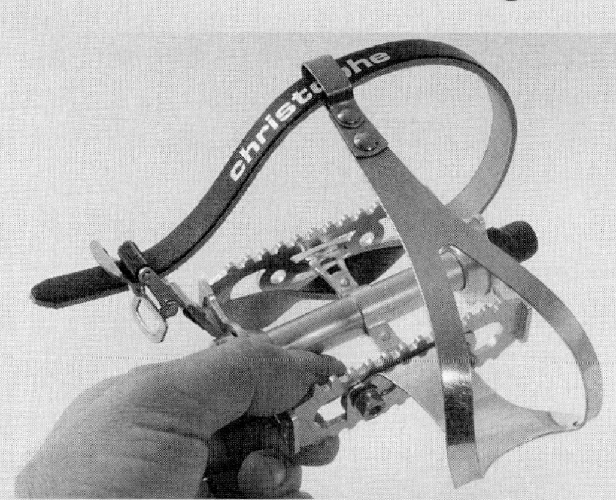

A correctly fitted toe-clip and toe-strap.

Toe-clips have a finite life due to continual flexing and scrapes; they are apt to break during a long tour. They are best attached with M5 allen bolts with Nylock nuts, or using Loctite thread compound. Small brass washers may also be useful.

Grease the bolts and put a washer under their heads. Put the bolts through the toe-clip's mounting slots, then screw into the pedal's mounting threads (if applicable; if not, loosely attach the nuts). Fully tighten the bolts, centralizing the toe clip and with it level with the top of the pedal cage. Fully tighten the bolts, then attach the nuts for additional security.

Thread the toe strap through the outer part of the cage fully, then through the first part of the pedal body; do this one step at a time or you will not be able to pull it through. Put a double twist in the strap (this prevents it pulling through) and then go through the second part of the body and then behind the retaining piece (road pedals). Ensure that the buckle ends up clear, but just above the pedal body. Then thread the strap through the toe-clip and into the buckle.

Shimano SPD Pedals

Disassembly

Summary – Shimano SPD Pedal Overhaul

⚒ 30 minutes

When?
- At overhaul intervals, sooner if you hear ticking or clicking sounds, or if the pedals do not spin freely or do so with a dry sound
- Adjust if play or stiffness is felt, rocking the pedal with your hand
- Use these instructions for all Shimano SPD pedals without dust caps, the Shimano 'Look'-type 1056 pedal and 1055 clipped pedals
- The M535 and M323 models with dust caps have a completely different bearing system that is best not disassembled without the expensive Shimano tool TLPD63; instead, injecting grease through a hole in a spare dust cap, from new, will ensure maximum life

Special Tools
- You will need the Shimano Pedal axle assembly tool TLPD40, which normally comes with the pedals or bike

Preparation/Notes
- Remove the pedals
- Disassembly of the axle assembly is not normally necessary or useful unless the parts are badly worn or corroded

Greasing and adjusting is usually sufficient without complete disassembly of the axle assembly. Slip the cartridge removal tool into a vice (or a large adjustable spanner) and tighten it. Put the pedal axle into the tool, engaging the knurled ring at the base of the pedal body. Unscrew the axle cartridge by pushing down on the pedal and turning the body anticlockwise for the left pedal, clockwise for the right. Keep unscrewing until the whole cartridge comes out; it will feel stiff at some points. If necessary use a big adjustable spanner on the pedal to obtain sufficient leverage. Clean the axle assembly with degreaser and let it dry.

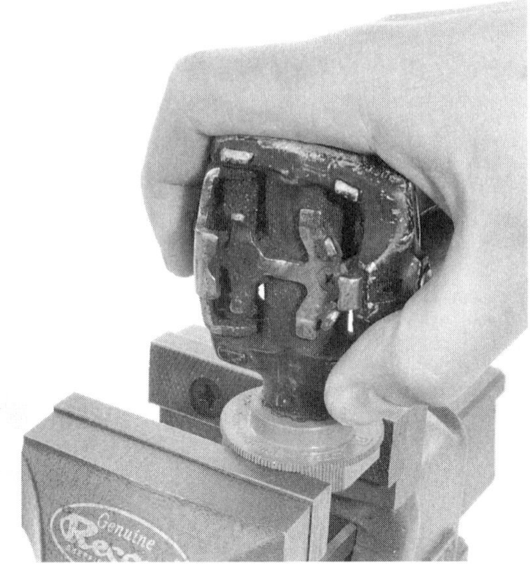

Removing an SPD axle assembly.

Disassembly and Reassembly of the Axle Assembly

Hold the cone with a 10mm flat spanner. Using a 7 or 8mm ring spanner (depending on model) undo the lock-nut at the top. Use your fingers to unscrew and remove the cone, followed by the bearing barrel with its two sets of loose ball-bearings, then the dished washer and resin core. Discard the ball-bearings. Wipe clean all the other components and the inside of the pedal body. Inspect the bearing surfaces of the barrel, axle and the cone. If these show

Adjusting SPD pedal bearings. This cone was between 9 and 10mm, and though not ideal, the vice Grip was the only tool I had to fit it – whatever the theories, sometimes needs must!

signs of pitting or other wear, buy a complete new cartridge assembly. Otherwise just buy new ball-bearings of the highest quality (44 × ⅛in); these are also available as a Shimano spare.

To reassemble, slide the resin core onto the axle, knurled end first. Now slide on the dished washer, facing up, and grease it. Grease the inner bearing races of the barrel and insert eleven bearings into each race. Slide the barrel onto the axle and position in either end against the dished washer. Screw on the cone, then the lock-nut finger tightly; then readjust as described below.

Pedal Adjustment and Assembly

Loosen the lock-nut and cone if necessary and set finger tight. Hold the cone with a 10mm spanner and nip the lock-nut tight. Test the barrel for play; it should turn as freely as possible without any side-to-side play when you grasp it with your fingers and rock it as hard as you can. Repeat until you find the best compromise.

Fill the bottom quarter of the pedal body with grease. Remembering that the right pedal has the axle assembly with the left thread, tighten each into the pedal body using the cartridge tool. As you do so, grease will be flushed through the complete assembly. Wipe off the excess grease and ensure that the axle assembly is tight.

The Cleat System

Shimano SPD type pedals get a lot of mud and crud into the spring system in particular. Clean out the loose mud using warm water and a tooth brush. When dry, spray a thick, heavy lubricant onto the spring mechanism and wipe off the excess.

Check the spring tension adjustment and cleats for wear from time to time. Using a 3mm allen key, tighten it to increase cleat tension, loosen to decrease, being certain not to unscrew the bolt from its retaining piece. Worn cleats or a worn pedal plate can make entry/exit from the pedals tricky and unpredictable; these should be replaced if necessary.

As you tighten the pedal assembly into place, the grease in the body will purge the bearings.

Clean and lubricate the cleat system, then use a 3mm allen key to adjust the cleat tension.

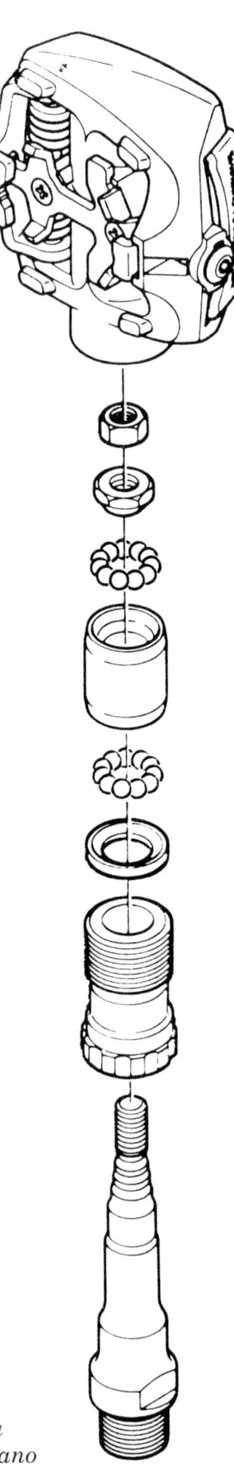

The internal assembly of a typical Shimano SPD pedal.

6 *The Derailleur Gear System*

A derailleur gear system consists of the rear cassette or freewheel with five to nine cogs, a rear hub compatible with the cassette or freewheel, the chainset with one to three chain wheels, the chain, and rear and front derailleurs to shift the chain between the cogs and chain wheels respectively. These are operated by gear levers and cables.

Modern derailleur gear systems are 'indexed', that is each rear cog, and in many cases, each front chain wheel, can be engaged almost immediately and exactly by a single click of the gear-shifter. Indexed gears are designed to work as a complete system. Though the parts may look the same, most of the components of an indexed gear system vary in detail, specifically to ensure that given movements of the gear-shifter produce an exact amount of movement of the derailleur cage, which must also correspond to the gap between each rear cog. A given groupset combines compatible parts together, though there is a fair degree of compatibility between most of a given manufacturer's range.

'Friction'-type gear systems were fitted to most bikes before the mid-1980s. These do not have preset gear lever positions for each gear. Instead the rider uses feel to obtain each gear, and normally a little readjustment of the shifter is necessary after each gear-shift to align the derailleur precisely and dispel irritating noises. Friction components are much less particular in their compatibly; most indexed gear components can be used within a friction system, with the exception of the shifter, which must have a friction setting.

The Shimano technical literature that comes with Shimano-equipped bikes and components often lists the compatible or best Shimano components to use in conjunction with the item in question. Campagnolo and Sachs equipment is generally interchangeable with any part of the same brand, except in the case of Campagnolo nine-speed systems.

A friction setting can be useful within an indexed gear system as it allows otherwise non-compatible parts to be used, an important consideration for tourists who do not want to waste their holiday finding an exact replacement part. Damage or excessive wear that can make an index system unusable may not affect a friction system. The compatibility of each component, and what you need to consider when buying a replacement, are covered alongside the maintenance of each of these items.

GENERAL DERAILLEUR MAINTENANCE

Derailleurs accumulate a lot of road grime, making the numerous pivot points sticky, especially after hard winter use.

Remove the wheels and use a degreaser and tooth and bottle brushes to clean all the inaccessible points inside and out; wipe off the excess. When dry, use a PTFE-based lubricant with its 'straw' to lubricate all the pivot points and moving parts. Then work the derailleurs fully back and forth a few times. Occasionally, a small amount of lubricant is useful on the gear-shifters, but never apply lubricant to a friction shifter, or one with a friction setting.

Operate the gear-shifters; if the derailleurs do not move with precise, steady and free movement in both directions then pay particular attention to cleaning the pivot points. Alternatively, the problem may be in the cables (*see* Cable Replacement, below). If the rear derailleur's sprung cage pivot is not free and smooth, try spraying a lubricant into it. If this does not work the cage can be removed from many models, then cleaned and regreased.

Over time the pulley wheel teeth and their bushings wear, causing less precise shifting and the danger of the chain coming off. Shimano and some Campagnolo models use a 'floating' top pulley with deliberate sideways travel, not wobble. While some pulley bushings are sealed to various degrees, the bushings are best cleaned and regreased at overhaul intervals. Pulley wheels utilizing cartridge bearings are also available.

Noting the order of the bushings, remove the assembly bolts, shielding plates and bushings. Buy exact replacements unless making deliberate modifications. Refit, taking care to ensure that the seals do not become trapped by the shielding plates. A spot of thread lock compound is a good idea.

Again over time, the chain can wear grooves on the inside of the cage plates on the front derailleur. These can catch and snag the chain. Play in the pivot points also leads to imprecise gear changing; test for this by trying to wobble the bottom end of the cage – you may need to compare it to a new one to gauge the degree of wear.

Clean and regrease the derailleur bushings at overhaul intervals.

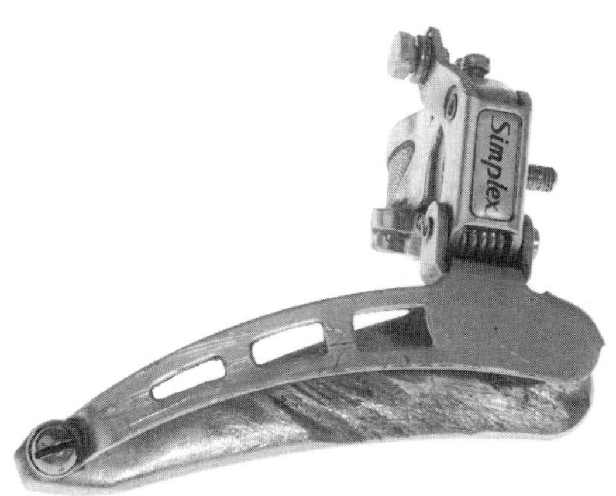

Worn cage plates such as these cause very poor gear changing.

THE FRONT DERAILLEUR

Fitting

Unscrew the bolt at the lower end of the cage, taking care not to lose the spacing piece, the tiny washer and nut if applicable. Carefully spring the cage open and past the chain, then refit these parts. Shimano XTR derailleurs have a hinged cage so the chain will need to be separated instead (*see* Chain Removal later in this chapter). Loosely attach the clamp around the seat tube, or bolt it to the braze-on fitting.

Many Shimano MTB models now mount behind the bottom bracket right side cup (except Shimano XTR bottom brackets, which have a separate lock-ring). Unscrew and remove the cup or lock-ring (*see* Chapter 5), position the mounting plate, refit the cup and tighten it firmly. These models do not require the careful positioning described below, but can only be used with chain wheels of a specific size.

Summary – Fitting and Adjusting the Front Derailleur

🔧 30 minutes

When?
- When replacing
- If you suspect positioning to be incorrect; positioning must be exact for it to function correctly
- Go through the adjustment routine at overhaul intervals and whenever gear changing is problematic

Positioning

If repositioning you will need to detach the front derailleur cable in most cases as it can pull the derailleur downwards.

Profiled cage plates can make alignment difficult to gauge – view the cage as a whole from above.

The front derailleur should clear the chainrings by 1–2mm.

(Below) *A Shimano bottom bracket-mounted front derailleur.*

With the attachment bolt a little loose, position the outer cage plate so that its closest point is 1–2mm above the larger chainring and parallel to it. Adjustment should be made by manoeuvring the body, not the cage. To view the alignment, you will probably need to pull the cage out by hand so that the cage plate is directly over the chainring; you can also use the low gear adjuster to do this (*see* below). If you have non-circular chainrings the clearance must be with the 'highest' point of the chainring.

Finally secure the clamp bolt, but note that tightening it can pull the derailleur position out; do not over-tighten this or you may crimp a thin-walled tube! To reattach the cable, *see* Cable Replacement later in the chapter, and Cable Adjustment below.

Adjustment Routine

The front derailleur has limit stop screws that preset the maximum inner and outer movement at the high (large chainring) and low end (small chainring) of the derailleur's travel. The screws are often labelled 'H' and 'L' accordingly. Their position is not always as shown in the photographs, as on some models the screw functions are reversed. If you are unsure which is which, slacken off the cable and unscrew each one – the one that causes the cage to move inwards is the low-stop adjustment.

Low-stop Adjustment

When adjusting the low-limit screw, first slacken off the cable to ensure that the limit screw and not the tension of the cable limits the inward movement of the derailleur. Slacken it off by either screwing in the adjuster on the gear-shift lever or the one on the down tube if applicable. If there is no adjuster, use the cable clamp on the derailleur instead.

Shift into the biggest rear cog. Repeatedly check the shift from the largest (or middle) chainring to the smallest. If the chain will not do this or is hesitant or rubs the cage, unscrew the low-limit screw until it does move without hesitation; this will normally be a matter of turning the screw half a turn at a time.

If the chain comes off, tighten the screw again a half-turn at a time until it shifts cleanly without doing so. The final adjustment can be as little as a quarter of a turn between the chain shifting cleanly or coming off – tune it as closely as you can so that the shift is clean but the derailleur moves no further inwards than is absolutely necessary. The screw is easier to adjust if you pull the cage out by hand to relieve the pressure on it. Reset the cable tension so that with the lever fully retracted it is just taut.

High-stop Adjustment

Shift into the smallest rear cog. Repeatedly shift into the biggest chainring. If the chain will not do this or if it rubs the cage (this may only happen when pedalling hard), unscrew the high-limit screw until it does so without hesitation; again this will probably be a matter of turning the screw a half-turn at a time. If the chain shifts too far and comes off, tighten the screw a half-turn at a time until it shifts cleanly. The final adjustment can be as little as a quarter of a

Adjusting the front derailleur's low-limit screw.

turn between the chain shifting cleanly or coming off – again tune it as close as you can to get the best results.

Cable Tension Adjustment (Indexed Systems)

Put the chain on the middle chainring and the biggest rear cog. Using the cable adjuster on the gear-shift lever or down tube set the inner cage plate 0.5mm from the chain – tightening it moves the cage outwards. If there is insufficient adjuster travel you will need to screw it (the adjuster) all the way back in, pull the cable through the clamp, and start again; *see* Cable Replacement below for more detail.

Adjusting the front derailleur's high-limit screw.

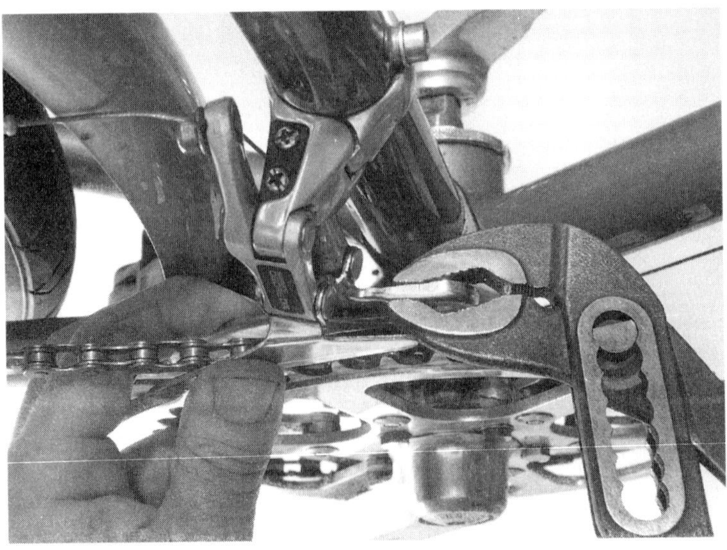

Toeing in the derailleur cage plates with a pair of slip joint pliers.

Last Resorts

If despite having made all the above adjustments you still have shifting problems then it may be helpful to toe in the cage plates; this can be of particular help with older derailleurs. Bend each cage plate in a little using an adjustable spanner or slip-joint pliers. The front tips of the cage will now nudge the chain down or up more easily.

In a few cases you may have trouble shifting to and from the middle ring, especially if you have exceeded the derailleur's capacity. Using slip-joint pliers, squeeze the lower to middle section of the plates in slightly. Finally, repeat the adjustment routine steps.

Buying a Front Derailleur

The performance of front derailleurs has improved greatly over the last few years but they are increasingly dedicated to specific chain wheel sizes. You should check the following if replacing the front derailleur or chain wheel.

Maximum Chainring Size

This is the maximum size chainring the derailleur is recommended for. Road models commonly take up to 54 teeth. MTB models vary more widely; current Shimano models take 42 teeth, except XT, which takes 44 teeth and XTR which takes 48. Current Sachs MTB models take 46 teeth. These figures can usually be exceeded by up to four teeth, especially if you do not exceed the maximum capacity and/or do not use the smallest chain wheel with the smaller rear cogs – the chain will rub the bottom of the cage.

Maximum Capacity

This is the maximum difference in teeth between the largest and smallest chainring the derailleur is recommended for. Current Shimano road models take 14 or 15 teeth, except for the triple chainset models, which take 20, 22 or 26 teeth. Current Campagnolo road models take 15 teeth and Sachs road models 16. Current Shimano MTB models take 20, 22, or 18 teeth, and Sachs 22 or 26 teeth. Front derailleurs can be 'half-step' for chainring differences less than 10 teeth or 'Alpine' for differences greater than 10 teeth.

Mounting and Cable Routing

Traditionally front derailleurs clamped around a 28.6mm seat tube, but alternative clamp sizes are available for wider seat tubes. Some frames have a brazed-on fitting for which specific models must be used. The latest Shimano MTB models attach behind the bottom bracket cup; these are designed for use with specific Shimano chainsets as they have little or no adjustment. Traditional and road models use a cable route pulling from below. Many recent MTB models are a 'top pull' design, which are considered to have a lighter action and are less prone to clogging with mud; choose according to the cable routing of your frame.

THE REAR DERAILLEUR

Fitting

Most modern frames take a derailleur that screws directly into its integral gear hanger. Use a 5mm allen key to mount it, ensuring that the B-tension bolt sits

Fitting and Adjusting the Rear Derailleur

30 minutes

When?
- When replacing
- Follow the adjustment routine at overhaul intervals and whenever gear changing is problematic

Preparation/Notes
- If fitting, you will need to break the chain (*see* Chain Removal and Replacement); alternatively, remove the pulley wheels as described above
- Many seemingly insurmountable gear problems are a result of the gear hanger not being perfectly aligned with the cassette (*see* Chapter 3)
- If your gear-shifter has a friction option, the high and low stops are best adjusted in this setting (*see* Gear-shifters page 99)

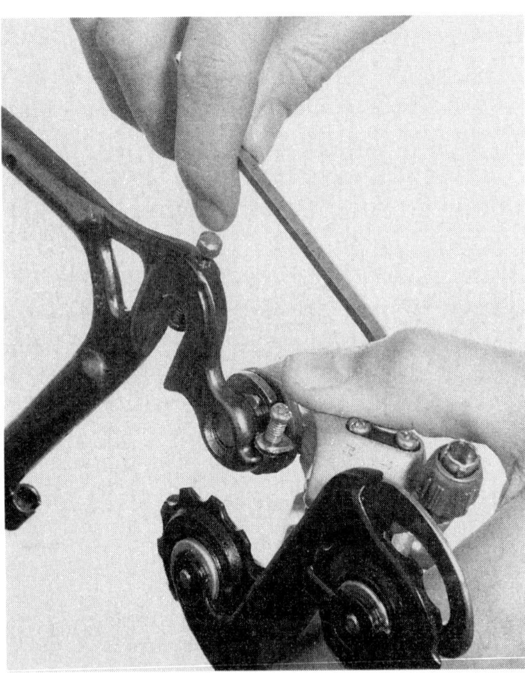

Tightening the derailleur fixing bolt; note the B-tension bolt clear of the tang.

behind the gear hanger tab before tightening, or you may irrevocably deform the derailleur. Be careful not to cross-thread it. Nip the bolt tight. Reattach the chain, ensuring that you thread it correctly through the cage.

If your frame has a separate gear hanger fit the nut at the back so that its curve fits snugly in the back of the dropout and the plate's tab fits within the dropout; a little filing may sometimes be necessary. Tighten the bolt and ensure that the gear hanger is flat against the dropout and parallel with the slot.

Adjustment Routine

B-Tension

This adjustment normally only needs to be made when fitting a new derailleur, altering the chain length or altering the chain wheel or rear cog sizes. With the chain on the smallest chainring and largest rear cog, use the B-tension screw to set the derailleur's top pulley/cage as close as possible to the largest rear cog but without its pulley or cage catching;

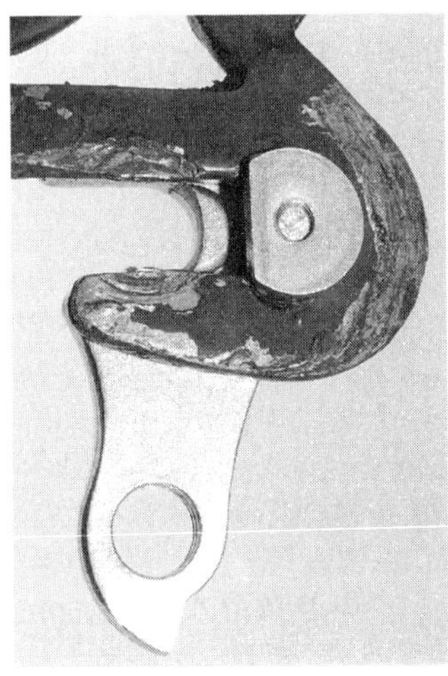

A separate gear hanger correctly fitted to an older frame.

Loosen the B-tension screw to minimize the gap between the derailleur pulley and the cogs.

turn the pedals backwards and forwards to test this. Now set the chain on the smallest rear cog and tighten the screw a little more if the pulley/cage catches.

The Limit Screws

Like the front derailleur, the rear derailleur has limit screws that preset the maximum inner and outer movement at the high (smallest cog) and low end (largest cog) end of the derailleur's travel. The screws are often labelled 'H' and 'L' accordingly. On Shimano and Sachs derailleurs the upper screw is the high-gear limit, on Campagnolo the upper screw is the low-gear limit. If you are unsure which is which, slacken off the cable, shift into the smallest rear cog and unscrew each limit screw; the one that causes the derailleur to move outwards is the high limit. As the cable tension also affects the derailleur's maximum travel, make adjustments in the order described.

Low-stop Adjustment

With the chain on the smallest rear cog, the gear cable should be taut or just taut; exactly how taut is not critical, but it should not be slack. Whilst turning the pedals, repeatedly shift into the largest rear cog, and tighten the low limit screw half a turn at a time until gear-shifting into the largest rear cog becomes hesitant. Next unscrew the low limit screw an eighth of a turn at a time until you obtain a clean shift; the chain should just shift into the largest cog, without excess travel.

Tighten the low-gear stop to reduce the derailleur's inward movement.

High-stop Adjustment

Make this adjustment with the cable slackened off – if it is too tight it can affect the 'resting' position of the derailleur for the purpose of this adjustment. Tighten the high limit screw until gear changing becomes hesitant, then unscrew it an eighth of a turn at a time until you obtain a clean shift, in the same manner as for the low-stop adjustment.

Tighten the high-gear stop to reduce the derailleur's outward movement.

Cable Tension Adjustment

If you have a friction system, the cable tension should just be taut when the gear lever is fully retracted with the chain on the smallest rear cog.

For indexed systems go through the following procedure if you have fitted a new cable, altered its tension, or if you have poor indexing with the chain chattering or miss-shifting.

With the wheel lifted and whilst turning the pedals, shift the chain onto the largest chainring. Shift the chain to the smallest rear cog; if it will not go, screw in the cable adjuster until it does – you may need to reset the cable in its clamp to allow sufficient adjustment.

Next shift the lever one click (to '2' if there is a visible indicator of the gear). If the chain does not shift to the second cog unscrew the cable adjuster (so tightening the cable) a little at a time and try the lever again until the chain does shift. If it jumps up to the third cog, screw the adjuster in until it only shifts to the second.

While turning the pedals, unscrew the adjuster until the chain chatters against the third cog. Slacken off until the noise only just disappears. The indexing should now be correct throughout the

Unscrewing the cable adjuster tensions the cable, moving the indexing points inwards.

range. If you have difficulty obtaining the largest cog, the low-gear stop may need to be unscrewed a fraction more.

Buying a Rear Derailleur

The rear derailleur has two jobs. Firstly it shifts the chain across the cassette; the amount of movement is jointly determined by the gear-shifter so the combination must be compatible for indexing to work correctly. Secondly, it keeps the chain under tension in all gear combinations. Shimano and Campagnolo models use a 'floating' upper pulley wheel, which generally offer the smoothest shifting and easiest adjustment.

You should check the following if replacing the rear derailleur or altering the chain wheel or rear cog sizes.

Derailleur Capacity

The maximum sprocket size of short-arm derailleurs intended for road bikes is typically 26 or 28 teeth. Long-arm 'MTB' derailleurs typically have a capacity of 32 or 30 teeth. The minimum sprocket size is usually 11 teeth for MTB derailleurs and 11 or 12 teeth for 'road' ones. The front difference is that between the largest and smallest chain wheel; 13 or 14 teeth is typical for road derailleurs and 20 or 22 for MTB. Finally the front difference and rear difference give the total capacity – typically 33–39 teeth for MTB and 26–28 for road.

Mounting Systems

Most derailleurs take a direct bolt fixing to the frame's integral gear hanger. Older and cheaper frames require a derailleur with its own gear hanger or a separate one to which a modern derailleur can be attached. Separate ones should be labelled 'index compatible' if you are using indexed gears.

FITTING GEAR CABLES

Fitting Gear Cables

⊓⊓ 30 minutes

When?

- Overhaul intervals
- When the casing is damaged or the cable does not pull freely – check by loosening the clamp bolts and pulling the cable in both directions
- The cable casing should be replaced yearly

Preparation/Notes

- Remove bar tape and casing if applicable

The Derailleur Cable

To avoid indexing problems it is best to use the cable and casing recommended by the manufacturer of the gear-shifter or groupset. Note the nipple type of the original cable as these can vary from the normal standard. Inner cables are normally 1.2mm in diameter, smooth to the touch and pre-stretched; the best ones are made from stainless steel and some are Teflon coated. Standard 1.2mm cables should be used in 5mm casing; 1.1mm cables are also available, which can be used in all casing diameters.

The outer casing is made with longitudinal reinforcing wires to prevent it from compressing. It is available in 3.6, 4, and 5mm outer diameters to suit the cable guides of your system. It usually has an inner nylon sleeve, but PTFE (Teflon,

Gore Tex) lined cables are also available. Spirally wound, brake-type casing should not be used in any index system. Shimano SIS SP casing is recommended for most Shimano systems. The cheaper Shimano SIS is recommended for use with Shimano Tourney components. SIS SP40 has sealed ends.

Cable ferrules (end stops) are usually factory fitted to the casing and should not be removed; these fit snugly into the cable stops and adjusters of your components and frame. If you need to shorten the cable, slide over a new snug-fitting cable ferrule. If the rear derailleur's section of casing is routed up the seat stay, a special 'rain cap' cover may be fitted to prevent seizure.

Preparation

Note the existing cable routing, all sections of cable casing, and its mounting under the derailleur's cable clamp. Shift the chain to the smallest front and rear sprockets, ensuring that the rear shifter is fully retracted – STI-type shifters should be clicked at least seven times to ensure this. Loosen the cable clamp, pull the casing free and, pushing the cable out of the lever to remove it, note its point of exit (*see* illustrations). Set the derailleur and down tube cable adjusters (if applicable) at two turns unscrewed. Cable casing lengths should allow the bars free movement and avoid sharp bends, but there should be no excess. Cut the cable cleanly with bicycle cable cutters, open up the cut end if compressed and fit end caps as necessary.

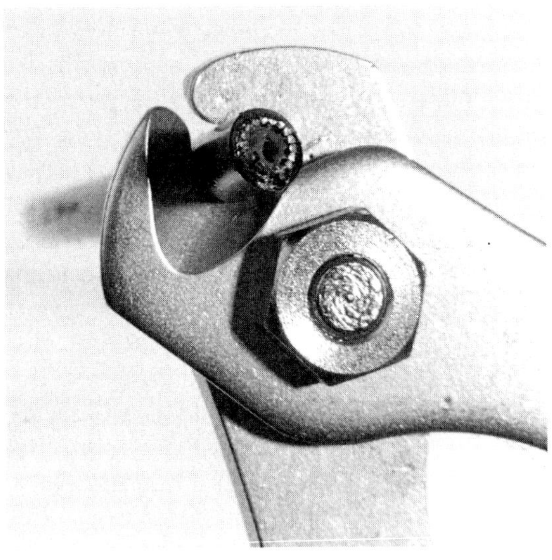

Use high-quality cutters to cut indexed cable casing.

Fitting

Ideally, use a grease gun to pump grease into the sections of cable casing and grease the inner cable and nipple. Note that Teflon-lined cables should not be greased; just grease the cable nipple.

Feed the cable into the gear-shifter (*see* illustrations). When the lever is fully retracted it should be possible to see a recess for the cable. If threading it causes the cable to be pulled at a sharp angle it will form a tight coil; it is best to thread it through in two stages.

Thread the cable through the first section of casing, through the down tube cable stop/adjuster and through the guide at the bottom bracket; the guide is above the bottom bracket on older bikes, under it on modern ones, or along the top tube for top-pull derailleurs. The front derailleur cable now goes directly to the cable clamp. The rear cable is threaded through the chain- or seatstay cable stop and an additional length of casing is fitted between it and the cable clamp.

Check that the shifter is fully retracted. Use a cable-puller or pliers

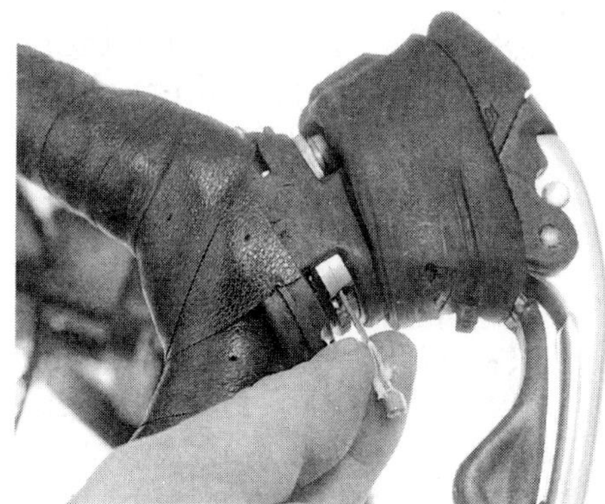

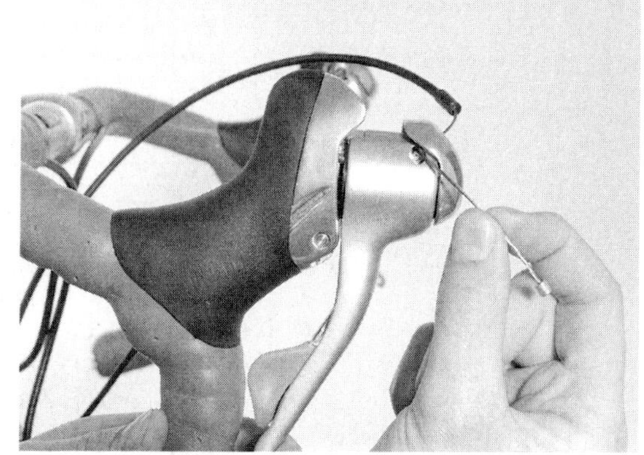

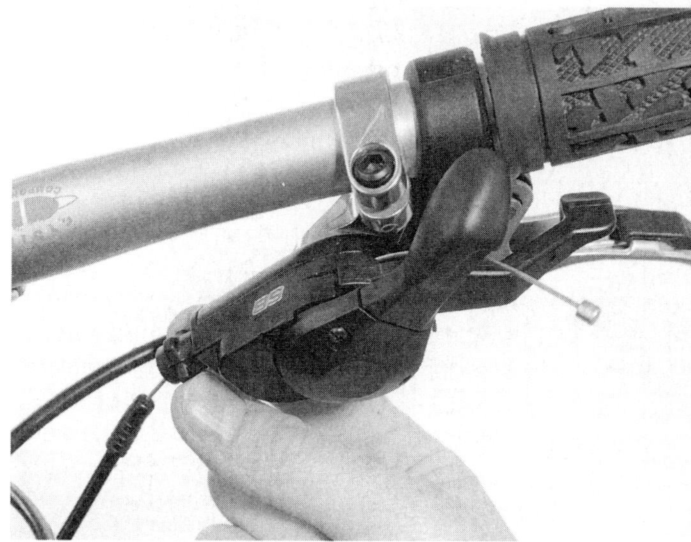

(Above left) *A Campagnolo Ergopower shifter; pull the lever hood forward to insert the cable.*

(Above) *A Shimano STI shifter; pull the lever back a little.*

(Left) *A Rapidfire shifter; note the cable adjuster on its left.*

(Right) *A handlebar-end shifter; thread the cable through in two stages.*

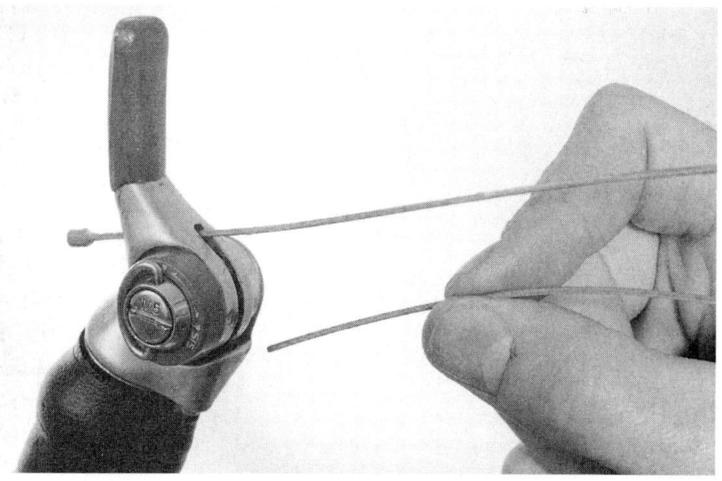

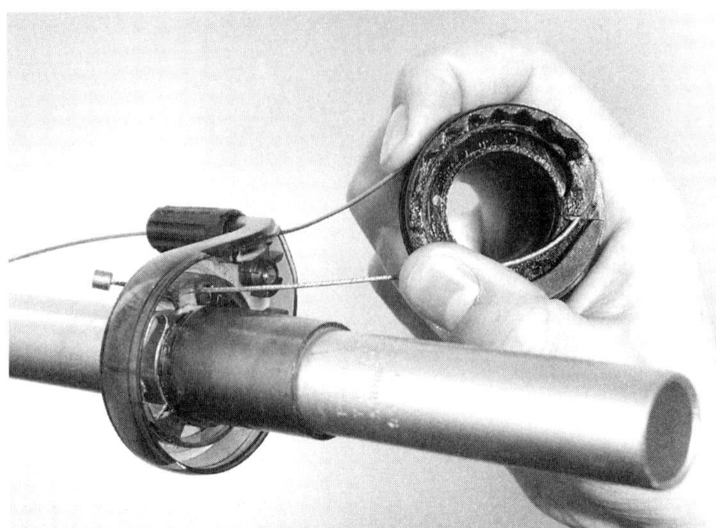

A gripshift system: remove the stationary grip and plastic washer behind it. Remove the screw that retains the small triangular cover and lift this and the grip off. Grease the 'detents' (shown under the forefinger) and spring in the shifter body with Gripshift 'Jonnisnot' or Vaseline. Thread the cable as shown and pull it through the adjuster, keeping it under tension as you reposition the grip in the housing – the detents should line up with the spring. Replace the cover and test the operation.

Using a cable puller makes it easier to tension the cable and tighten the cable clamp simultaneously.

✔

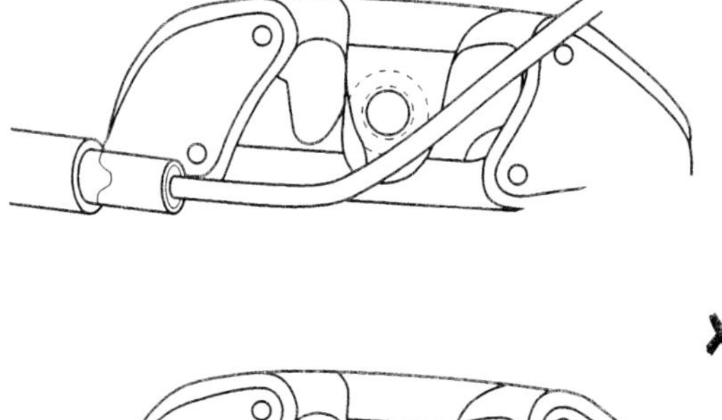

✘

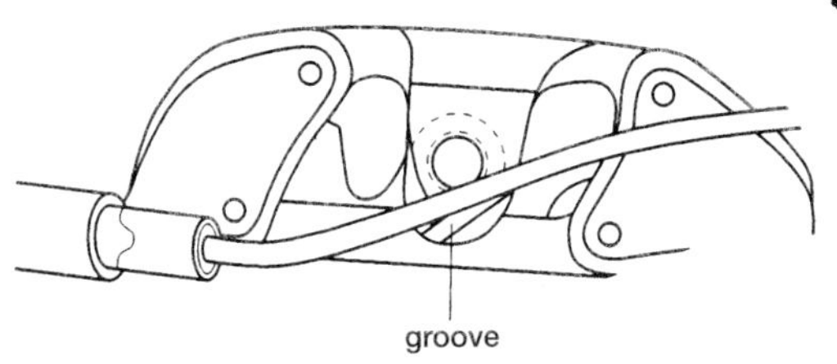

Clamp the cable correctly in its groove.

to take up the slack firmly, release it slightly so that the cable is just taut and tighten the clamp. Cut off the excess and crimp on an end cap with a pair of pliers. Now go through the adjustment routine described earlier in the chapter.

GEAR-SHIFTERS

Indexed gear-shifters must be compatible with both your derailleur and cassette (both with regard to the spacing between the cogs and the number of cogs). The shifter should be the same brand as the derailleur unless specifically stated otherwise. Shimano Dura Ace shifters are not compatible with non-Dura Ace derailleurs.

Friction Gears

Turn the ring to change the gear, ensuring that the setting marks align; the friction setting is sometimes indicated by an 'F', while the indexed setting of Shimano systems is indicated by 'SIS'. If the ring will not turn easily, loosen the central bolt in the first instance. A friction lever depends upon friction to stop the derailleur moving by itself. Increase the friction by tightening the centre bolt, but do not tighten it any tighter than necessary to prevent unwanted movement of the derailleur. Never oil it!

Removal and Fitting

Dual Brake and Gear-shifters

See Chapter 8 for further information.

Down Tube Shifters

Put the lever in its most forward position, remove the central bolt and slide off the lever. The plastic mounting plate can then be prised up. Replace the mounting plate with its protrusion facing forwards, slide on the lever so that it mates with the protrusion and secure it with the central bolt. Clip-on shifters are mounted butted up against a protrusion on the underside of the down tube to prevent them from slipping.

Handlebar End Shifters

Set the lever in its bottom-most position. Remove the lever from the body by removing its central screw. Prise off the mounting plate and remove the back portion of the mounting nut left in the

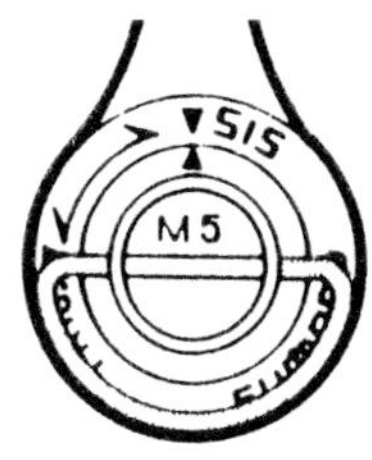

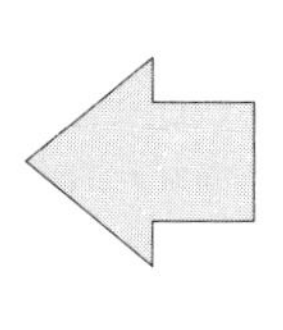
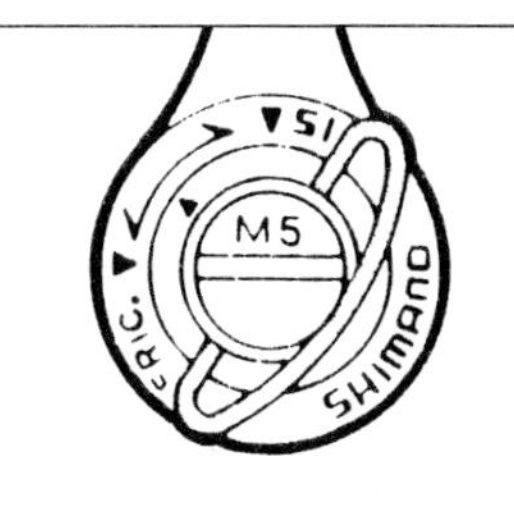

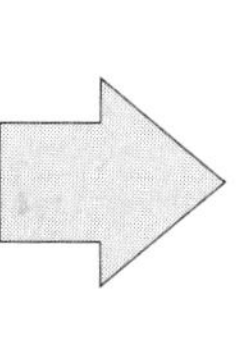
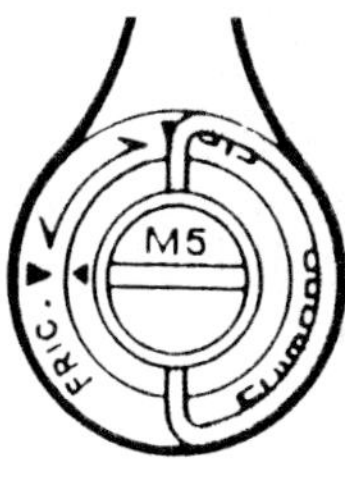

(Above) *Setting a Shimano bar-end or down tube lever to Friction or Indexed (SIS).*

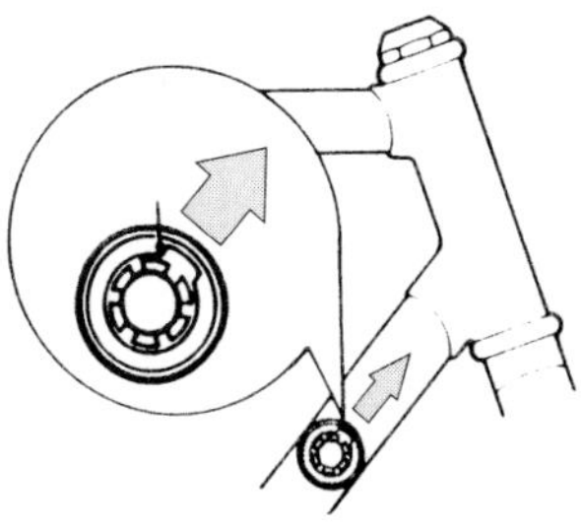

(Right) *Shimano down tube levers must be correctly aligned to their mounting plate.*

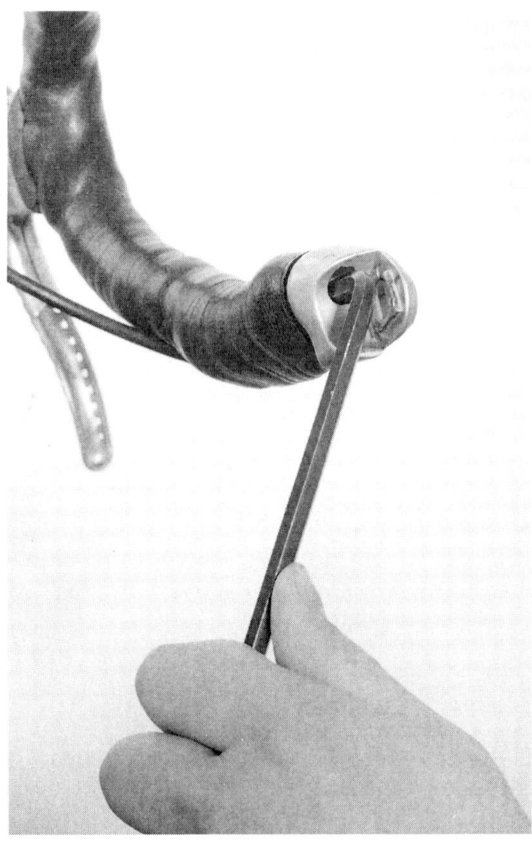

Removing a bar-end shifter.

body. Use an allen key to turn the expanding clamp in the bar clockwise to loosen it as it has a left-hand thread. Refit the mounting plate's protrusion in the six o'clock position and replace the lever in its bottom-most position so that it aligns with the protrusion.

Thumb Shifters

These remove and fit in to their mounting in a similar manner to down tube shifters. The mounting plate can sometimes be repositioned to improve their comfort and ease of use.

Gripshift

These are secured by the 3mm allen bolt within the shifter body. Position so that the cables do not have to bend sharply.

TRANSMISSION WEAR AND CHAIN MAINTENANCE

In wear terms, the chain, cassette (or freewheel), and chain wheels (cogs) should be seen as a complete system. In use the grit in and around the chain wears down the chain's bushings and the cog teeth; the effect is that the gaps between the chain-links increase as well as those between the cog teeth. To some degree the effect is self-cancelling as the components wear in and wear out together.

However, some cogs normally receive more use than others, and smaller ones wear more quickly than larger ones. What then happens is that the chain only engages a single tooth of the cog at a time instead of spreading the pedalling force over a group, thereby greatly increasing the wear rate on all the cogs – and jumping of the chain often occurs. At this stage the backs of the teeth begin to wear down too, causing the characteristic hooked shape seen when teeth are severely worn. Gear-shifting and efficiency also suffer greatly and the chain may come off unexpectedly.

Therefore, keep your chain clean and correctly lubricated, and check it for wear on a regular basis. Replacing the chain before it is worn can greatly extend the cassette and chain wheel life. If the chain is unworn and the cassette presents no problems it is generally safe to assume that the combination is fine.

(Above left) *A worn chain only engages a single tooth at a time.*
(Above right) *A new chain engages a group of teeth equally.*

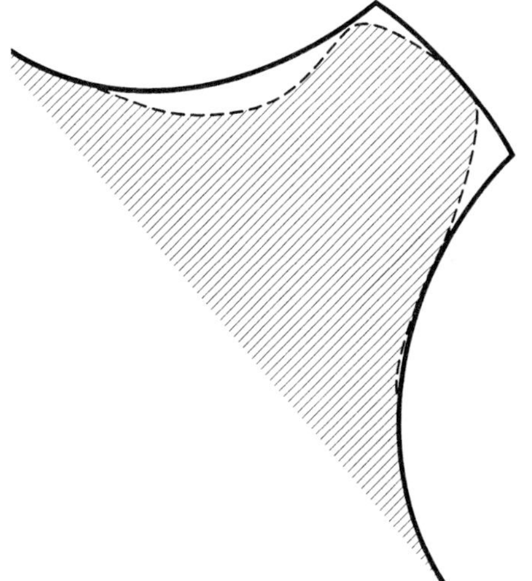

(Left) *A new cog gradually wears into a hooked shape, especially if the chain is worn.*

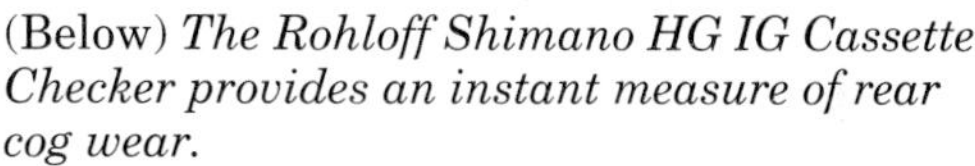

(Below) *The Rohloff Shimano HG IG Cassette Checker provides an instant measure of rear cog wear.*

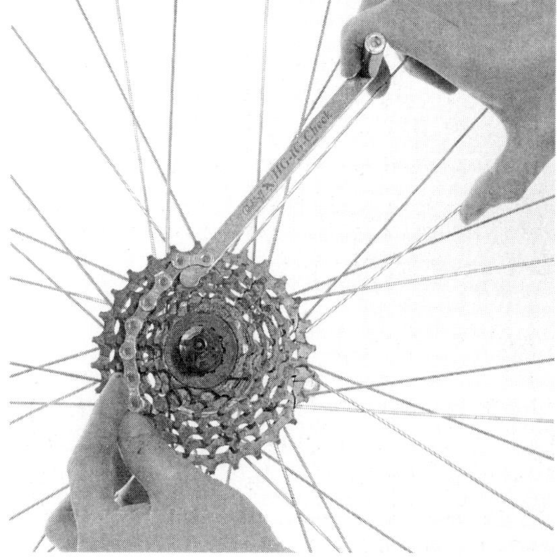

Shimano HG and IG cogs can be checked with a Rohloff cog checker. Wrap the chain section around the cog to be checked and tension with the handle. If the last link will not push down behind its tooth, the cog is worn and should be replaced.

A ruler can also be used to measure chain wear. Measure twenty-four links of the chain (rivet centre to rivet centre), held under tension. If the distance is 308mm (12⅛in) or longer the chain is worn out.

Chain Cleaning

If using a cleaning device, fit it as per its instructions, and fill to the line with degreaser. Hold up to the chain and close the unit, thus attaching it. Put the hook behind the derailleur. Pedal backwards for fifteen revolutions or so. Take off the unit and wipe the chain dry, then lubricate. Very dirty chains may need the process repeated with fresh degreaser or require removing and soaking overnight. You can leave the old solvent to settle, filter it and use it again.

Using a ruler to measure chain wear.

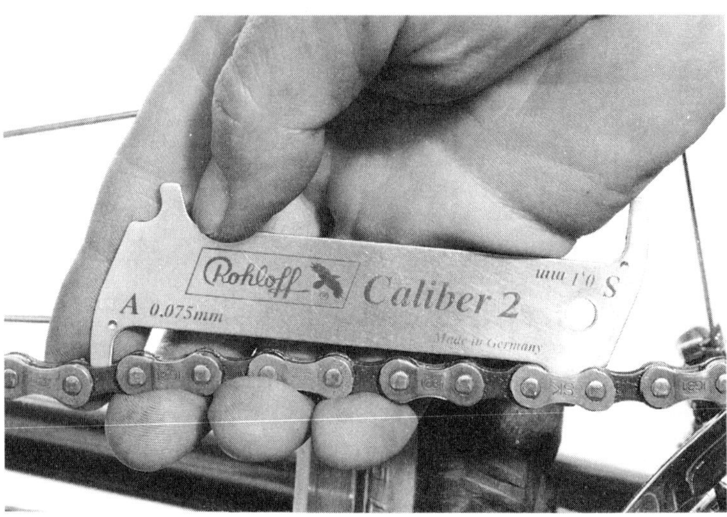

The Rohloff Chain Caliber provides an instant measure of chain wear – a worn chain fits over the hooks.

Alternatively, if the chain is clogged up but dry, a stiff wire brush works well. Crud also tends to collect between the cassette cogs; the chain then compacts this into the gaps until eventually the chain is prevented from seating fully. Scrape out the worst with a knife or spoke, spray on a degreaser and clean out with strips of cloth; also clean the derailleur jockey wheels and crud from around the chain wheels.

After cleaning lubricate according to the lubrication guidelines in Chapter 2. Lubricate the chain when it becomes dry, or begins to sound noisy, with impaired shifting and 'hissing' as you exert pressure (also a sign of wear). If setting out on a longish ride, lubricate the chain before you go, especially if you plan to go off-road or ride in dusty or wet conditions.

Use a chain-cleaning device for best results and least mess; the alternative is a toothbrush and dish.

Chain Removal and Fitting

Summary – Chain Removal and Fitting

🔧🔧 20 minutes

When?

- Replace when worn; do not remove without good reason
- To adjust length if rear derailleur, or any max./min. chainring or cog has been replaced by a different size
- To free a jammed chain
- If you use different cassettes/freewheels on the same bike, it is best if these each have their own chain

Preparation/Notes

- Shimano HG and IG chains require a special Shimano chain rivet to reconnect them, so keep a couple spare
- If fitting a new chain you will almost certainly need a new cassette, or at least smaller sprockets to prevent the chain from jumping

Chain choice used to be simple: any derailleur chain could be used with any derailleur system component. This is no longer the case if chain, rear cogs and chain wheels are to work properly together. Use the table below to choose a suitable chain.

The chainset generally causes few problems beyond noting that Shimano chain wheels can be of the HG or IG type, which are labelled as such. IG type chain wheels work best with IG chains so you may want to ensure that your rear cogs are also IG compatible, or vice versa, and go for a more flexible system.

For other components, ask your dealer's recommendation.

Removal

Normally the chain can be separated at any point, but note that Shimano black connecting rivets should not be removed. Sachs chains with a single black side plate (SCM90 and SCM55 chains) should only be removed by the rivet on this side plate, by its dimpled end; the other rivets should not be removed except to shorten the chain.

Put the chain on the smallest chain wheel and cog. Fully retract the chain extractor's pin. Put the rivet to be removed on the tool's rear 'saddle' (if it has two). Screw the pin in towards the rivet. As it begins to touch, check that the pin is fully aligned with the rivet and that the rear of the rivet is not obscured. Continue to screw in the pin; it will be tight at first but should then give. Push the rivet four-fifths out, or remove completely if the chain is a Shimano HG or IG one. Retract the pin and lift out the chain. Bend the chain as illustrated to part it. If the chain does not part easily push the pin out a little more.

	Sachs chains					*Shimano chains **		
	SCM90 (MTB)	SCR80 (road)	SCM55 (MTB)	SCM40 (general)	TM20 (friction)	IG type	HG type	UG type
Cog type								
Shimano IG	✓	✓	✓	✓	X	✓	X	X
Shimano HG	✓	✓	✓	✓	X	O	✓	O
Shimano UG	O	O	O	✓	O/X	O	O	✓
Campagnolo Exadrive	O	✓	O	O	X	O	O	O
Sachs Power Glide	✓	✓	✓	✓	X	X	X	X
Sachs Aris freewheel	✓	✓	✓	✓	O/X	X	X	X

✓ = Good performance; O = acceptable, second-best or poor value choice; X = not recommended

* Shimano make a range of chains of each type, according to the quality of the groupset; it is best to choose one of similar quality.

To part the chain, push the rivet out four-fifths of the way, or remove completely in the case of Shimano HG and IG chains.

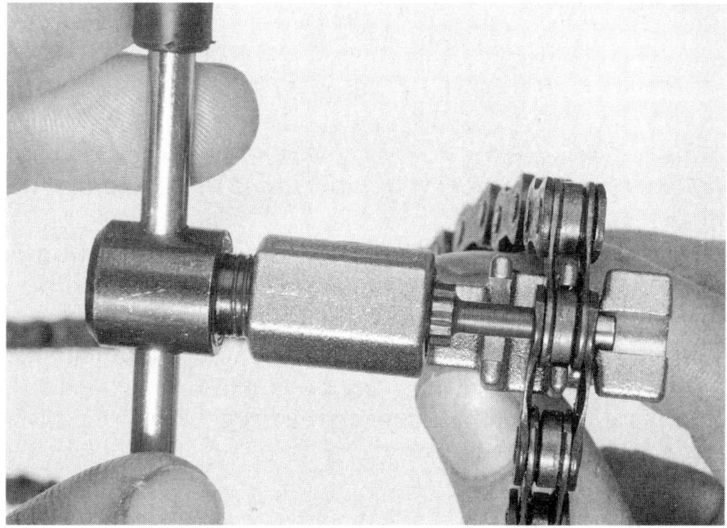

(Below) *Bend the chain to part non-Shimano HG and IG chains.*

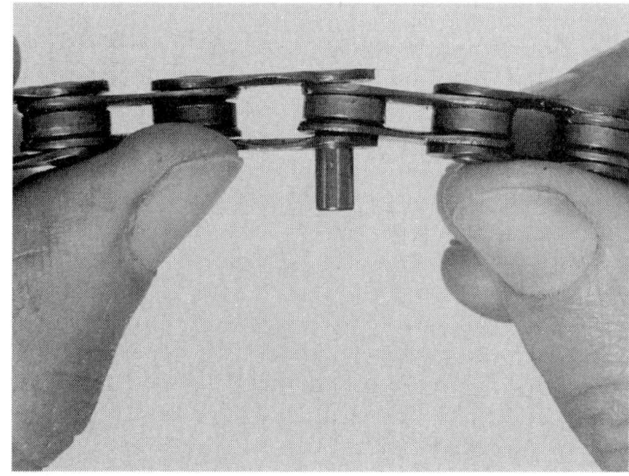

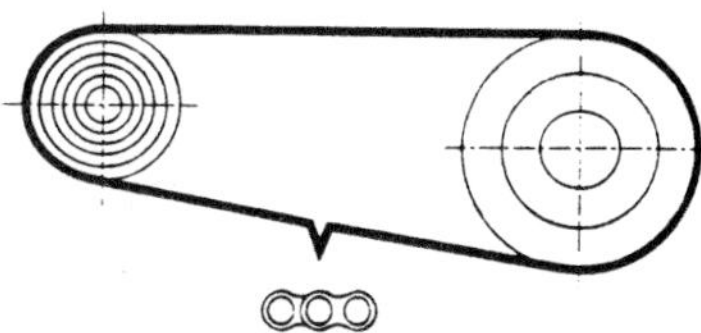

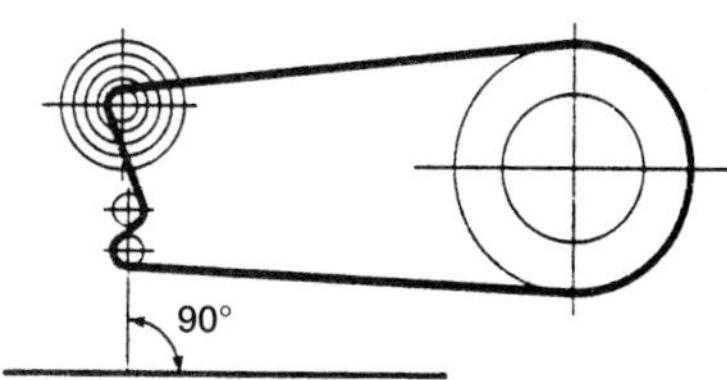

The chain should be the correct length.

Fitting

If fitting a new chain, determine its correct length. If using a long-arm 'MTB' derailleur put the chain around the biggest chainring and rear sprocket, pull it taught and add two links. If using a short-arm 'road' derailleur, set the length so that the cage is at 90 degrees to the ground.

If the chain needs to be shortened, remove links from the end of the chain with the inner link (or from either end for Shimano HG and IG), pushing the rivet right through. Thread the chain through the derailleurs; take particular care around the top jockey wheel that the chain goes between it and any lips on the cage.

Thread the chain correctly through the rear derailleur.

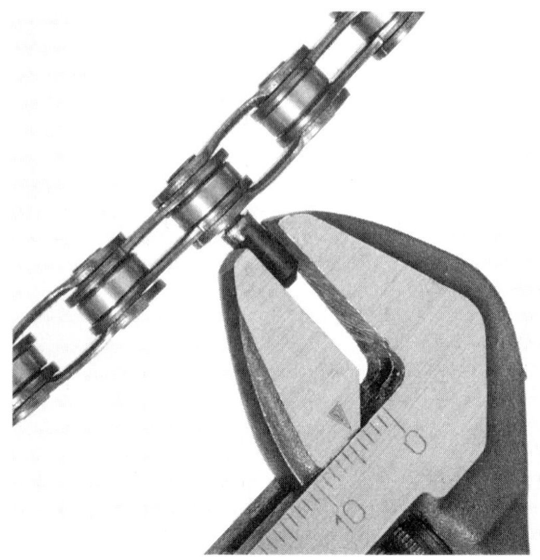

A fitted Shimano HG or IG chain pin. Now break off the protrusion.

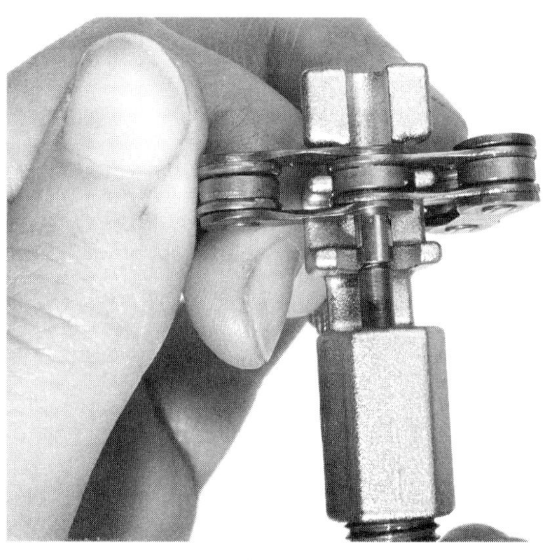

To join the chain, push the rivet back through until it protrudes equally on both sides of the chain.

If connecting a Shimano HG or IG chain, take a special Shimano connecting rivet and push the pointed end through the two links to connect them. Put the link in the tool's rear 'saddle'. Tighten the pin until it makes contact with the rivet. Check that the rivet can pass out of the back of the tool and tighten until the fatter half of the rivet is exactly equal on both sides of the chain plates. Unscrew the pin and remove the chain. Take a pair of pliers to the protruding part of the rivet and snap it off with a gentle twist.

For all other chains, push the unconnected links together, letting the stub of the removed rivet snap back into place. If this was pushed too far out to do this, put the links into the extractor tool, keep them in place with your thumb and screw in the pin, making sure it is aligned.

(Right) *Use the tool's near slot to free stiff links.*

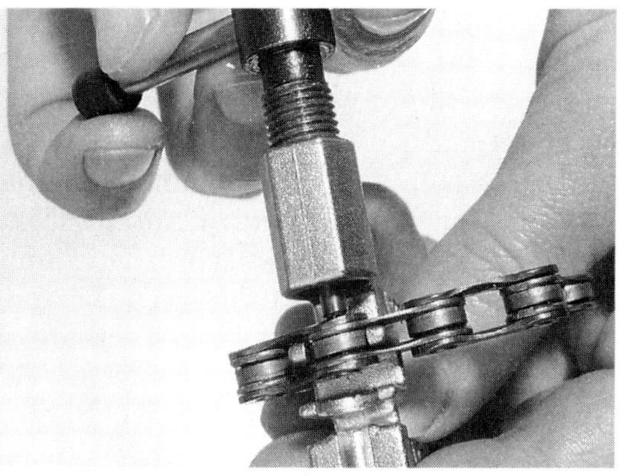

If you suspect a stiff link and need to find it, turn the pedals backwards; the stiff link will jump or stand proud as it passes around the bottom derailleur jockey wheel.

Ensure that the rivet's exit is clear to avoid damaging the link. Continue screwing until the rivet protrudes equally on both sides of the outside plates.

If the link is stiff, put the chain on the tool's near 'saddle' and use the pin to very gently nudge the chain's plates open a fraction.

CASSETTES AND FREEWHEELS

Cassettes

Most modern rear hubs are what are known as 'freehubs'. These combine the freewheel mechanism within the hub – identified visually by a bulged section of

Cassette/Freewheel Removal and Replacement

1 hour

When?

- If the chain is worn, it is normally necessary (and good practice) to fit a new cassette as well; if you do want to try fitting a new chain only, ride putting a lot of pressure on each cog, and try to detect any sign of jumping, as the cogs that jump will need replacing
- When modifying gear ratios
- To fit a spoke
- Hub overhaul

Preparation / Notes

- Some older cassettes do not have a conventional lock-ring with splines; instead the smallest cog is unscrewed the hub shell just behind the right-side spokes. The 'cassette', or set of cogs, slides over a spline and is held in place by a special lock-ring. There are two main systems available, which are not compatible: Shimano and Campagnolo. These use different splines and different cog spacing. Both Campagnolo's and Shimano's top-end nine-speed systems use different cog-spacing from any of their other systems. Shimano and Sachs seven- and eight-speed cassettes all use the same cog spacings.

Cassettes normally come as a complete set and each cog is usually profiled in such a way that the chain will change easily from one cog to the next. Campagnolo cassettes can be easily rearranged to provide custom gear ratios but unless prescribed sets are used the gear-shift quality may be impaired. The latest Sachs cassettes are held together by a clip system, enabling easy replacement of individual cogs.

Shimano cassettes allow less freedom to adapt as the cogs are normally bolted or riveted together. These can be removed and the cogs rearranged, however, without replacing the rivets. Conversion kits of four cogs are available to enable you to change the ratios of any Shimano cassette. While these and individual cogs are available and can be used to modify the cassette ratios, these will not always give the smoothest shifting if a different sequence from the original is used. Note that Shimano's MTB cassettes with 11 tooth cogs can only be used on Shimano MTB and RSX groupsets, while those 12 teeth upwards fit all hubs. Shimano make both IG and HG cogs; as they are recommended for use with different chain types, do not mix them.

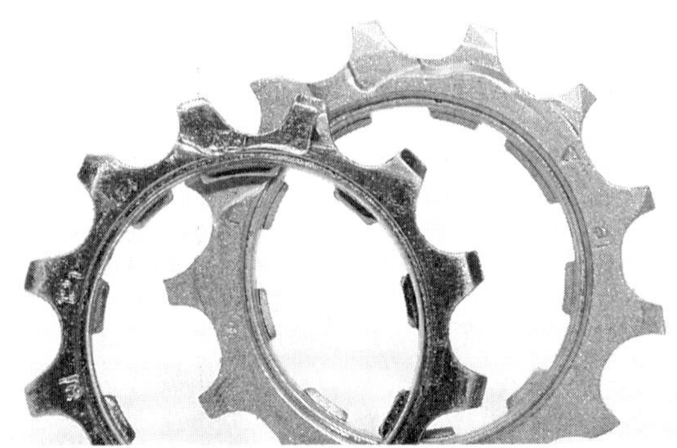

Left, *a Shimano HG rear cog;* right, *an IG cog. Note the IG cog has more detailed profiling and ramping – do not mix them.*

Removal

Remove the quick-release by unscrewing the knurled nut. Slide the lock-ring removal tool into the splines of the lock-ring, ensuring that at least 2mm of spline engage. Refit the quick-release without its springs, or use a wheel nut to keep the tool fully seated.

Working from above, position a sprocket remover on the left side of the second largest cog so that you are pushing down and clockwise. Use a large adjustable spanner on the lock-ring tool to act the opposite way. Position them so that you can press down on the two against the floor and push until the lock-ring gives.

Remove the quick-release and spin the lock-ring free. Lift off the smallest cog, the second cog and any shims. Slide off the cassette body or further individual cogs, taking note of the arrangement.

Replacement

Ensure that the cogs and their spacers and the cassette body are thoroughly clean; debris might prevent them from

The cassette lock-ring removal tool correctly fitted.

(Below) *When you are ready to remove the cassette, push hard against the floor to free the lock-ring.*

Fitting a Shimano or Sachs cassette.

sitting flat or prevent the lock-ring from tightening properly. Do not swap spacers between different makes or between seven-, eight- and nine-speed cassettes.

With Shimano and Sachs cassettes, align the ▽ mark on top of the cassette body (or on the individual cogs, followed by their spacers) with the wide spline, then position the shim (if applicable), then the top cog.

With Campagnolo cassettes, slide on the largest cog (or cassette body), then a

A fitted Campagnolo cassette; this is not a perfectly matched set so the 'O' marks stagger between the third and fourth cog.

spacer and the next cog and so on. Keep the △ marks of each cog in line. Matched sets of cogs will have the O marks spaced evenly clockwise.

With all cassettes, finally grease the lock-ring threads, then screw the lock-ring on using its tool. Refit the quick-release to keep the tool in place and tighten firmly with a large adjustable spanner until you hear/feel a number of positive clicks. Alternatively put lock-ring tool in a vice and turn the wheel clockwise.

Freewheels

Traditional rear hubs with a screw thread take a separate freewheel combining the cogs and freewheel mechanism. Exceptions to the standard thread are rare; almost all freewheel-type hubs and freewheels in Britain use British or ISO threads, which are compatible. Italian threads are also sufficiently compatible but not French ones.

Freewheels vary in width according to the number of cogs and their spacing. Replacements need to be of similar width so that neither the freewheel nor the chain foul the frame. The cog spacing needs to be compatible for use with index systems. Fortunately all modern seven-speed freewheels can be used

Removing the sprockets of a Sachs Aris freewheel.

with Shimano and Sachs systems. Five- and six-speed freewheels use a wider spacing for indexing – buy one that says it is index compatible if that is what you need. The Sachs Aris freewheel allows individual choice and replacement of the separate cogs, allowing its life to be extended and gear ratios to be customized. The individual sprockets of these may be removed by using a pair of sprocket removers. Use one on the second largest cog to press the freewheel forward and use another on the smallest to unscrew it.

Turn the removal tool anticlockwise to remove the freewheel.

Removal

Fit the removal tool in the same manner as the cassette lock-ring tool described above – you may need to remove the lock-nut and spacing pieces to do this. Use a large adjustable spanner on the remover flats to unscrew the freewheel; you may need to give it a sharp thrust to get it going, or better still, put it in a vice and turn the wheel anticlockwise. If you installed the quick-release or nut, unscrew the remover just enough to loosen the freewheel before continuing to remove the quick-release or nut.

Fitting

No tools are required. Grease the threads, then carefully align the freewheel body with the hub's threads and screw it on just a turn. Check that you have not cross-threaded the freewheel as this is very easy to do. If everything is all right, spin the freewheel on the rest of the way – it should go on easily. Once fitted to the bike, stand on the pedals in a low gear to tighten it, then check the gear adjustment.

Sometimes a spacer is fitted behind the freewheel. This is only necessary if the derailleur would otherwise touch the spokes, or the derailleur has trouble engaging the biggest cog, or to otherwise improve the chain-line, and should not be used otherwise.

Maintenance

Occasionally run a viscous oil, but not grease, into the freewheel body between the body and outside section, and lie the bike on its side. If the freewheel mechanism slips or sticks and running lubricant in has not worked, the freewheel is normally best replaced. A special Stein injector and lubricator may help but the cost of this tool is prohibitive; a shop may do the job for you.

If there is more than 1mm of play in the freewheel (often noticed as a knocking sound as you use a high gear), internal spacers can be removed to allow the top race to tighten down further. This is usually a fiddly and time-consuming job that is not particularly recommended as the myriad ball-bearings inside will be dislodged. You will need to hold the pawls (ratchet levers) in place as you lower the upper section back into place; use a length of fine thread wrapped around the pawls as you do this and pull it free after you have reassembled the freewheel.

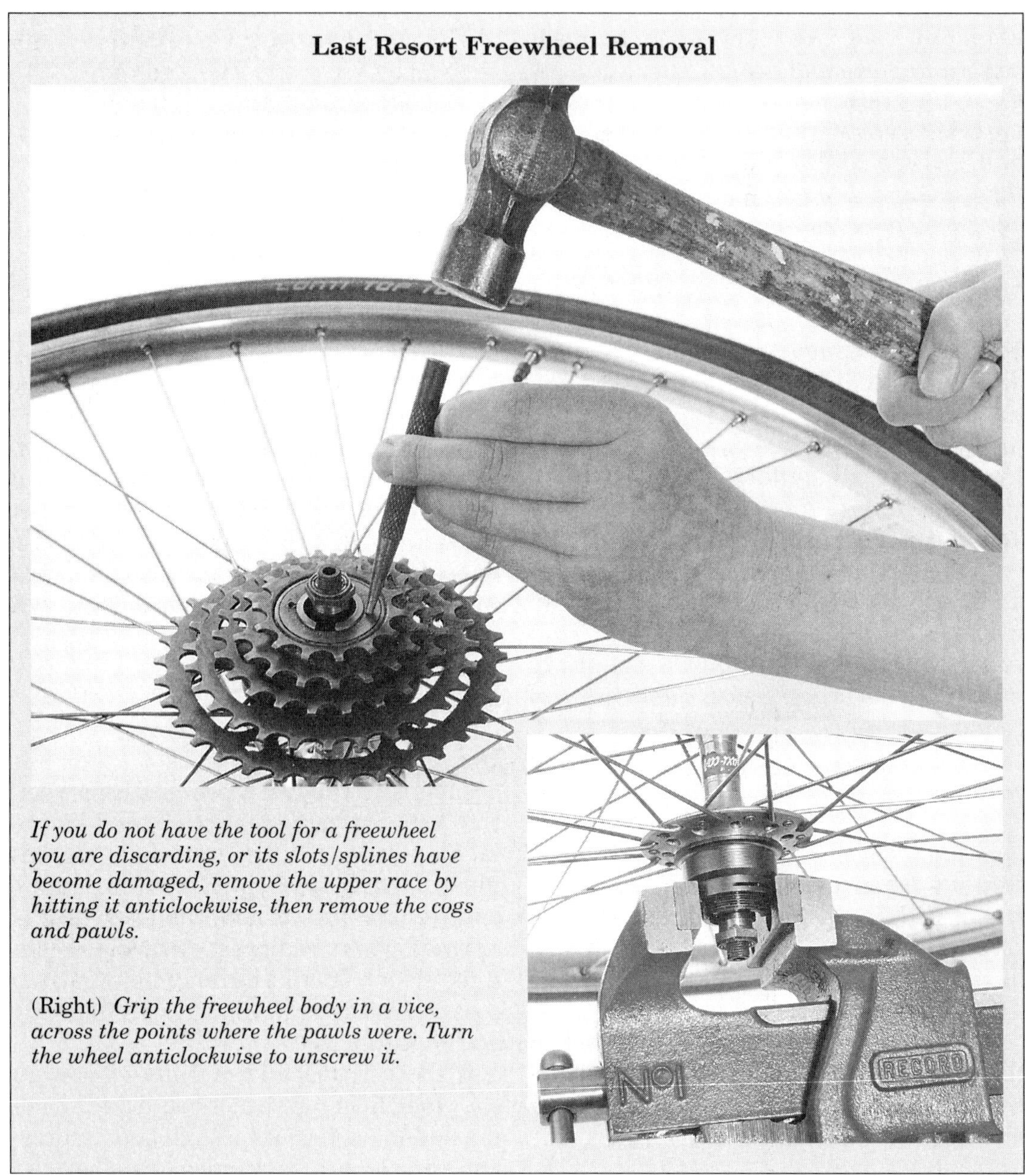

Last Resort Freewheel Removal

If you do not have the tool for a freewheel you are discarding, or its slots/splines have become damaged, remove the upper race by hitting it anticlockwise, then remove the cogs and pawls.

(Right) *Grip the freewheel body in a vice, across the points where the pawls were. Turn the wheel anticlockwise to unscrew it.*

7 Hub Gears

Hub gears enclose their complete mechanism within an enlarged hub shell, giving it exceptional protection from dirt and water. The internal parts of modern hubs are usually lubricated with long-life greases so will generally last several years before disassembly of the hub becomes necessary. The exception are older Sturmey Archer hubs with an oiling port on the main barrel identified by a plastic cap (metal in the case of very old hubs). With these add 5ml (one teaspoon) of Sturmey Archer oil once a month. Do not use any other lubricant as this can be either too viscous, or gum up, stopping some of the internal parts from functioning correctly.

Whenever you shift gear the cable pulls on a clutch-like device that engages different sets of intermediate gear wheels between the axle and the outside of the shell, or a direct drive without a gear wheel. To complete the shift, you most momentarily ease the pedalling force, or if stationary it can help to turn the pedals back a little, allowing the parts to move into their new position.

The clutch must exactly align with a given part of the hub's components to work properly. If it does not, the clutch will only engage the edge of a component and may sheer off its edges. Once this happens, the clutch is even more likely to slip as it has less to grip by; if this is repeated, a given gear (or all the gears if the clutch itself is worn) will slip. It is therefore vitally important that the hub gear is always kept in correct adjustment.

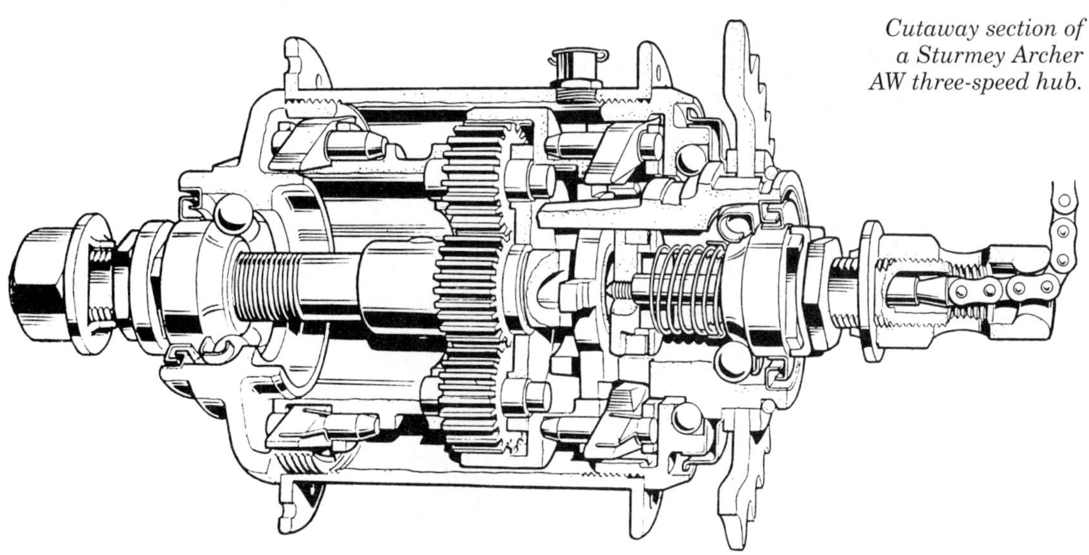

Cutaway section of a Sturmey Archer AW three-speed hub.

Apart from the correct cable adjustment and maintenance of the cable system in general, hub gears require little attention. You should ensure that the chain is tensioned correctly, as it must be adjusted every time you fit the wheel (this is explained below). Any adjustment of the wheel will also require the cable adjustment to be redone.

The chain (and rear cog and chain wheel) used with most hub gears is wider than a derailleur chain (½ × ⅛in as opposed to ½ × 3/32in). The transmission wears in the same manner as a derailleur set-up (*see* Chapter 6). Replacement of the hub cog and chain are covered later in this chapter.

THE HUB GEAR WHEEL

The nuts for hub gears are often deliberately made of a softer metal and often have a different thread from other hubs to distinguish them, because of the complexity of replacing the axle, should it be damaged. If you should over-tighten the nuts normally only the nut's thread will be stripped. For this reason you should use the manufacturer's specific nuts. In any case, the right-side nut is often dedicated to the cable fitment.

Removal

Cable systems attach/detach using four main systems as described below. Most systems must be removed before adjusting the wheel nuts. Remove the wheel by loosening the wheel nuts, prising back any washers left stuck to the frame, and sliding the wheel out. For additional information on removing wheels *see* Chapter 9. Note that a single-speed and fixed gear wheel is also removed/fitted on the same principals as a hub gear wheel with regard to chain tension.

Indicator/Toggle Rod Models

Disconnect Sturmey Archer three- and five-speed models by unscrewing the

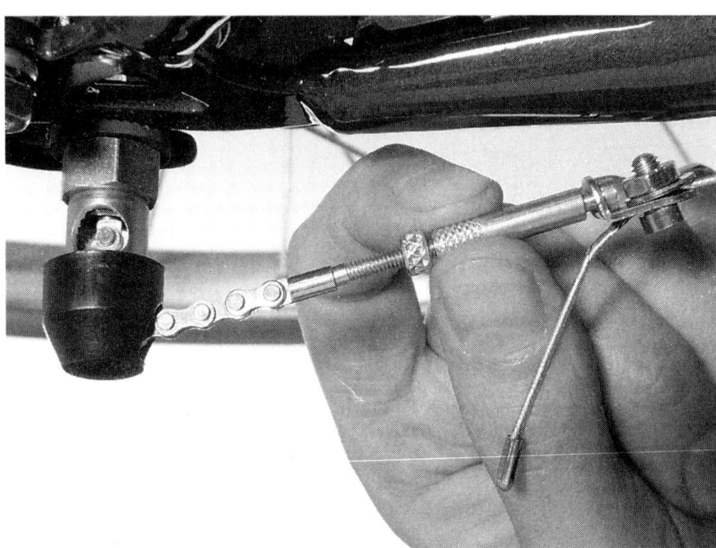

A Sturmey Archer three-speed cable connector and adjuster. The chain connects to the indicator rod inside the hub.

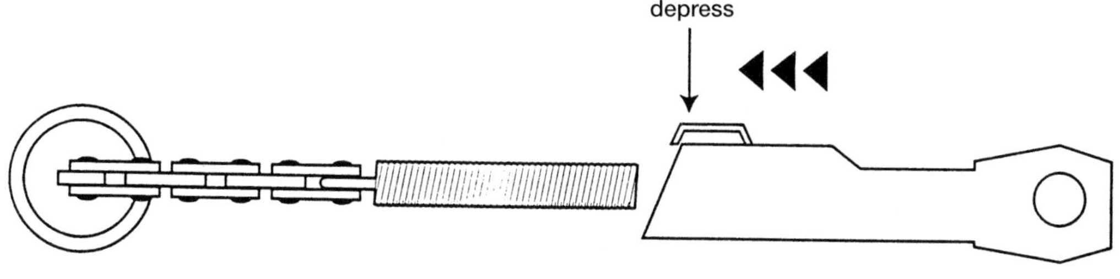

Sachs three-speed cable connector and adjuster.

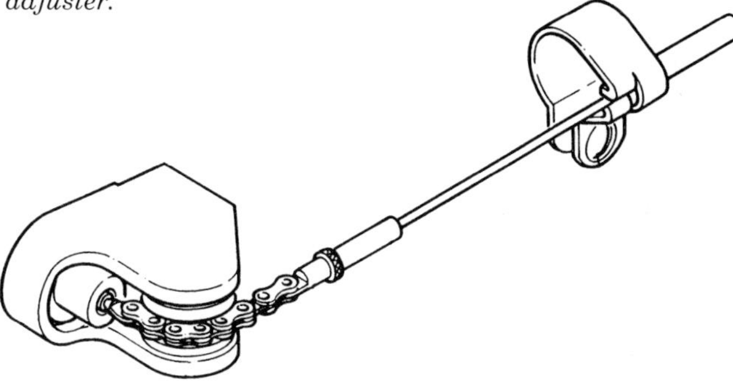

Sturmey Archer five-speed cable connector and adjuster.

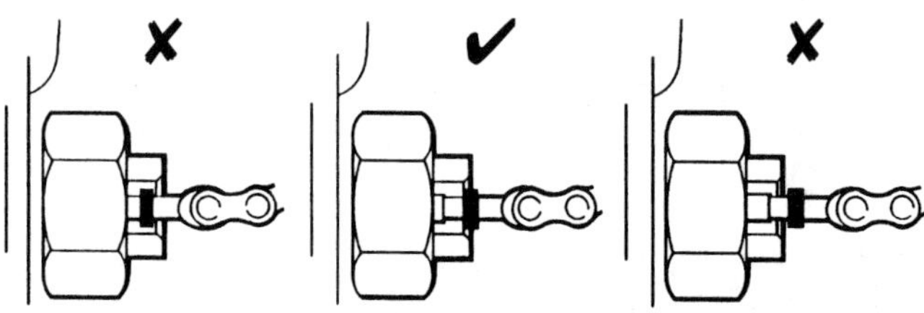

adjuster lock-ring and then the adjuster, taking care not to twist the chain as you do this. If the adjuster is tight you may need to use two pairs of pliers. Sachs models have a catch on the side of the adjuster, which you depress and pull off. Remove the indicator's plastic guard cap (if applicable). Unscrew the indicator completely and then pull free. Some Sturmey Archer five-speed models have a second cable on the left side that must also be removed in the same manner.

Sachs Click Box Models

Most Sachs five- and seven-speed models have a 'clickbox'. Unscrew the retaining bolt with your finger or a Phillips screw-driver and simply lift it off. Remove the guide sleeve and inner and outer push rod (as applicable) from the end of the axle.

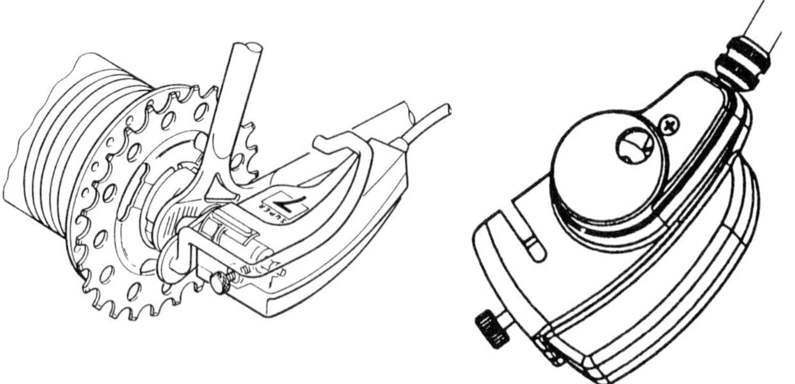

Sachs click-box cable connector with adjustment window.

Shimano Models

To remove the gear cable, select the top gear, push the cable cartridge right down and pull the inner cable fixing nut out of its holder to free it. Pull the cable housing free from the cartridge arm. As Shimano Nexus hubs incorporate a hub brake you will also need to release its cable and remove the torque arm securing bolt. To release the cable, push in the brake link to release its tension, and pull the brake inner cable fixing nut free. Please note that more detailed information on Nexus hub fitting and adjustment should have been supplied with your bike or hub.

Sturmey Archer Sprinter-7

Sturmey Archer seven-speed models use a cable drum that normally remains attached to the hub. Remove the right-side nut, the fulcrum lever (metal plate) and unscrew the loose end of cable leaving the hub from the main cable.

(Left) *The Shimano Nexus gear cable and cartridge assembly.*
(Right) *Releasing the cable from a Shimano Nexus brake.*

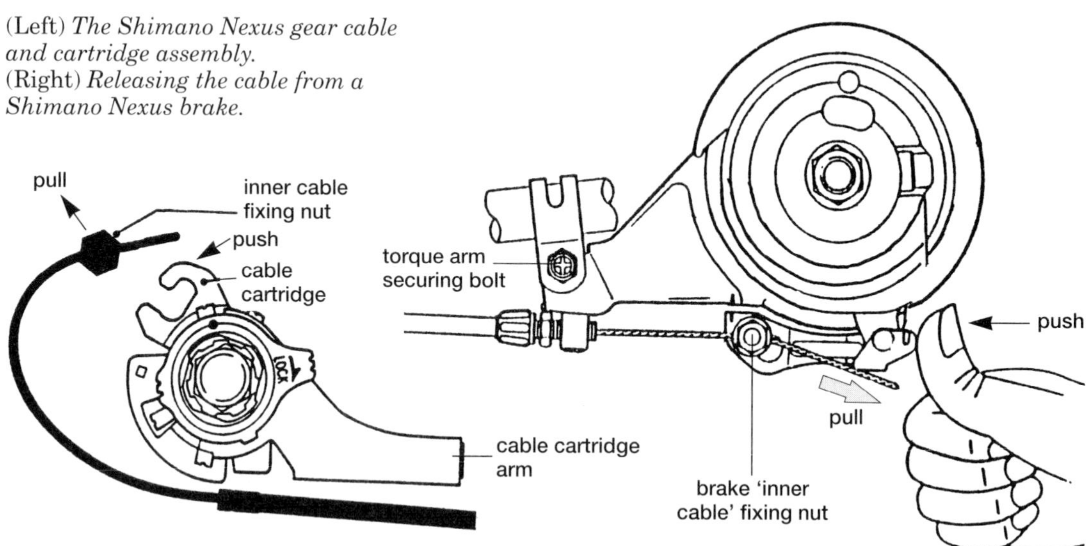

Sturmey Archer seven-speed hubs have a cable that must be separated before the outer 'fulcrum lever' (metal plate) is removed.

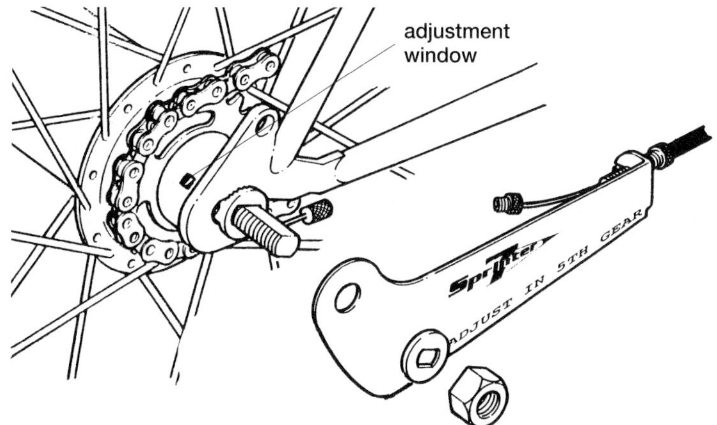

Fitting

If you have a Shimano or Sturmey Archer seven-speed hub, the cable should first be reattached. For all hubs you should have the correct special 'lock washers' fitted under the wheel nuts with their groove/tang facing in. These help ensure that the axle cannot rotate or move in the dropouts. Sometimes serrated washers are used instead but these are less effective. If the wheel did move, the cable adjustment would be thrown out, and the chain become loose.

Position the wheel centrally between both the seatstays and the chainstays. Pull the wheel back so that the chain is almost taut. As you do this, nip the nuts tight and check that the wheel is still central. Check the chain tension and ensure that when the wheel is tight and properly centred in the frame there is 1.5cm (½in) of free play at the midpoint of the chain. If it is too loose the chain may come off, if it is too tight the chain will put tension on the freewheel mechanism, making it stiff and rough.

Some trial and error will usually be needed to tension the chain correctly. The easiest way to do this can be to loosen one side of the axle at a time, easing each side forward or back a few millimetres to ease the wheel into the correct position. Just nip the nut to tighten it until alignment is correct, then tighten fully.

The freewheel mechanism will also feel stiff if the cones are incorrectly adjusted; the cones are adjusted in the same manner as in conventional hubs described in Chapter 9. Make all adjustments from the left. The right (drive side) cone is factory set in a precise position and not designed for adjustment.

Cable Fitting and Adjustment

Indicator/Toggle Chain Models

Lightly oil the indicator rod, and press it in gently as you use its chain to screw it in. Go carefully as after about six turns it will become finger tight; do not go beyond this point or you may strip the internal axle key. Now unscrew the rod to the point where the connecting chain is pointing towards the cable. Refit the indicator guard. Some five-speed systems use an axle-mounted pulley wheel.

Put the shifter into second gear and turn the pedal back to ensure the mechanism has changed gear.

On Sturmey Archer three-speed models, now use the cable adjuster to align the end of the rod (the shoulder where it meets the chain) exactly with the end of the axle.

On Sturmey Archer five-speed models, align the centre of the red recess at the end of the axle so that it is level with the end of the axle. Tighten the lock-nut down onto the adjuster. You may wish to nip the lock-nut tight with pliers to prevent it working loose, but this will also prevent easy adjustment on the road.

Damage can sometimes occur to the indicator rod or toggle chain through the bike falling over or through being overtightened. In some cases the rod can become bent. This can contribute to poor gear changing, so it is best to replace it if in doubt. As the indicator rod serves as a visual indicator of correct cable adjustment it must be the correct model as the rod length can vary. To check if yours is the correct model put the shifter in the highest gear (third or fifth as applicable), and turn the pedals back a turn to ensure the gear is engaged. Adjust the cable tension to just take up the slack. It should be to within 2mm of the correct adjustment described above.

On Sachs toggle chain models put the shifter into third gear and turn the pedals back. Adjust the cable tension so that it is on the verge of pulling taut, but not quite exerting any movement on the chain/rod.

Sachs Click Box Models

Replace the cleaned and greased guide sleeve and inner and outer push rod (as applicable) in the end of the axle. Slide the click box onto the hub axle; it will help to have the shifter in first gear. Tighten the knurled/Phillips screw so that it aligns in the groove at the axle end. For trigger-operated gears no further adjustment is necessary. Gripshift models require adjustment at the click box. Put the shifter in third gear (five-speed hubs), or fourth gear (seven-speed hubs). Rotate the adjuster at the front of the click box so that the arrow in the window aligns with that on the body.

Shimano Nexus Models

Replace the cable in the cartridge, ensuring it seats correctly in its channel. Set the shift lever to the fourth position and turn the cable-adjusting barrel to the right of the hub (alternatively, on the gear-shift); align either of the two sets of red setting lines on the cassette joint bracket with the pulley. You may also need to readjust the brake.

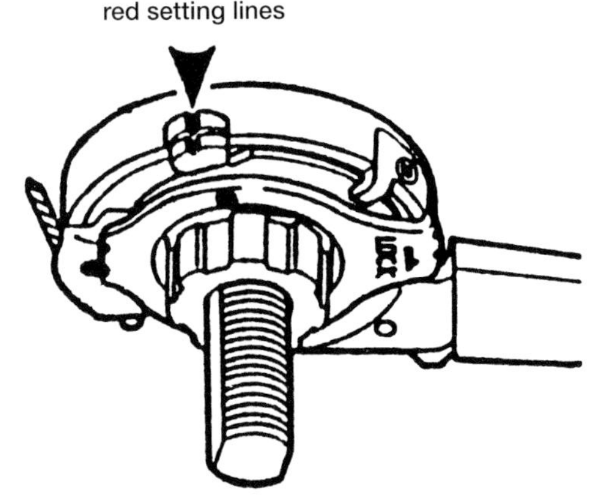

Shimano Nexus gear cable adjustment; align the red setting lines.

Sturmey Archer Sprinter-7 Models

Select fifth gear from fourth gear and use the adjuster at the end of the fulcrum plate to align the white mark in the adjuster window of the cable drum cover with the rear sprocket.

All Models

Finally, run through all the gears to check them. If it is found that they are not working properly, double-check the adjustment, as the cables may have bedded down.

CABLE REPLACEMENT

Gear-shifters not described below are generally sufficiently similar to derailleur gear cable replacement not to require any further instruction (*see* Chapter 6). When removing a cable take careful note of its route through the shifter and to the hub if it is unfamiliar. As a general practice with all systems, back-pedal the cranks to ensure that the highest gear is engaged and clamp the cable with the gear-shifter in the highest gear position. The initial cable tension should be on the verge of pulling taut but not quite – then make the final adjustment as described above.

Click Box Models

These are semi-rigid and come as a complete item with the box for attachment to the shifter. They cannot be shortened. Ensure that there are no kinks when fitting.

Sturmey Archer and Three-Speed Sachs Models

These systems have a fulcrum clip (cable stop) on the chainstay, seat tube or down tube. Some systems may have a small pulley wheel to guide the cable, which should turn. These fitments must be securely mounted so that their position does not creep in use. These should guide the cable by the smoothest route possible to the end of the toggle chain.

Spare cables for Sturmey Archer hubs are bought as a complete unit of inner, outer, and adjuster cable. Grease the inner cable and cut the casing to length in the same manner as for a brake cable (*see* Chapter 8). Unscrew and remove the adjuster from the chain. Turn the pedals back a turn to put the hub in top gear; third, fifth or seventh gear (as applicable).

Sturmey Archer Three-Speed Triggers

Pull the trigger right down to lift the spring within the top of the trigger. This will open up a gap within the trigger, enabling you to pass the greased inner cable through it. Position the cable in the groove at the rear of the trigger, its long, thin nipple pulled up into the end of this groove. Pull the cable from the back of the trigger to tension it, keeping it in place, and shift the trigger into third gear. Slot the special cable casing ferrule into the keyhole exit at the rear of the trigger to secure it. Thread the inner cable through the cable guides to the indicator chain, secure in the cable clamp so that the adjuster engages the indicator chain by about 1cm, and the cable is just taut, then adjust as described above.

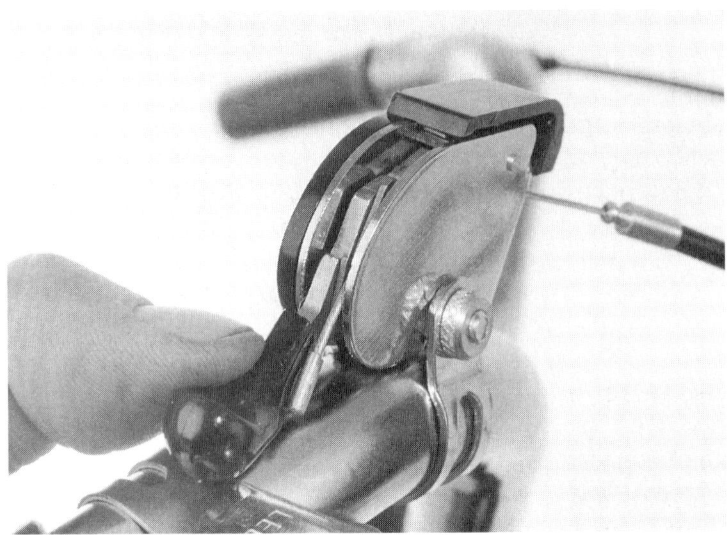

A Sturmey Archer three-speed trigger pushed down to accept its cable.

CHAIN REMOVAL AND FITTING (½ × ⅛ TYPE)

Summary – Chain Removal and Fitting

When?

- If worn and needing replacement
- If sprocket or chain wheel sizes have been altered, requiring links to be added/removed

Preparation/Notes

- 'Split' links are normally used on ⅛in chains on single-speed and hub-geared bikes only. They must not be used on any derailleur-geared system or with other chain-tensioning devices

Removal

Find the chain's split link. Remove the link spring clip by using a pair of pliers to squeeze the horseshoe-shaped spring-retaining clip back against the chain rivet. Be careful, however, as it might catapult away. Now lift off the plate and remove the back part of the clip. If you cannot find a split link, remove and fit the chain as described in Chapter 6.

Fitting a split link spring retaining clip.

Fitting

Assemble the back part and plate and slide over the clip so that it points backwards as you pedal, positioning it so that its open end rests against the back rivet. Now squeeze on the clip in the same way that you removed it.

Chain Length

Ensuring that the chain completely wraps the rear sprocket and chain wheel, pull the wheel back into the dropout. With the wheel roughly centred in the frame, the axle should be approximately in the middle of the dropout slot. If it is too far back you may not get the chain taut enough (especially later as it wears). If it is too near the front of the dropouts, the washers may have insufficient grip on the frame. In both cases, the tyre may rub the mudguard.

The chain length links are removed in the same manner as for derailleur chains. In some cases removing or adding a whole link can prove to be too much. In this case obtain a special 'cranked' link.

SPROCKETS AND CHAINSETS FOR HUB GEAR USE

Many hub gears come with a sprocket for use with ½ × ⅛in chain. Sachs and Shimano hubs may come with a sprocket for ½×3/32in chains (as used on derailleur gear bikes). The sprockets are generally interchangeable between brands. Almost all chainsets are designed for use with ½ × 3/32in chains, except some basic steel, cottered models and expensive models designed for track-racing use. There is generally no problem in using a ⅛in chain with a 3/32in chain wheel. If you have a chainset with a 50.4 or 130mm BCD, replacement chainrings are available manufactured by TA (*see* Chapter 5).

More so than with derailleur gear systems, the chain must travel in a straight line to the rear cog. Poor alignment will cause the chain to feel rough as you pedal, wear itself and the sprockets prematurely and possibly come off. Sturmey Archer hubs allow 7mm (⅓in) adjustment of the chain-line through the positioning of the

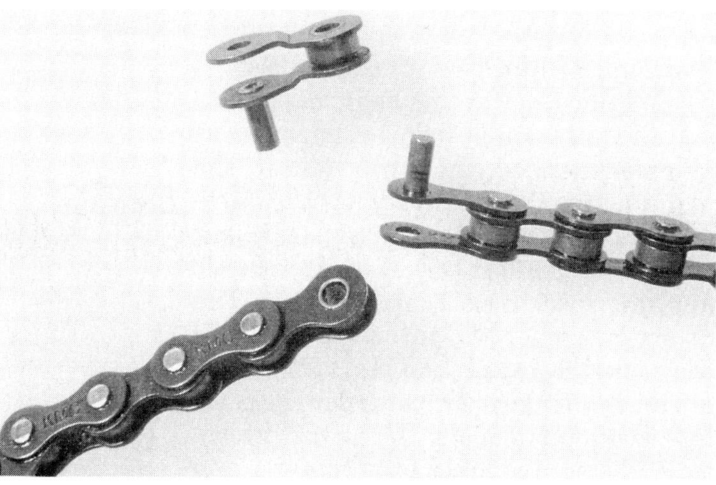

A 'cranked' link can be used to shorten the chain by half a full link, but they are hard to find.

sprocket spacers and by the nature of the dish-shaped sprocket, which can be used either way up. *See* Chapter 5 for more information on the chain-line.

Sprocket Removal

To remove, position a small, flat-bladed screwdriver in the spline nearest the open end of the clip. Gently prise the clip up a little, then move the screwdriver round a bit further, twisting it to spring the clip off. Lift off the spacing pieces, noting their order and which way up the sprocket is. Clean all the parts you intend to reuse.

Sprocket Fitting

Reassemble the sprocket and spacers in the same manner as before unless you want to alter the chain-line – if so, the parts can go in any order. Position the clip with your thumb over the open end. Use a screwdriver to lever over the clip – it should snap into place in a single operation. If the clip has become distorted and does not sit snugly in its groove, replace it.

HUB GEAR OVERHAUL

Overhaul of hub gear internal parts is beyond the scope of this book; disassembly and reassembly can be tricky so it is recommended that you follow the manufacturer's own instruction literature. Sturmey Archer supply excellent instruction leaflets (*see* Manufacturers), and few special tools are required. The Sturmey Archer AW three-speed hub is the easiest to repair, and most good dealers stock the parts or can order them for less common models. Technical literature is also available for Shimano and Sachs hub gears. Parts for these will need to be specially ordered. Note that complete internal units are also available and can be the most cost-effective option if a lot of the parts are worn and the rest of the wheel is in good condition.

Springing off a Sturmey Archer cog circlip.

Springing the circlip on; note that the sprocket has been turned up the other way to alter the chain-line.

8 Brakes

Brake designs vary more than perhaps any other part of the bike. It is beyond the scope of this book to cover less common designs, but generally similar principles hold true when setting up other rim brake types. If your brake is not exactly like those described, check the details of those shown that have similar design elements. I have divided this chapter into given stages of work on the brakes, covering the relevant detail for common types as I go.

A rim brake system consists of brake callipers or cantilever arms, the brake blocks, wheel rims, cables and brake levers. The system requires frequent maintenance to keep it at its most effective. By ensuring that braking is smooth and progressive yet powerful when needed you also improve safety.

In wet conditions more pressure must be applied to the brake levers, increasing cable stretch. Winter grit tends to clog the brake blocks and wear the rim, and the increased pressure used makes this effect all the worse. Water also tends to enter the cables, making them stiff and subject to greater strain. A poorly maintained cable is much more likely to fail, and in just the conditions where you need it most.

Before working on any rim-operating brake you should ensure your wheels are fully seated in their dropouts and centralized in the frame/forks. A rim over to one side, or out of true, will make centralizing the brake difficult or impossible. Braking is best on clean rims. Clean them with hot water and dish detergent to remove the black rubber/aluminium deposit that tends to collect in winter.

BRAKE QUICK-RELEASES

When working on brakes or removing a wheel it is often very useful to release it so that the brake blocks temporarily opens out wider, but can be quickly reset to their original adjustment. Various systems are used but if there is no obvious method (as is the case on many older brakes) you may have to screw in the cable adjuster. Always remember to reset the brake afterwards.

Most Shimano and many other calliper brakes have a small lever by the cable clamp bolt; lift it to release the brake.

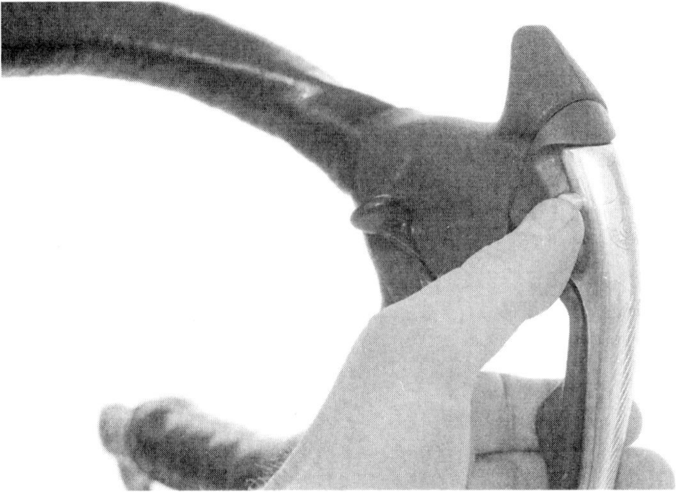

Campagnolo brake levers have a small button at their top, which you have to press across to release the brake.

(Below right) *Most cantilever systems release by unhooking the straddle wire. Hold the brake blocks in with your hand while you do this, pulling the end tab to lift it out of its recess.*

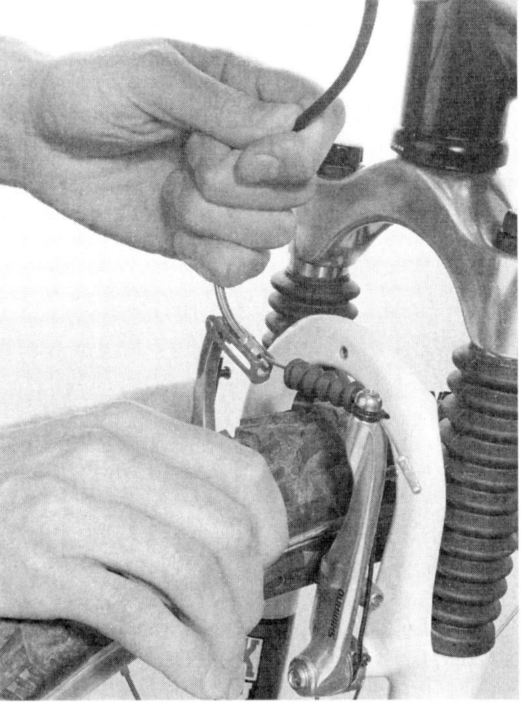

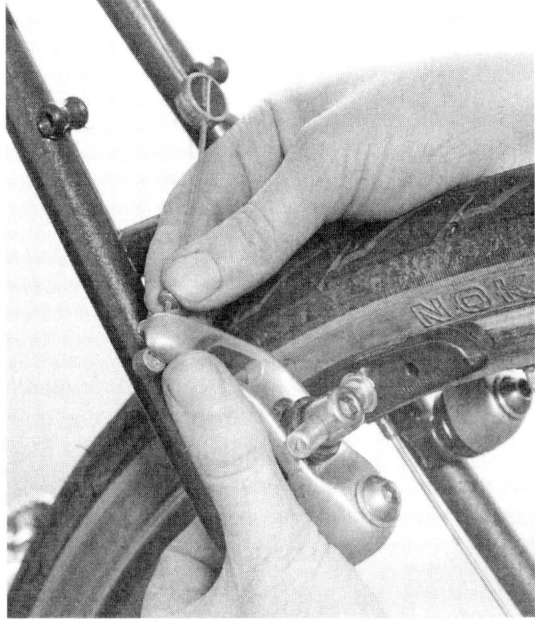

(Left) *'V' brakes are released by unhooking the cable from the swinging bracket.*

BRAKE LEVERS

Brake levers should be attached firmly, positioned as the mirror image of each other and within easy reach.

Straight-bar Levers

Most of these have an allen key clamp on the underside of the lever body. Some have the attachment clamp bolt hidden

The hand reach can be adjusted on some straight-bar brake levers – look for a small bolt on the lever body.

behind the cable routing, always ensure the lever is tight before fitting cables. Some MTB brake levers have adjustable reach; use the adjustment bolt or screw on the lever body.

Drop-bar Levers

Most drop-bar and some straight-bar levers have a 5mm allen bolt inside the lever or, in the case of Campagnolo Ergopower and Shimano STI levers, under the hood. You may need a large screwdriver or box spanner for older levers.

Loosen the clamp enough so that it will not mark the bars, but not so much that it falls apart; check the arrangement before you start in case it does. Slide each lever into position and nip each clamp firm. Check that the levers are in a comfortable position for you, and that they are level by running a straight edge across them and ensuring that it is parallel with the bars. Reposition as necessary. Tighten the clamp but be careful not to overdo it and break it! Check that the brake levers cannot be moved when twisted.

Brake Lever Compatibility

Modern brakes have become increasing dedicated to specific levers to work properly. Low-profile cantilever brakes are designed for use with MTB brake levers: the lever's cable pull matches the geometry of the brake unit. Drop-bar levers designed for calliper brakes generally have too much cable pull for low-profile cantilevers, resulting in a spongy feel and the need to have the brake blocks right up against the rim. This type of lever should be used with the former wider profile cantilevers.

'V' brakes should be used with their own special levers. These have a 'servo-wave' that pulls the brake in quickly at first, then more slowly to increase the power. This means that the brake blocks can be positioned further from the rim. This is adjustable on some models – just loosen the locating bolt and slide into one of three positions.

Check drop-bar levers are level with a straight edge.

(Below) *The clamp bolt of Shimano STI levers is hidden under the hood.*

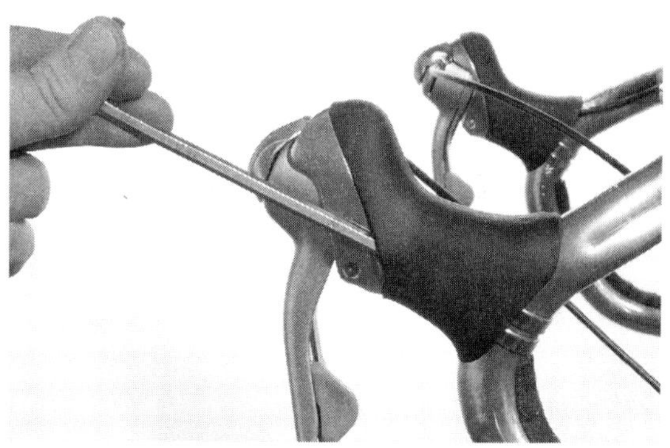

BRAKE BLOCK REPLACEMENT

Summary – Brake Block Replacement

Calliper brake 🔧🔧 15 minutes
Cantilever brake 🔧🔧🔧 45 minutes

When?

- When the block's pattern has worn away, or the wear line is reached. 'V' brake blocks can be used until the edge of the shoes is reached.

Preparation/Notes

- Cantilever brakes should have their cable arrangement correctly set up before fitting brake blocks
- Screw the cable adjusters in fully in order to slacken the cable and bring the brake blocks out

Brake blocks tend to collect grit and aluminium particles that wear the rim and impair braking. Pick these out with a pointed implement, particularly when the braking feels rough (imagine sandpaper), or is otherwise poor. A brake block that overhangs the rim will wear into an 'L' shape, although if such wear is minor it can be trimmed back into shape.

Check the orientation of new brake blocks and their shoes. Arrows indicate that the blocks should face the same direction as the wheel rotation. Some Shimano brake shoes have an open end to aid block replacement only – the open end must face backwards. If your rim has neither indication, it should go with its broader base at the bottom, so that the block sits at 90 degrees to the rim.

All brake blocks should be positioned so that the front touches the rim 0.5–1mm

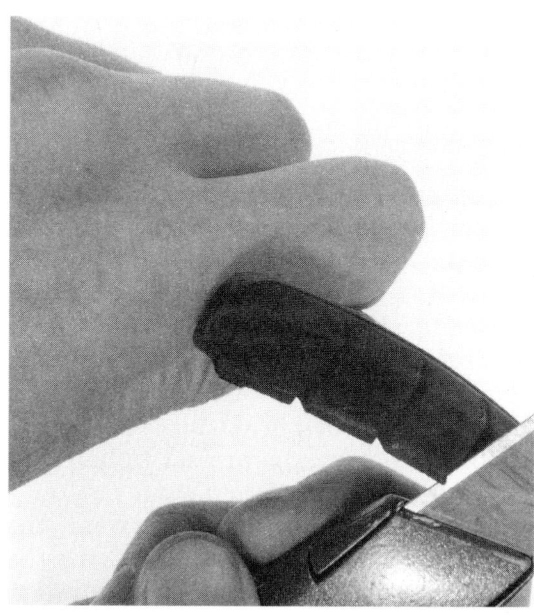

A brake block that has worn unevenly can be trimmed back into shape if the wear is minor.

before the rear. This 'toe-in' prevents squealing and vibration and improves the power.

Calliper Brakes

Remove the old brake block by removing its attachment nut. Position the new one with the spherical washer (if applicable) on the inside and the plain washer on the outside of the arm. The spherical washer allows the angle of the brake block, and thus the toe-in, to be adjusted.

As the blocks wear, the calliper arms start pointing upwards, which may make the blocks rub the tyre; therefore position them so they follow the curve of the rim, and as low as they will go on the rim braking surface without overhanging it. Tighten the bolt as you keep the alignment; it may help to pull the brake 'on' to stop it moving, or hold it with an adjustable spanner or slip-joint pliers.

Cantilever Brakes

Loosen the brake bolt attachment nut with a 10 mm spanner; you may need to hold the front part of the bolt with a 5 or 6mm allen key. Fit the new brake block

Fitting a brake block to a calliper brake.

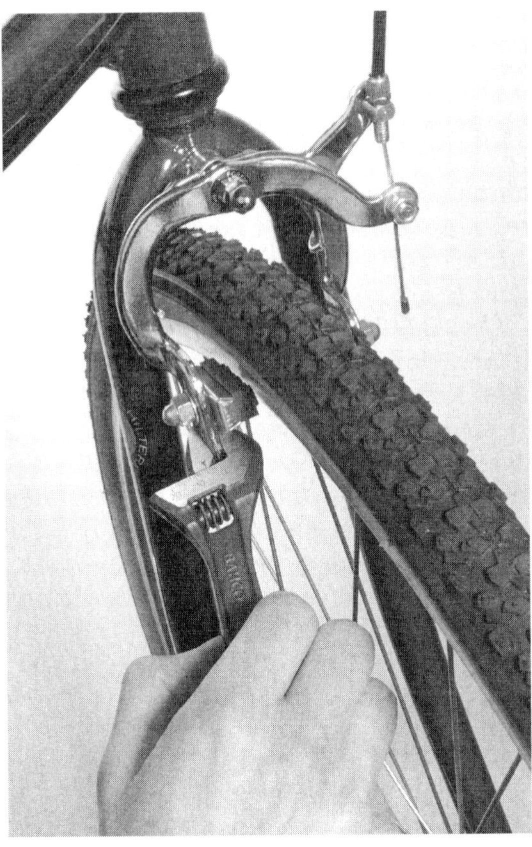

'peg' through the 'eye' and finger tighten the nut to keep things in place.

Now align the block with the rim. You have the up/down adjustment in the arm, the angle of the block's approach, the alignment with the rim curve, the in/out movement of the block on its peg, and the toe-in to deal with – quite a handful! The brake blocks should hit the rim squarely in all respects except toe-in and be set on their pegs about 2mm from the rim. Some older cantilevers have a 'tab' on the dished brake block mounting washers that can be pre-set to help you adjust the toe-in.

As cantilever brake blocks wear, the arms begin to arc further in, with the danger of the brake block under-hanging or even missing the rim. Therefore position them with 1mm clearance under the tyre so that they will miss it but have the maximum of room for wear. Finally tighten the mounting bolt firmly. The brake block mountings should look symmetrical.

The brake blocks can be toed in by careful bending of the brake arm. Use this method if there is no alternative.

The final tightening of a correctly positioned cantilever brake block.

'V' Brakes

Before removing the original brake blocks note the arrangement of the spacing pieces on either side of the brake arm. Take off by removing the allen bolt at the back of its mounting stud. Fit the new block with the spacing pieces in the same positions. Align the brake block in the same manner as for a cantilever brake block, though this is much easier.

It is worth making the following check: with the blocks pulled against the rim, measure the distance from the horizontal hinged bracket to the other brake arm. It must be between 39mm and 55mm. If not, use the thick and thin mounting washers to reposition the blocks to adjust the gap as necessary. If the gap is too small the brake may not apply fully.

All Models

Finally, unscrew the cable adjuster to position the brake blocks about 2mm from the rim, or 3mm for 'V' brakes. You may also need to centralize the brake (*see* General Maintenance below).

BRAKE CABLE REPLACEMENT

Brake cables come with either 'pear' or 'barrel' nipples for drop- or straight-bar levers respectively, but check the original. Some 'universal' cables have both types; cut off the one you do not want with a good pair of cable cutters.

Take note of the original inner cable and cable casing routing and remove the old cable. Along the top tube it may have rubber 'donuts' fitted; reuse these as they stop the cable rattling against the frame. Ensure that the cable adjusters of the lever, brake unit and cable hangers (as applicable) are fully screwed in and that the cable quick-release is closed (if applicable).

Cut the new cable casing sections you will need allowing a little for smooth bends, but without excessive length. Use

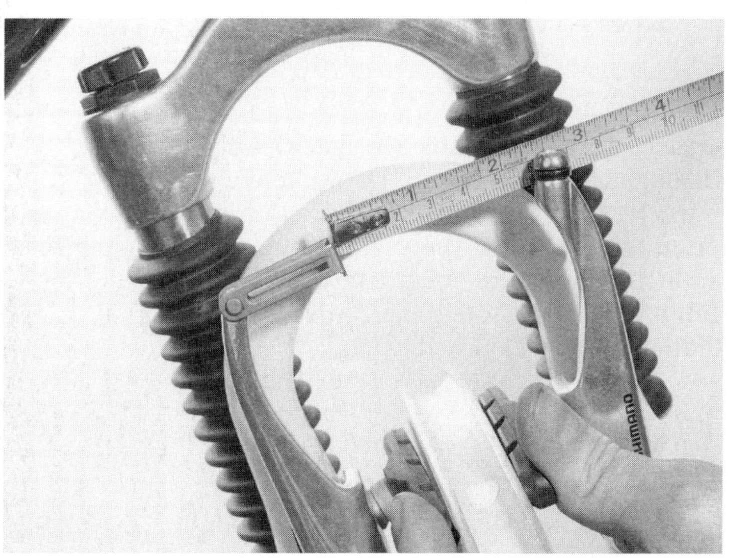

Measure the gap as shown to be sure the brake functions correctly.

Summary – Brake Cable Replacement

Calliper brake 🔧🔧 15 minutes
Cantilever brake 🔧🔧🔧 45 minutes

When?

- Overhaul intervals
- When cables no longer pull and release without hindrance or start to have a dry feel
- If the cable casing develops kinks or the cable shows signs of fraying; the cable clamp is commonly a starting point of fray as the clamp bites into the cable
- If you have low-profile cantilevers the cable system should be set up correctly before the brake blocks are adjusted

Special Tools

If you have Shimano '90–'92 cantilevers the correct Shimano Pro-Set is desirable.

Preparation/Notes

- If you have cantilever brakes *see* the panel on Straddle Wires
- Remember that in the countries that drive on the left the front brake cable attaches to the right brake lever; this is so that you can slow down safely when turning right. This convention also insures against unwelcome surprises! The reverse is true for nations that drive on the right.

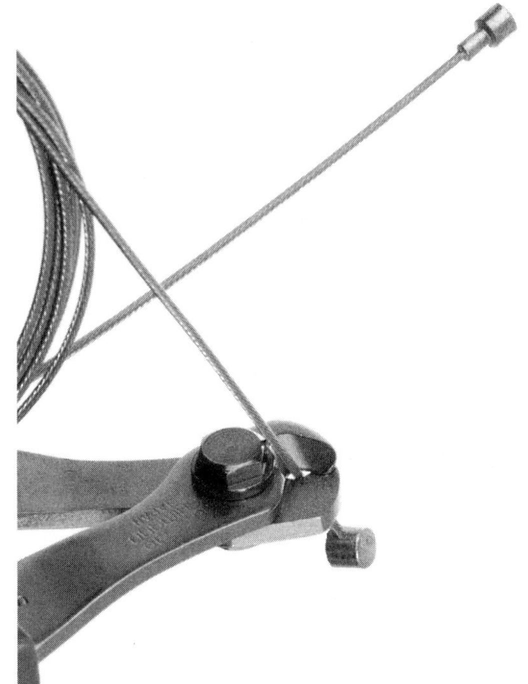

side cutters if possible to cut cleanly through the metal spiral. Do not leave a burr. It can help to use a grease gun to pump grease down the casing from the end that you will be inserting the inner cable into. You should not grease PTFE (Teflon, Gore-Tex) lined cables.

(Top right) *Cutting the barrel nipple off a universal brake cable.*

(Bottom right) *Using side cutters to cut the cable casing.*

Left: *the left cable casing is burred over and should be cut again.* Centre: *the casing has been cut cleanly and is acceptable.* Right: *for perfection a clean cut has been filled down flat.*

Liberally grease the inner cable and nipple and thread through the brake lever cable hook (it may be reversed, so spin it round and check that the nipple will seat firmly in it) and out through the cable exit or adjuster. Use ferrules (end caps) on each cut end of casing unless these will not fit into the appropriate recesses of the lever, adjuster, frame cable stops and so on. Thread the cable through to the brake unit, then follow the specific instructions below that apply to your type of brake.

Calliper Brakes

Thread the inner cable through the cable clamp eye or slot and tighten the bolt until it grips the cable very lightly. Use pliers or a cable puller to pull the cable tight, take up all excess cable and seat the cable casing. Release to bring the blocks out to about 1mm from the rim. Now fully tighten the clamp, then go to the Final Checks detailed below.

Cantilever Systems

There are three main cantilever designs. Examine the photographs to determine

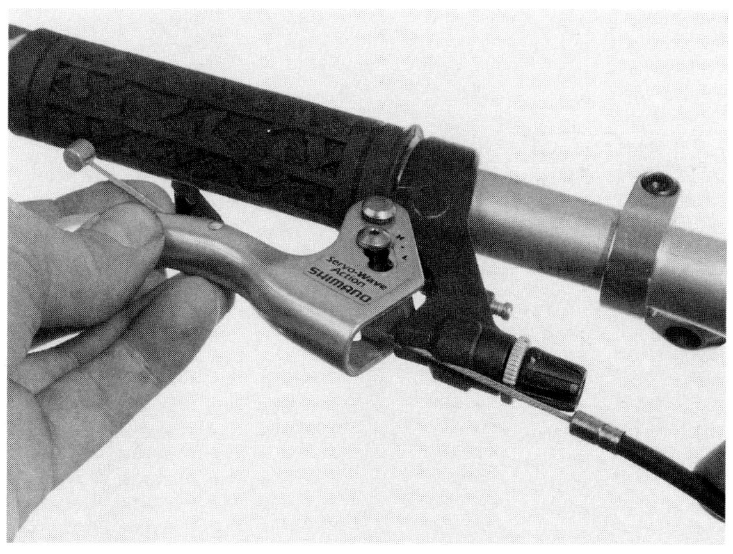

Straight-bar levers have slotted adjusters to make cable maintenance easier. Line up the slots with those of the lever body to remove and fit the cables quickly.

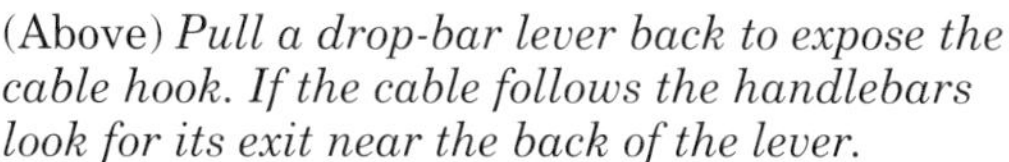

(Above) *Pull a drop-bar lever back to expose the cable hook. If the cable follows the handlebars look for its exit near the back of the lever.*

(Right) *Use ferrules on all cut ends of cable casing if at all possible. Here the adjuster is fully screwed in ready for the new cable.*

(Below) *Tensioning a calliper brake cable by a cable puller and tightening the cable clamp.*

Traditional wide-profile cantilevers; here the cable is set up correctly and is now being clamped.

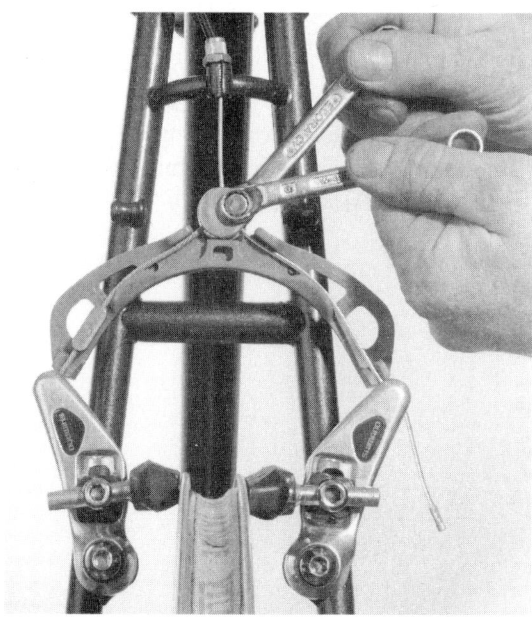

(Below) *Shimano low-profile '90–'92 cantilevers with their plastic 'banana' fitted.*

what type yours are and follow the instructions accordingly.

Traditional (Wide-profile)

Check the length of the straddle wire linking the two brake sides, as you may need or want to adjust it (*see* panel page 136). Check that the straddle wire cable clamp on the brake unit is tight. Pass the inner cable through the cable carrier's clamp – there is a washer immediately either side of the carrier. Replace the cable over the straddle wire – it may help to unhook it. Pull the cable tight as shown but release a little before tightening the clamp fully.

Shimano '90–'92 (Low-profile)

Loosen the cable carrier's clamp bolt and pass the cable through to the cantilever cable clamp. Set up the brake with the correct Shimano Pro-Set 'plastic banana' as shown (the accompanying literature explains which one to use). Pull the main cable through the brake unit clamp and tighten it – the brake blocks should be right against the rim. Tighten the cable carrier clamp and remove the banana. If you do not have the banana try to get the arrangement symmetrical with the straddle wire 90 degrees to the brake unit for maximum efficiency.

Shimano M-System (Low-profile)

On the back of the cable carrier there are two slots: one to feed the cable through without bending it and the other to seat it in after setting up. Feed the inner cable through the cable carrier, then through the short sleeve, then through the cable clamp on the brake unit. Pull the cable through until the short cable aligns with the line on the cable carrier, then tighten the cable clamp's pinch bolt. Finally reposition the main cable in its 'fixed' narrow slot on the carrier.

'V' Brakes

Thread the cable through the curved metal cable link tube and through the cable clamp. Pull the cable through the clamp, ensuring that the cable link is seated properly in the hinged bracket, and taking up the slack. Let the brake blocks rest about 2mm from the rim and tighten the clamp. Note that a 90-degree metal cable link tube is used for a cable coming from the opposite side, and a 130-degree type for a cable from same side; this avoids acute bends of the cable housing and snagging.

Final Adjustment and Checks

Pull hard on the brake lever ten times to bed in the cables and test the cable fit. This normally results in the blocks moving a little further from the rim. Use the cable adjuster to bring the blocks back in if necessary. The blocks should be about 2mm from the rim, or 3mm in the case of 'V' brakes. However, the most important consideration is that the brake is easy to apply, yet will develop full power if necessary, with a little extra pull available should something slip.

Shimano M-system cantilevers with an alignment-type cable carrier are the most common variety.

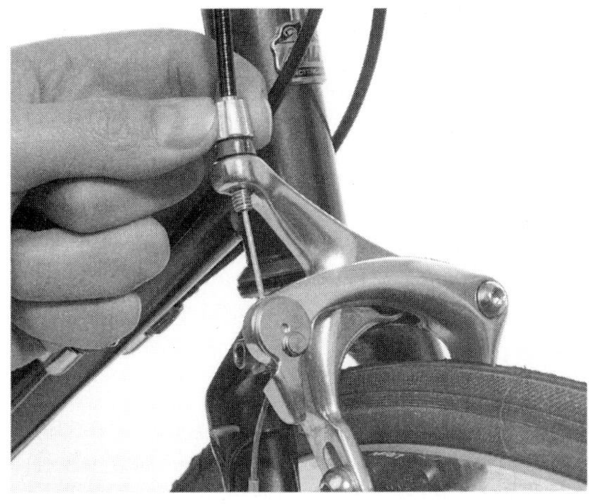

Making the final adjustment to a calliper brake using its cable adjuster.

Cut off excess cable with cable cutters and crimp on a cable end cap by gently using pliers or cable cutters.

(Above) *For frames without cable guides, electrician's zip-ties work well.*

(Right) *On open (ladies') frames the cable approaches the brake from below. Water can drip down into it, causing it to seize, so seal its end with grease.*

Cantilever Straddle Cables

Most Shimano cantilevers use dedicated link cables. Their length (and the sleeve of M-System types) is crucial to the correct operation of the brake – replace with the same model number (stamped on the cable nipple or finger hold), or measure it and find an identical third-party replacement – Clarks make a wide range. If you are in doubt, quote the brake part number (on its reverse) to your dealer. You can if you wish fit a straddle cable intended for traditional cantilever brakes in accordance with the diagram below. Traditional cantilever designs (usually wide rather than low profile) use a one-piece straddle cable, which should be used in combination with either a reflector bracket or mudguard; if the main cable broke, the straddle cable could grab your tyre with potentially lethal consequences. For maximum efficiency, set it up so that the straddle cable is at 90 degrees to a line through the centre of the brake arms.

To improve the feel of cantilever brakes used with drop-bar levers intended for calliper brakes, the straddle cable length can be increased to make the braking less 'spongy' and allow the brake blocks to be set further from the rim. However, increased hand pressure will be required when working the brakes as the effect is partly to pull on the brake mountings. If increasing the length of the straddle cable be sure that the distance between the cable carrier and underside of the cable hanger is at least 20mm.

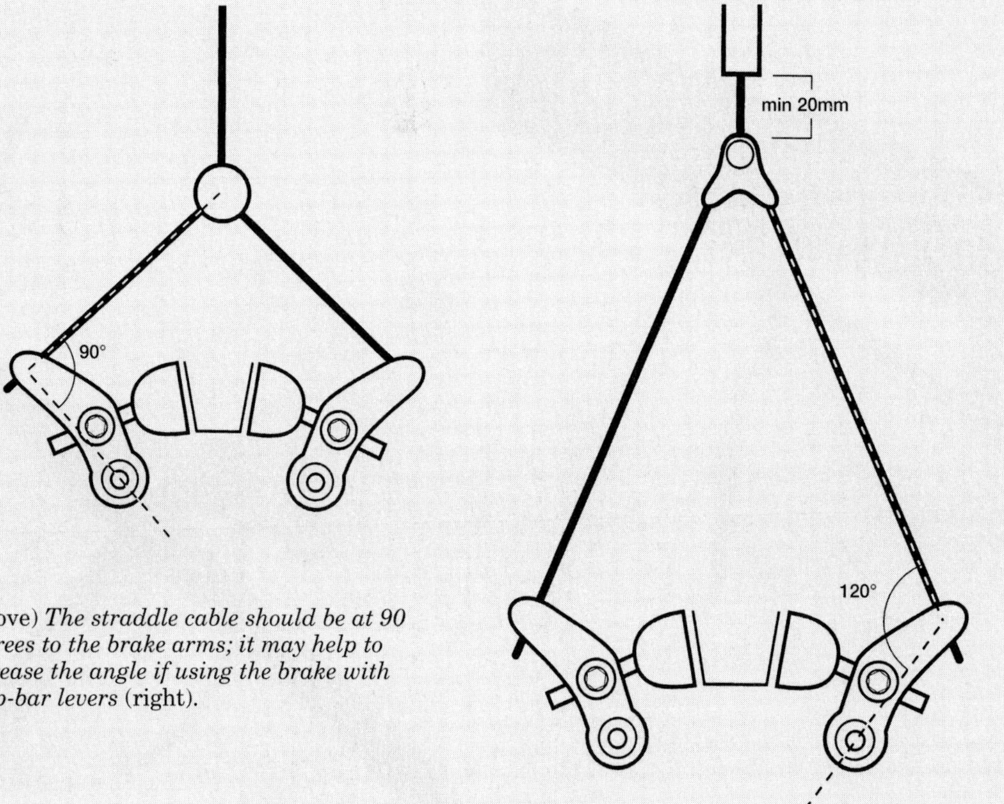

(Above) *The straddle cable should be at 90 degrees to the brake arms; it may help to increase the angle if using the brake with drop-bar levers* (right).

GENERAL BRAKE MAINTENANCE

Calliper Brakes

Calliper brakes are fitted to almost all modern road-racing bikes, some fast tourers and many sports and utility bikes. Single-pivot models generally offer better control and are lighter, but the longer arms are more flexible – leading to squealing. Dual-pivot models are now the norm and are much more powerful. They are also easier to set up and adjust. On quality bikes most calliper brakes are now fitted by recessed allen bolts. Older brakes are fitted by a Nylock-nut; note the curved mounting cups used on the bolt to fit it securely against the frame and help prevent it from going off-centre.

Keep on eye on the pivoting points as these can work loose or become stiff, especially on older and cheaper models. Loosen the outer lock-nut, adjust the nut behind to remove play but allow the pivots to move freely, then tighten the lock-nut against it. A small amount of lubrication will help but avoid getting it on the brake blocks or rim. You may need to strip the brake and regrease the moving parts. If you do this, take note of the shims and washers, which reduce friction in the system.

If the pivot assembly is correctly adjusted and lubricated but the brake fails to reopen fully after use, the tension of the spring should be increased. A new spring may help. On some brakes this can only be done by pulling out the spring, bending it up a little and refitting it, do this equally to both sides. Many Shimano brakes have their spring secured in a plastic block; reverse these to increase the tension.

Centralization

Better-quality brakes have a built-in method designed to make the brake's centralization easy. Some have flats for a

A recessed allen bolt is used to attach modern calliper brakes; centralize the brake as well as you can before tightening.

Adjusting the pivot of an older-style calliper brake.

(Below) *To increase the tension of most Shimano brakes reverse the plastic blocks.*

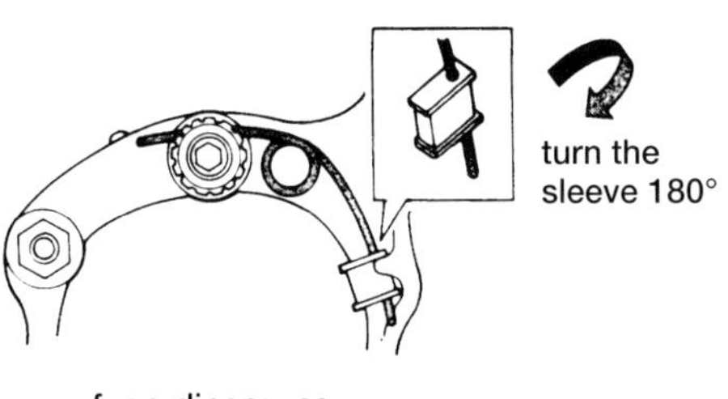

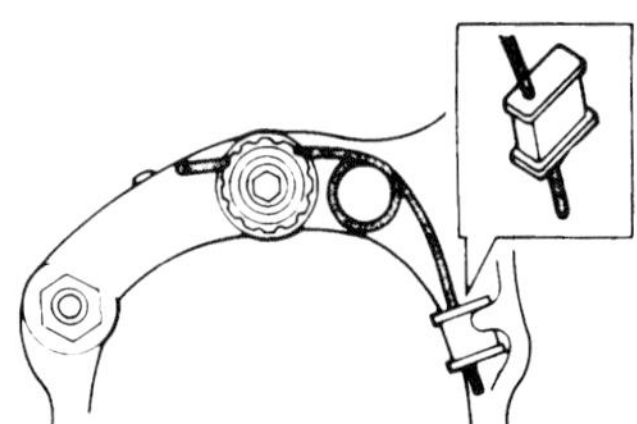

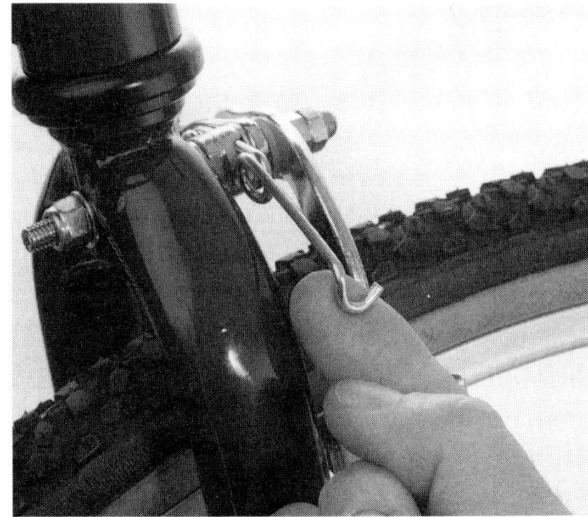

Increasing the spring tension of a cheap brake.

thin spanner (a cone spanner or dedicated model) near the back of the front part of the brake. Use the spanner as a lever to tilt the brake one way or the other to centralize it. Brakes can also be centralized by loosening the attachment nut, positioning the brake and retightening it. Sometimes a one-eighth turn of this nut will reposition the brake without loosening anything. Older Weinmann brakes use a special key on the front of the pivot to centralize them.

Centralizing an older Shimano brake by the flats near its back, using a spanner designed for this.

(Right) *Using the side adjustment screw to centralize a Shimano dual pivot brake.*

Shimano dual-pivot brakes have a centralizing mark on the brake unit (by the front of the fork crown). It should point directly up; loosen the attachment bolt, reposition the brake and retighten as necessary. If adjustment is still necessary, tighten the adjustment screw to bring the brake arms towards you or loosen it to push it away.

Older or cheaper brakes may need more drastic measures. If the brake sticks on one side, try pulling the spring out, bending it out a little and then refitting it. Also try gently hitting the spring

Centralizing a more basic brake design is a bit crude.

with a hammer and drift on the opposite side to that sticking.

Cantilever and 'V' Brakes

If the arms do not pivot freely and spraying lubrication into the pivot does not work, note the hole used in the frame (one of three), then remove the brake arms by removing the central bolt. Note that the coiled spring is separate on older models and is fitted with its shorter end in the brake body and the longer end in the frame's spigot; do not mix the springs between the left and right unit. If the spring has 'Normal' and 'SLR' settings these are intended for use with conventional (unsprung) and Shimano SLR levers and cables, which can offer a lighter response. Clean and grease the pivots and

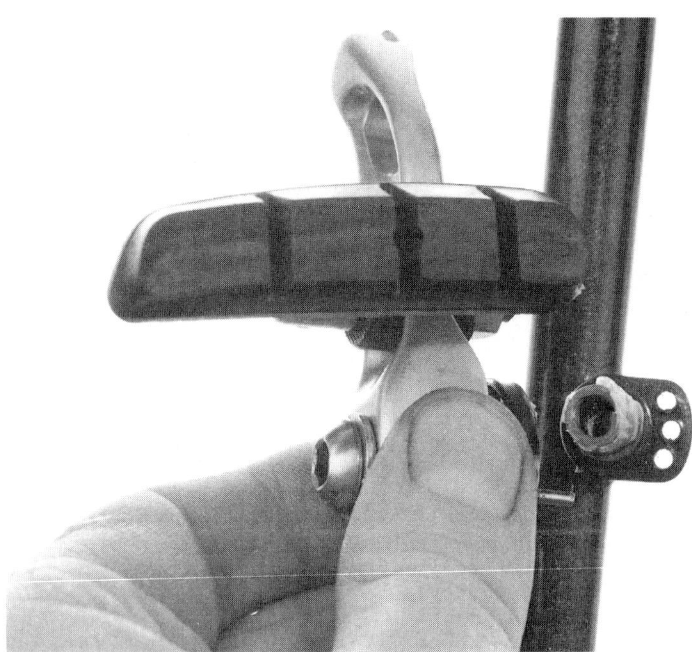

Positioning a cantilever brake arm.

Most cantilever and 'V' brakes have a centralization screw on their side.

remount the cantilevers. Alternative spring mounting holes can be used to alter the brake tension – it should spring back without hesitation but should be as low as possible to ensure a light feel.

Centralization

Most better cantilever brakes have some built-in form of adjustment to make centralization easy. If there is no obvious provision, remove the wheel and bend the brake unit that sticks back; this 'winds up' the spring so that it rests further out. Brake blocks can also be adjusted on their pegs. Most Shimano models have an adjustment tilt screw or 2mm allen bolt on the right cantilever. Tightening the screw pivots both brakes away from you, loosening does the reverse.

Some arms such as Sachs have a concealed spring. Mount them first, just nipping the mounting bolts tight. Then use a cone spanner to increase and balance the spring tension of each unit, finally tightening the mounting bolt firmly.

Adjusting the spring tension of a Sachs cantilever arm.

Brake Hangers

All cantilever and centre-pull brakes (but not 'V' brakes) require a front and rear brake hanger. This is an anchor point for the cable casing and it is from here that the bare inner cable runs to the brake; it should have an adjuster if there is no provision at the brake lever. It should be as solid as possible to avoid flexing wasting your efforts and leading to a spongy feel. The rear brake hanger is normally brazed onto the frame and is rarely problematic – except that an adjuster is not always fitted, so you may wish to add one.

Front hangers normally fit under the headset lock-nut. They were traditionally made from pressed steel but these are usually too flexible. Modern 5mm thick aluminium ones are much better but see the notes regarding stack height in Chapter 3, Buying a Headset. Brake hangers that fit around the stem are helpful, providing extra stack height.

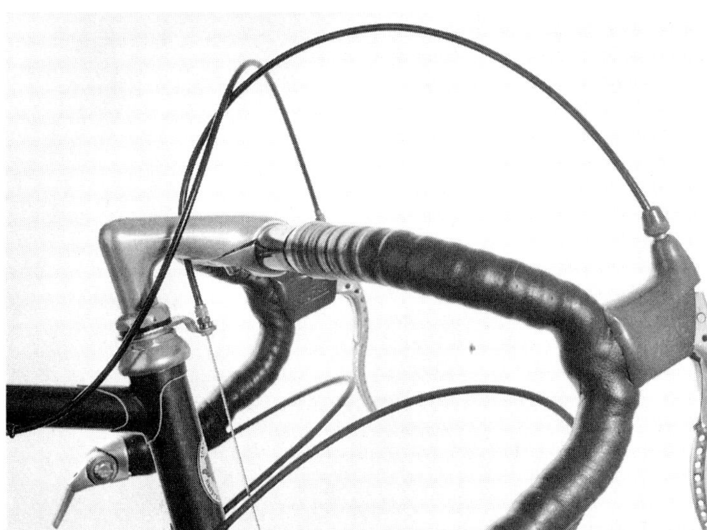

A traditional brake hanger is used here. Note also, the arrangement of the cables if using 'non-aero' levers such as these.

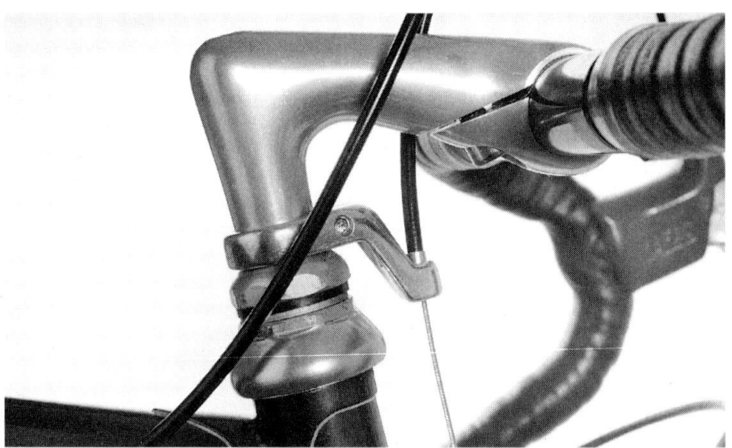

A more solid stem-fitting brake hanger, but note the lack of a cable adjuster.

9 Wheels and Tyres

Wheel maintenance breaks down into the following areas: rims and spokes (wheel build quality), hubs and tyres. Cassettes and freewheels are covered in Chapter 6.

After the frame, the wheels and tyres have the greatest influence on the feel of the bike. Like the frame, they need to be relatively stiff for good control. A loosely built wheel will make steering slack and unpredictable. An under-inflated tyre also causes this and leaves the rims with less cushioning; they can be literally pounded against bumps in the road causing rim damage such as flat spots, dents and 'snake bite' double punctures.

Most wheel problems result from a lack of maintenance, or from using an unsuitable wheel for the use given. The needs of tourists and tandemists should be carefully thought through; with the weight of a load, problems are more likely to occur, and, when they do, help may be far away. The components need to be particularly well chosen and built.

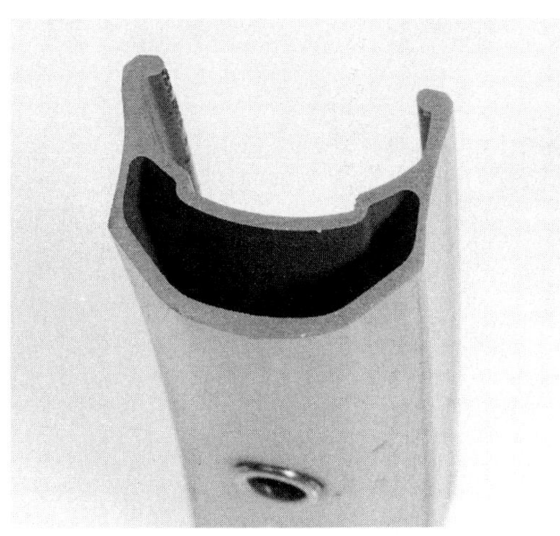

This worn rim has been replaced before problems occurred.

While wheels can often be continually repaired (spokes, bearing parts, axles and rims can all be replaced), there comes a point of diminishing returns, especially in the case of cheaper wheels, and especially if there is more than one major problem. Not only do things become uneconomic, but it is a sign that the wheel is coming to the end of its useful life – another problem may be just around the corner.

A very much neglected problem is rim wear. Modern aluminium rim walls can be as thin as 1.2mm and wear down through braking. Take care to pick grit out of the brake blocks after off-road rides. A worn rim could suddenly split. Look for deep grooves or concaving of the braking surface. If more than 0.5mm appears to have worn away, replace the rim or wheel. Ceramic-coated rims are available that resist wear, which are expensive to buy but perhaps prove to be cheaper in the long run. Alesa Apollo and X-plora rims intentionally wear through along a safe channel before safety is compromised.

When working on a wheel, work in the following order of priority to avoid wasting your time: hub first, then spokes and rim, then tyre. For example, you cannot true a wheel properly with play in the bearings, and if the hub needs replacing, efforts to true the wheel will be in vain.

WHEEL REMOVAL AND FITTING

Summary – Wheel Removal and Fitting

15 minutes

When?

- Being able to remove your bike's wheels is one of the most essential skills you will need; you will need to remove it to clean it effectively, repair punctures, replace worn tyres, pack the bike for carriage and a host of other less frequent maintenance jobs

Preparation/Notes

- Wheels are attached by either conventional nuts, or a quick-release mechanism fitted through a hollow axle
- For all bikes without derailleur gears, *see also* Chapter 7, Hub Gears, Hub Gear Wheel Removal and Fitting
- It will help to open up the brake's quick-release to avoid the tyre snagging against the brake blocks
- After fitting a wheel check the brake block alignment with the rim (*see* Chapter 8)
- If you have a derailleur with its own gear hanger plate, the rear wheel nut will attach over the top of this; ensure it is mounted correctly (*see* Chapter 5, Fitting a Rear Derailleur)

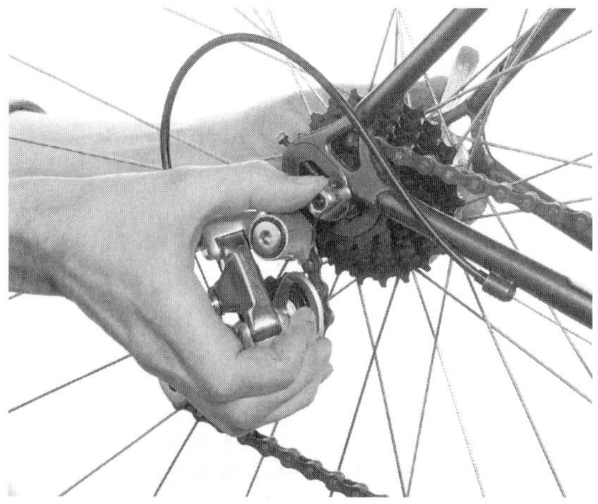

Removing a rear wheel should be a smooth operation if done properly.

Some front forks have 'safety lips', indicated by the pen.

Quick-Release Models

Wheel Removal

In the case of rear wheels, shift the chain to the smallest front and rear sprockets. Pull the quick-release lever back 180 degrees, fully opening it; if it is curved, the curve will face outwards. Lift the bike if necessary, pull the chain and rear derailleur back a little to clear and let the wheel drop out. A small thump on the tyre may be necessary.

Front wheels are removed in a similar manner, but you may need to contend with 'safety' dropouts. These have retaining lips that require you to open the quick-release fully, then loosen off the knurled nut on its opposite side a few turns to clear the lips.

Wheel Fitting

To fit a wheel fully open the quick-release first; if you are not sure that it is fully open, operate the lever back and forth and watch the lever's base move in and out. By convention both front and rear levers are always on the left of the bike.

The rear gear-shift lever should be fully retracted. Lift the top part of the chain over the smallest cog and let the bottom part hang below. Keeping the derailleur back, pull the wheel into the dropouts. Keeping the wheel fully in the dropouts, close the quick-release so that the lever points back and up or rests between the framestays. This should feel firm but not require excessive force. Leave enough finger space for when you next open it. If you need to adjust the amount of force, open the lever; tighten or loosen the knurled nut on the opposite side to increase or decrease it.

Close the front wheel's quick-release against the fork so that there is a small gap between it and the fork blade; this helps prevent the lever from being knocked accidentally yet leaves space for your fingers to open it next time. If you have 'safety' lips you will need to re-adjust the quick-release by tightening the knurled nut a few turns and testing the force needed to close it.

If your dropouts and frame are perfectly aligned your wheels should

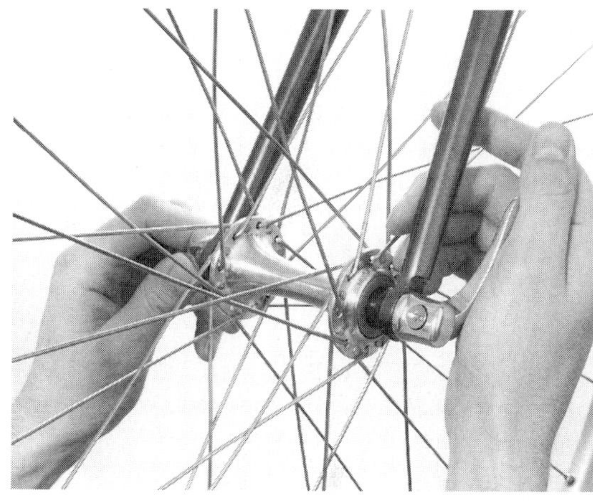

(Above) *Keep the wheel firmly in place as you close the quick-release.*

You may need to adjust the nut (left) *so that the lever closes with the correct amount of force.*

Horizontal dropouts should have adjusters that can be preset to allow easy wheel alignment.

automatically centralize. If a wheel does not centralize, hold it in alignment as you close the quick-release.

Nut Models

Removing a nutted wheel is normally quite straightforward. Use a correctly fitting spanner that is not too short (at least 20cm/7¾in) or you will not obtain sufficient leverage. If the axle turns with the nut, try tightening the other side's nut first to lock the axle. Loosen the nuts, then pull the washers clear before sliding the wheel out. Note that some washers locate in the dropout or hook over it.

When replacing the wheel, note that the washers go on the outside of the dropouts; locate them correctly, then tighten the wheel nuts. Many wheel nuts have an integral serrated washer, so do not use these with additional washers. It can sometimes help to use a spanner on both nuts at once.

WHEEL AND TYRE SIZING

Wheel and tyre sizing can be a complicated matter with several different

Loosening the nut of a hub gear wheel. The cranked ring spanner offers maximum grip and clears the frame.

systems in common use (often different for each country, even if expressed in what appears to be the same system). The table below shows the useful measurements for wheel sizes common in the UK. The British sizes in inches are nominal, the second figure is an additional reference for the tyre diameter; for example a 26 × 1⅜in tyre will not fit a 26 × 1¼in rim. The ISO size is the only foolproof and internationally accepted method of comparison.

With tyres the ISO's first figure indicates the tyre section, the second the rim/tyre's bead seat diameter – the point where the tyre sits in the rim. Where an ISO marking is used for a rim, the first figure is the rim's inside diameter between the flanges. Most road bikes use 700C wheels and almost all adult MTBs use 26 × 1.75in wheels; however the width of these rims varies widely.

Tyre section (width/depth) must be matched to the rim. The stated tyre

British Size	*ISO*	*Metric tyre marking*	*Rim outside diameter*	*Approx. tyre radius*	*Common use*
20 × 1.75*	44-406 to 54-406		422mm	244–253mm	BMX and folding bikes
20 × 1⅜	32-451 to 37-451		463mm	260–265mm	older shopping & folding bikes
24 × 1.75*	40-507 to 57-507		523mm	295–304mm	small MTBs
24 × 1⅜	32-540 to 37-540		552mm	304–309mm	older child's bikes
	28-541 to 37-541	600A	554mm	305–310mm	French child's bikes
26 × 1.75*	40-571-47-571	650C	585mm	333–336mm	mountain bikes
26 × 1½	32-584 to 47-584	650B	599mm	327–342mm	some roadsters & French touring bikes
26 × 1⅜	28-590 to 40-590	650A	602mm	335–338mm	classic British roadster
26 × 1¼	32-597	650	609mm	333–338mm	older sports bikes
700C (28 × 1⅝...)	20-622 to 47-622	700C	634mm	334–361mm	most road and hybrid bikes
27 × 1¼ × 1in, × 1⅛in	20-630 to 37-630		642mm	338–348mm	older UK and US sports touring & racing bikes

** Compatible rims and tyres (commonly fitted to MTBs) can also be marked × 1.5, × 1 .75, × 1.9, × 2, × 2in, × 2.125.*

Typical tyre markings of a 700C tyre. The 23-622 marking is the ISO size.

section (in millimetres) should be approximately 1.45 to 2.25 times the rim width as measured between the insides of its flanges.

The tube size must be correctly matched to the tyre, though most do cover a small range of tyre sections (check its box). A tube that is too narrow will be overstretched and liable to split or puncture. A tube that is too wide is likely to trap under the tyre bead and may blow off the tyre.

If you have a hybrid bike note that fitting a wider-section tyre may reduce the distance between your feet and the tyre/mudguard to the point where you may catch your foot when cornering, which can be dangerous. This is especially the case on smaller models.

Front suspension forks must have sufficient clearance under the tyre so that in the worst case scenario the tyre is not jammed up against the fork crown, throwing you on your face. This is normally 5cm (2in), but check with the manufacturer.

TYRE REMOVAL AND FITTING

Summary – Tyre Removal and Fitting

30 minutes

When?
- To replace a tyre that is worn or where the tread or side wall is damaged
- To repair a puncture or replace the tube
- To replace spokes or true the wheel

Preparation/Notes
- Remove wheels!

Removal and Checks

Completely deflate the tube and remove the dust cap and retaining ring, although not all valves have the latter. Push the valve right up into the tyre to help free it. Insert a tyre lever opposite the valve under the tyre bead (its edging) and hook it over a spoke. Fit another about 15cm (6in) to its side, slide it around the rim lifting off one complete bead and pull the tube free.

If you had a puncture, find and remove its cause by carefully feeling inside the tyre until you find it (thorn, glass and so on) or are sure nothing is there. Look for cuts, damage, and embedded debris in tyre treads and side walls. Also check for and file smooth protruding spokes and any rough edges.

Fitting

Ensure that the rim tape covers the full width of the rim well, is centred and in good condition to avoid punctures from the spoke heads and rough edges. Thinner tapes can make tyre fitting easier as there is more slack in system, but the risk of a puncture can increase. If the tyre is loose and will not centralize, try using a thicker tape or two tapes.

Fit the tyre by one bead. Inflate the tube till it is just round and fit the valve through the rim, lifting the tyre back over it. Push the tube neatly into place, keeping the valve straight.

Starting at the valve, use your thumbs to fit the second tyre bead. If it is tight deflate the tube a little. Push the valve up into the tyre to seat it correctly. Using your thumbs only, slide the last bit of tyre on.

Check that the tube is not caught under the tyre bead and free it if necessary. Inflate to about 1.5bar (20lb) and spin the wheel. If the bead line does not follow the rim edge push and pull the tyre into place. Inflate to the pressure recommended on the tyre wall. Replace the retaining ring and dust cap.

(Left) *Use two or three tyre levers to start removing the tyre.*

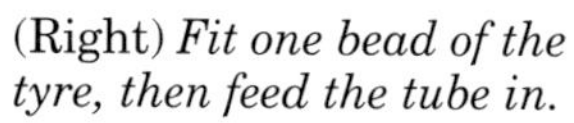

(Right) *Fit one bead of the tyre, then feed the tube in.*

(Below) *Use your thumbs to work the last bit on; conventional tyre levers will nip the tube.*

(Below right) *This special Var tyre lever is designed for fitting tight, narrow tyres without damaging the tube.*

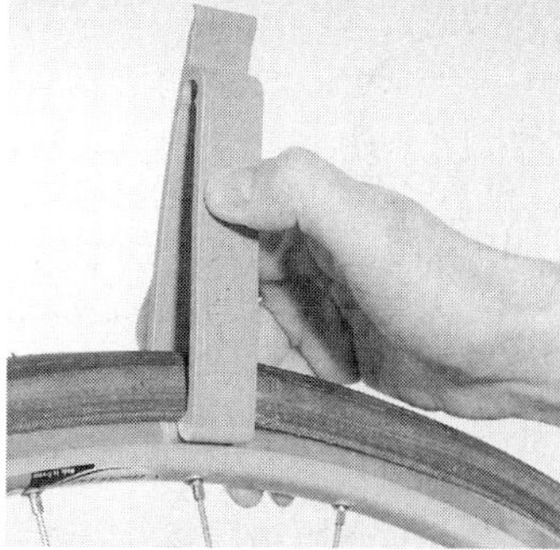

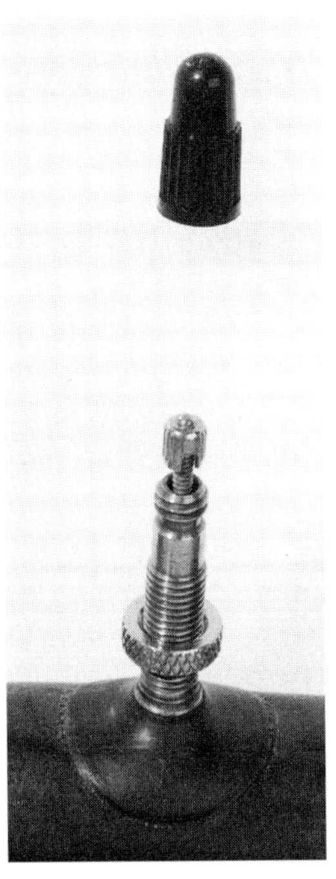

(Above left) *A Presta valve with its retaining ring and dust cap.*

(Above) *A Schrader valve, with the core and a pronged dust cap used to screw in the core.*

(Left) *A Woods valve with its retaining ring; the core, core-retaining collar and dust cap have been removed.*

VALVES

Three types of valve are used.

Presta

These are typically used on better-quality bikes, and particularly for higher tyre pressures as they are the easiest to inflate. Presta valves can be used in rim holes intended for Schrader valves but it is advisable to use a special adapter. Adapters are also available to convert a Presta to a Schrader valve. Presta valves cannot generally be replaced.

To inflate, fully loosen the top lock-nut and connect the pump. You must keep direct-fit pumps at 90 degrees to the valve, or you may bend it. After inflation fully tighten the lock-nut and replace the dust cap.

Schrader

These are identical to those used on cars and tend to be used on cheaper MTBs and utility bikes. Car pumps can be used but filling station air lines are not advised as it is too easy to over-inflate the tyre and risk blowing off the rim. A Schrader valve cannot fit through the rim hole for a Presta valve unless enlarged to 8.5mm.

To replace the valve, use a special pronged dust cap to unscrew the valve core and screw in the new valve, ensuring that it is tight.

To inflate, simply screw or push on the connector; do this briskly to avoid air loss.

Woods

These used to be common on utility bikes. The same rim hole size as a Schrader valve is used. You will normally need an old-fashioned style pump with a dedicated connecting tube. A direct-fit pump intended for Presta valves will sometimes work. The valve can be easily replaced by removing the retaining collar and pulling the valve core free. Use a modern replacement, not those that depend upon a short rubber tube as these are very hard to inflate.

To inflate, ensure that the valve retaining collar is tight, then screw on the connector tightly. When removing the pump, ensure that the valve retaining collar does not unscrew.

TUBE REPAIR

Find the hole by inflating the tube to twice its normal size and listening or feeling for escaping air. If you cannot find the hole, hold the tube and the valve under water and look for bubbles; these may come at the rate of one a second if it is a slow puncture. Keep track of the hole by drawing on lines that converge on it. Fully deflate the tube and ensure that it is completely dry.

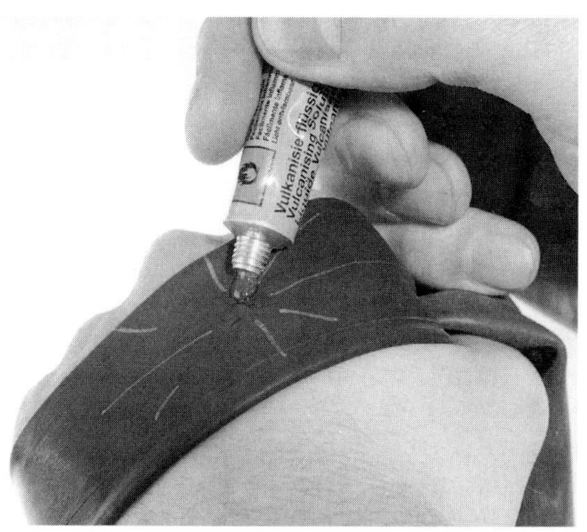

Summary – Tube Repair

⏱ 30 minutes

When?
- Loose patches, very hot weather, or repairing anything other than a very small hole may result in the patch blowing off, or slow deflation
- If in any doubt about a repair ensure you have eradicated any possible cause and fit a new tube

Preparation/Notes
- Remove wheels and tyre
- Tube repair takes some care, and needs to be done properly to avoid later frustration
- I recommend Tip Top puncture repair kits with feathered patches, which can be overlapped if necessary
- Glueless patches such as Park work well on MTB-size tubes but are less successful on narrow road tubes; they are likely to prove less reliable and are best seen as an emergency measure to get you home

Roughen an area twice the size of your patch. If there is old rubber on the tube from a previous repair attempt, peel and sand off as much as you can, then use cellulose paint thinners to remove the rest back to the bare tube. Apply two thin films of rubber solution, letting each touch dry.

Peel off the backing and centre the patch on the hole. Rub it down firmly from the centre outwards. Fold and crack the cellophane and peel off from the centre outwards. Dust the repair with chalk powder, talc, or anything similar to mop up the glue – flour works well! You can inflate the tyre to full pressure right away, but do not inflate the tube beyond the just round stage while

Applying a thin film of solution.

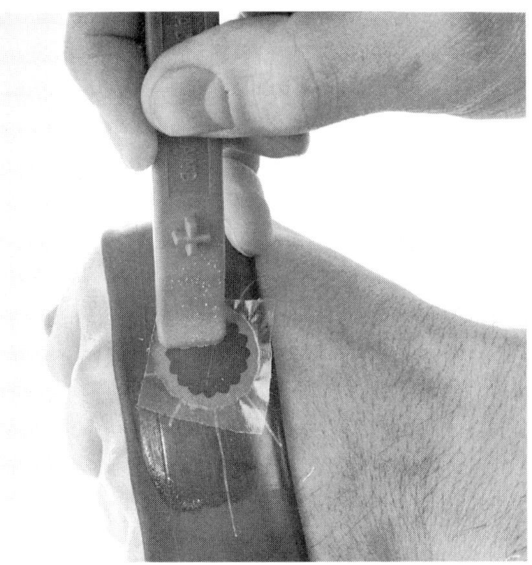

Firm out the patch until the cellophane backing cracks.

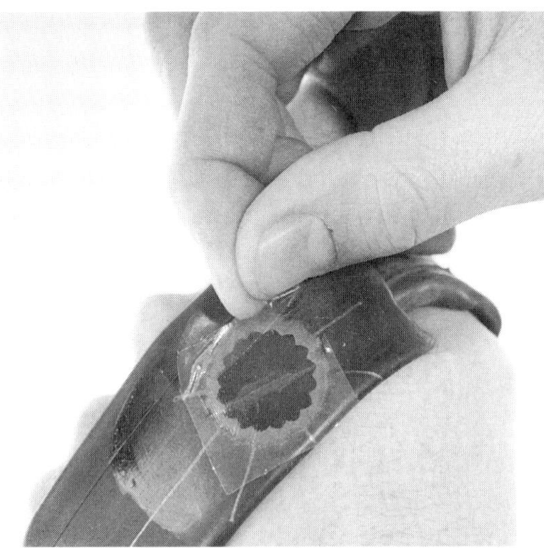

Peel back the cellophane from the centre outwards.

it is still outside the tyre or the uncured patch may lift off. If the repair has been unsuccessful you must remove the patch and start again.

TUBULAR TYRE FITTING

Tubular tyres are just that: tyres where the inner tube is completely hidden inside a sewn-up tyre casing, the stitching being hidden by a protective tape. They are mounted to special rims without the deep well of a conventional rim. I will not go into their repair but if you are patient you can peel back the tape, cut away the stitches and repair the tube inside in the normal way; specialist services are often available for this. Normally a special tubular rim cement is used to stick the tyre to the rim. Special double-sided tape may also be used, which is cleaner but less suited to hard use. A new tubular should first be fitted to an unprepared rim and then inflated to stretch it.

Clean off all old cement and tape with paint thinners and buff the surface with a wire brush. Apply a thin layer of cement to the concave rim well, avoiding the braking area. Leave it to dry and apply a second layer. Inflate the tubular until just firm and apply cement to its base tape.

When the cement has dried to something between being sticky and tacky you can fit the tyre. Inflate it until it is just round and start at the valve. Keeping the valve straight, work downwards, keeping the tyre taut as you go. Work equally around each side of the rim. Use your thumbs to get the last bit on. Align the tyre with your thumbs, pulling it about as necessary so that when you spin it, it appears straight. Check and correct again after inflating it until it is firm. Leave the tyre for a few hours to cure before riding and inflating it to full pressure.

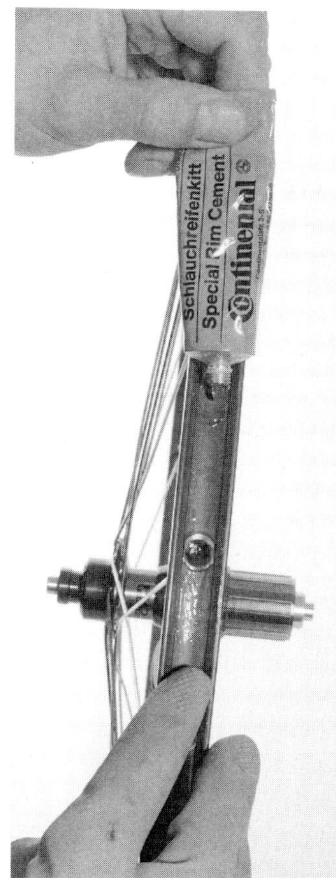

(Above) *Mount a tubular tyre by working downwards, with the tyre under tension.*

(Left) *Applying rim cement to the rim well.*

HUB OVERHAUL (CUP AND CONE TYPE)

Disassembly

Remove the quick-release skewer if applicable by unscrewing its knurled nut end. Holding the left-side cone with a cone spanner (front hubs either side) and using a second cone or conventional spanner as appropriate, loosen the lock-nut. Remove it and the plain and the lock washers as appropriate, and the cone below it. Take note of any seals so that you can refit them properly. Pull the axle out from the other side.

Shimano MTB hubs have a rubber dust cap that must be pulled back to give access to the cone and lock-nut.

Hub Overhaul

🔧🔧🔧 30 minutes to 1 hour

When?

- At overhaul intervals or when ticking sounds or roughness are noticed when the correctly adjusted axle is turned
- When play is felt at the rim and if the axle feels tight/rough if turned by hand
- Do not neglect hubs, because although the cones are normally replaceable, the hub's inner races are usually not: once these have worn, the hub is at the end of its life and a complete new wheel, or as a minimum, a complete wheel rebuild is needed
- Campagnolo inner races can be replaced. Once the axle and bearings are removed they are tapped out from behind with an old axle or drift. They are fitted in a very similar manner to cartridge bearing units, by careful pressing in; *see* Replacing Cartridge Bearings below.

Special Tools

A vice and axle vice, as shown on page 156, are useful but by no means essential

Preparation / Notes

- To carry out any job on a freehub or a rear wheel with separate freewheel (beyond simple bearing adjustment) the cassette or freewheel must first be removed (*see* Chapter 6)
- Campagnolo freehubs can be quite tricky to reassemble, so injection maintenance makes sense and some hubs come with provision for this; if disassembling, see the additional instructions applicable to these hubs
- A front hub is easier to overhaul

Hold the cone spanner still while you loosen the lock-nut.

Remove and discard all the old ball-bearings but count how many were in each side and check their size. These will be easier to remove without the dust caps. Use a broad screwdriver tip to lever these up. Shimano XTR dust caps unscrew instead, so use a small, adjustable peg spanner. In some cases the dust cap may deform before popping free; if it starts to do this leave it alone and work around it.

Campagnolo Freehubs

Keep the axle pushed in from the right side as you undo the cones. The axle lifts out complete with the cassette body. Use your other hand to safeguard the three springs and pawls that might catapult

You may need to rest the screwdriver on a support to avoid crushing the dust cap.

out as you do this – keep these safe. Be aware of the O-ring seal around the base of the cassette body.

Removing the Cassette Body

Shimano

Only remove the cassette body if it needs replacement, that is, when the free-wheeling mechanism has become stiff, developed play or has become unreliable. It has no serviceable parts. Insert a 10mm allen key into the freehub body and unscrew anticlockwise. You might need some extra leverage. Sometimes there is a thin washer behind the bolt, which you will need to safeguard.

Fit the cassette body in the same manner that you removed it, greasing the bolt and remembering to replace the

Removing a Shimano cassette body.

(Right) *Replacing a Shimano cassette body.*

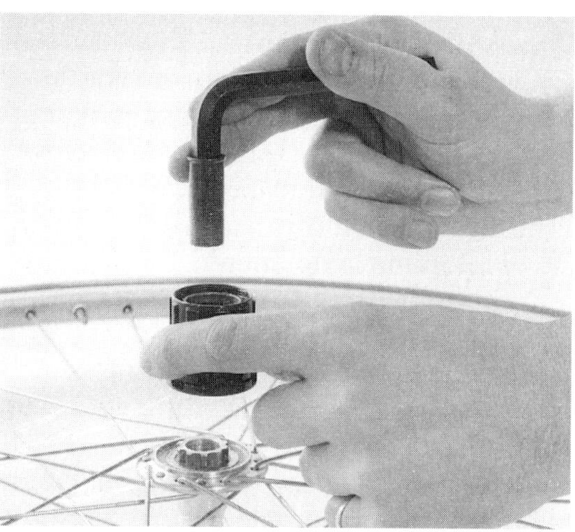

washer under its head. Make sure the bolt is tight, applying a little extra leverage if necessary.

Campagnolo

You will need to remove the cassette body from the axle in order to check the axle for straightness. Use a 2mm allen key to loosen the right-side lock-nut's grub screw. Holding an unthreaded part of the axle in a vice or mole grips (or use an axle vice), unscrew the lock-nut with a 17mm spanner. Lift off the plain washers and spring washer, then the cassette body. The remaining cone is an integral part of the axle. Do not remove the cartridge bearings from within the cassette body.

To replace, slide the cassette body onto the axle, pawl end first, followed by the spring and plain washers and lock-nut. Holding the axle's centre, tighten down the lock-nut to compress the spring washer, then tighten the allen key grub screw. Ignore the pawls for now.

Reassembling a Campagnolo cassette body; note the lock-nut with its allen key grub screw – the small protrusion to the left.

Cleaning and Inspecting the Parts

Wipe out excess grease and clean the ball races and recess. Freewheel-type rear hub axles frequently bend, as can freehub axles. Check by rolling the axle over a glass surface and looking for wobble, it is best replaced if this is more than 2mm. A replacement axle should be the same length and thread type. Replace the cones if pitted, scoured or if there is a noticeable ball track worn into them. If the hub's inner races are similarly worn, the hub is nearing the end of its life. If replacing the cones, remove the right-side cone from the axle and fit the new cone, washer/s and lock-nut so that the same amount of axle protrudes as before. In the case of quick-release axles this should be 5mm. For axle nuts, enough axle should protrude beyond the dropout for all the threads to engage.

Assembly

Apply grease to the bearing cups and fit new ball-bearings. In the case of most front hubs this will mean ten $\frac{3}{16}$in ball bearings, and in rear hubs nine $\frac{1}{4}$in ball-bearings. (Some Campagnolo front hubs use nine $\frac{7}{32}$in bearings.) Campagnolo freehubs use ten $\frac{7}{32}$in bearings on the drive side and nine $\frac{1}{4}$in bearings on the

(Above) *The left cone is new, the middle has had some wear but is serviceable, while the right one is badly pitted and should be discarded.*

(Left) *A quick-release axle should have a 5mm protrusion beyond the lock-nut.*

left side. When the bearings are fully seated shoulder to shoulder in their track, there should be a space of half a bearing width remaining. Cover with a little extra grease and gently tap the dust covers back into place.

Push the axle through from the drive side, taking care not to dislodge any of the bearings. Ensure that any seals that were removed or disturbed are refitted correctly. Keep the right side pressed in while you refit the cone, lock and spacing washers as appropriate and the lock-nut. Do these up finger tight.

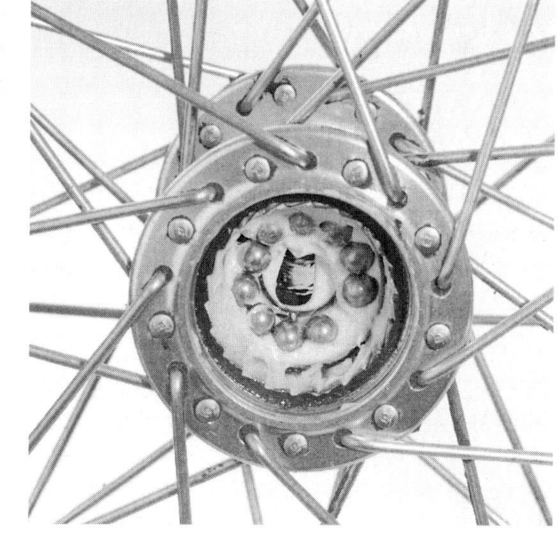

The replaced bearings, in this case in the cassette side of a Campagnolo freehub.

Replacing the cone, washers and lock-nut; all that remains now is the final adjustment.

Campagnolo Freehubs

Grease the three recesses of the cassette body and position a pawl in each recess with their sharper corners facing outwards. Position the cassette spring in the cylindrical hollow of the recess and the pawl. Keep everything in position and lower the assembly into the hub shell. As the pawls touch the hub, press them in gently with a screwdriver tip, while rotating the cassette body slowly backwards – it should drop down into place. While pressing it down, turn it backwards and check that the mechanism is working correctly. Also see the photos on page 162 which show the final assembly of the very similar Hope cassette body.

Fitting the pawls to a Campagnolo cassette body.

Adjustment

Hold the cone with a cone spanner and tighten down the lock-nut onto it, trying not to let the cone move. Check that the axle turns with free movement without side-to-side play when you grasp and try to wobble it; some trial and error and readjustment is normally necessary. In the case of quick-release hubs a trace of play can be desirable as it will usually disappear once the quick-release is closed (and the bearings are compressed). Check by wobbling the rim and readjust if the play remains.

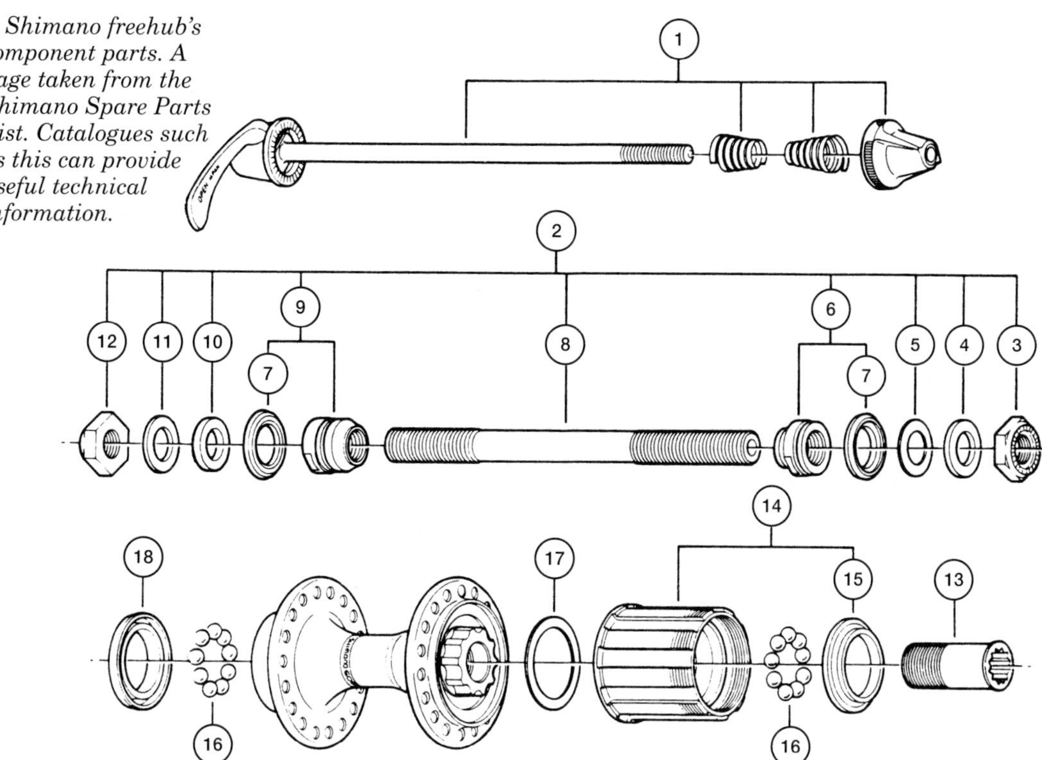

A Shimano freehub's component parts. A page taken from the Shimano Spare Parts List. Catalogues such as this can provide useful technical information.

- Use with CS-7401-8.
- Over Lock Nut Dimension: 130mm ($5\frac{1}{8}$in)

A: Same parts.
B: Parts usable, but differ in materials, appearance, finish, size, and so on.
Absence of mark indicates non-interchangeability.
The table indicates the adaptability of conventional parts to FH-6402-8.

Item No.	*Description*	*Interchangeability* FH-7403	FH-6401
1	Complete Quick Release 161mm ($6\frac{11}{32}$in)		B
2	Complete Hub Axle 141mm ($5\frac{9}{16}$in)		B
3	Right Hand Lock Nut 3.5mm		A
4	Right Hand Washer 1.9mm		A
5	Right Hand Washer 0.5mm		A
6	Right Hand Cone (M10 × 12mm) & Seal Ring		A
7	Seal Ring	A	A
8	Hub Axle 141mm ($5\frac{9}{16}$in)	B	B
9	Left Hand Cone (M10 × 15.1mm) & Seal Ring		A
10	Left Hand Washer 2.3mm		B
11	Left Hand Washer 1.5mm		A
12	Left Hand Lock Nut 4.5mm		A
13	Freewheel Body Fixing Bolt		A
14	Complete Freewheel Body (B.C.34.6) w/Right Hand Dust Cap		
15	Right Hand Dust Cap		A
16	Steel Ball ($\frac{1}{4}$in) 18pcs	B	A
17	Freewheel Body Washer		A
18	Left Hand Dust Cap		B

CARTRIDGE BEARING REPLACEMENT

Summary – Cartridge Bearing Replacement

🔧🔧🔧🔧 30 minutes to 1 hour

When?
- When the cartridges are worn (*see* Chapter 2)
- Do not attempt to remove the cartridges unless worn, as doing so will destroy them

Special Tools
- Tools designed to seat and press the cartridges (Hope tools are shown); you may be able to improvise substitutes

Preparation/Notes
- The following hubs use cartridge bearings: Hope, Mavic, Ringlé, Suzue, TNT, some Sachs models, '97 Campagnolo Record front, and some Sturmey Archer hub brakes

The exact design between models can vary considerably, mainly in the external detail, though most use a stepped axle over which the cartridges are press fitted; once you have access to the cartridges you may choose to regrease them rather than replace them.

Prising off the external spacer from a Hope hub.

Disassembly

Most models have a number of external parts and spacing pieces: note their exact arrangement, then remove them. Dust covers are often unscrewed using an adjustable peg spanner. Circlips prise off; try a screwdriver tip under the 'closed' end, or, if this is not accessible, two screwdriver tips pushing at each end. Use your hand to safeguard the clip, as it can catapult itself some distance.

Outside pre-load nuts are normally removed with cone or conventional spanners as appropriate. Some axles take an allen key in their end, preventing it from rotating. Various packing pieces may need to be removed; some are a press fit and will self-remove when you knock the cartridges out, others are held on by tiny grub screws, typically taking a 1.5 or 2mm allen key.

Once all the external parts are removed, hit the axle through using a soft-faced hammer; it should come free with the cartridge from the opposite side. Sometimes this can only be done from one direction so do not hit it too hard until you have tried both directions. If this does not work, pour a kettle of boiling water over the hub shell to expand it and try again.

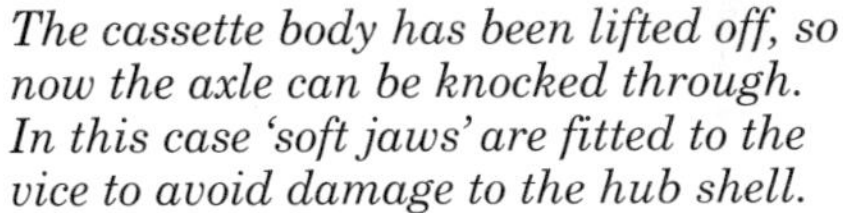
The cassette body has been lifted off, so now the axle can be knocked through. In this case 'soft jaws' are fitted to the vice to avoid damage to the hub shell.

Support the cartridge and hit the axle to remove it.

Support the cartridge on the axle and knock the axle through it. Remove the remaining cartridge from the hub using the axle or a drift. Discard the old cartridges as they will now be permanently damaged.

Assembly

Scrupulously clean out all specks of debris from the inside of the hub, the axle and new cartridges. Insert the axle and slip over the cartridges, one on each side (a few use three cartridges, two on the drive side). Support must now be offered to the outside race (or outside and inside race equally) of both the cartridges, but this must not interfere with any other part of the hub or you will damage it. Use tools designed for this, or an appropriately sized socket, nut, or similar item. Some freewheel and cassette removal tools are the right shape.

The cartridges must now be squeezed into place. Either use a hammer, or put the whole arrangement in a press or vice. As you fit the cartridges, ensure they stay square to the hub, and continue until they are fully seated.

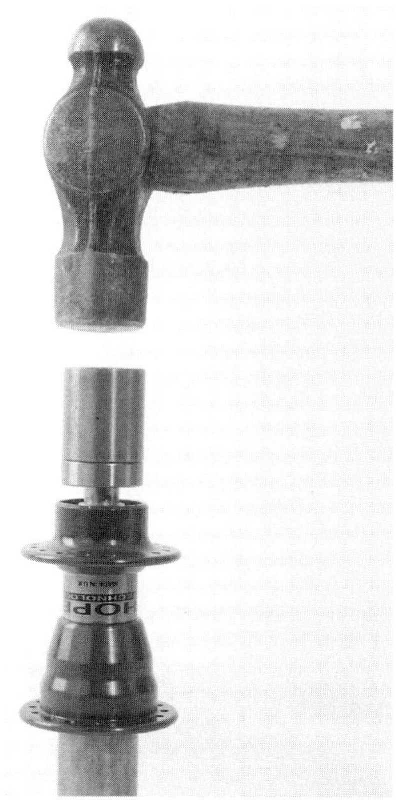

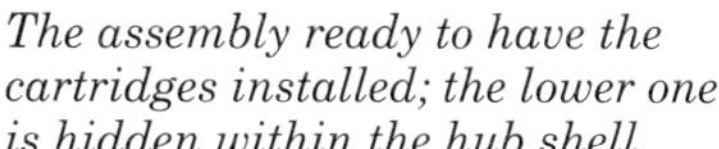

The assembly ready to have the cartridges installed; the lower one is hidden within the hub shell.

Replace the cassette body. You may need to press in the freewheel pawls.

Reinstate the cassette body and external parts as applicable. If the pre-load on the cartridges can be adjusted by outside nuts, a small amount of play is essential if you have a quick-release; it will take this up. A trace of play at the rim is in fact quite normal. Tighten the pre-load with care – overdo it and the cartridge bearings will be ruined!

SPOKED WHEELS

A bicycle wheel is exceptionally efficient in that it will support a great many times its own weight. Your weight and the bike's are amplified as the bike hits irregularities in the road's surface and when you lean or corner. This exerts a compression load on the rim and the spokes. In a well-built wheel the spokes are sufficiently tight to prevent them from bending under this load and so are able to resist side forces on corners, and are durable and stay true.

Spokes rarely break from an overload of tension but from metal fatigue. Over time, spokes bend back and forth millions of times, once with every wheel revolution, which naturally weakens them. Slack spokes will bend further and so build up metal fatigue much more quickly. Often, when spokes begin to break, it is a sign that the complete set is coming to the end of its useful life. Spokes that are excessively tight make an unstable wheel prone to sudden collapse, especially if highly dished – a term I will explain under Wheel Building later in the chapter.

The spokes in any given wheel can vary in number, gauge (diameter), material, and in their lacing, that is their spoking pattern. These can all be varied according to specific requirements. Increasing the number of spokes increases reliability, as the load is spread more widely, both over the spokes and the rim. However, more spokes increase weight and wind resistance.

In general, bicycle wheels use thirty-six spokes, both front and rear. Thirty-two spokes front and rear has become the norm on better MTBs and racing bikes. Reflecting the weight distribution on a bicycle, older British bikes used forty spokes in the rear and thirty-two in the front. Though this practice almost died out, forty spoke rims and hubs (and even forty-eight for tandems) have now become more readily available again.

Spoke Types

Plain-gauge spokes are the same thickness throughout their length. These are normally 14-gauge (2mm thickness) and are the typical basic spoke. Tandems sometimes use 13-gauge (2.3mm), but these are more difficult to tighten and tension correctly.

Double-butted spokes are typically 14-gauge at their ends but taper to a central section of 16-gauge (1.6mm). They are used on most good-quality wheels as they have the advantages of reducing weight and wind resistance. They can be tensioned more easily than plain-gauge spokes but are more prone to 'wind-up' (described under Wheel Building below). They can also stretch, so wheel building takes more patience. The greater tension helps to stop them unwinding and losing tension so generally they build the most reliable wheels. However, if one spoke does break it will allow the rim to deflect further out of true than it would if a plain-gauge spoke broke.

Single-butted spokes are typically 13-gauge at the hub end with the remaining section being 14-gauge. These offer strength where it is needed yet still allow the spoke to be tensioned sufficiently. Single-butted spokes are recommended for tandems and the rear wheels of heavily laden touring bikes. Bladed and elliptical spokes are used on many racing wheels to reduce wind resistance. These also resist the 'wind-up' problem. Special hubs are needed for bladed spokes.

Spoke Materials

So called 'rustless' spokes are made from galvanized high-tensile steel wire and are the cheapest and least exotic. They are thought to be the most resistant to metal fatigue. They do tend to oxidize, particularly on salted winter roads, leading to poor looks and the nipple freezing to the spoke. This can make subsequent retruing very difficult as each spoke you touch snaps as you try to adjust its nipple.

Stainless steel spokes are used on almost all quality bikes. These can stretch more than rustless spokes, making truing more difficult. The quality of stainless-spokes can vary and it pays to use a respected brand such as Sapim or DT.

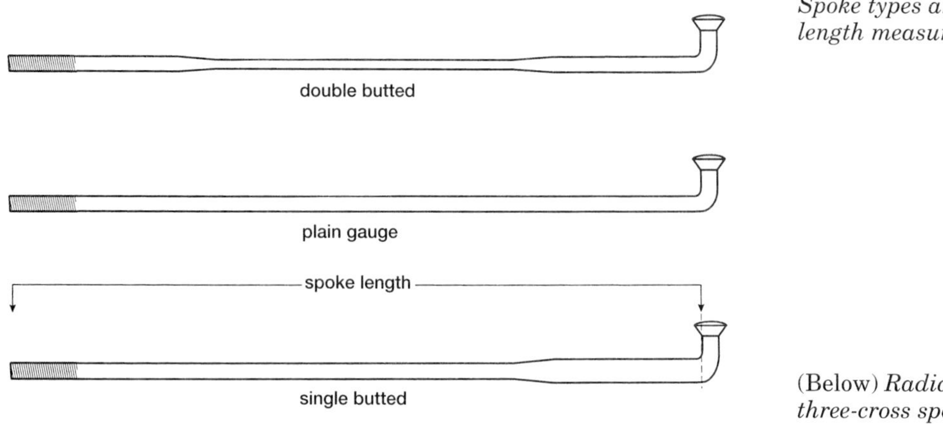

Spoke types and spoke length measurement.

(Below) *Radial and three-cross spoking.*

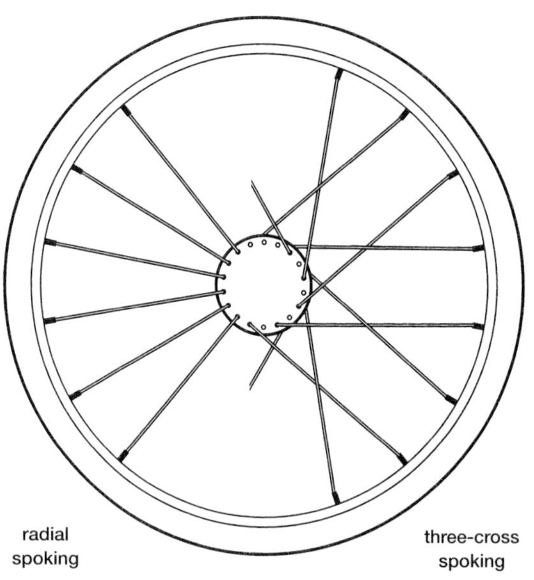

The spoke is connected to the rim by a screw-on nipple either made from plated brass or aluminium alloy for marginal weight saving purposes.

Spoke Fit

Spokes must have a snug fit in the hub flange to avoid excessive movement and build-up of fatigue. The bend at the head of the spoke (shoulder) can vary greatly but should be 90 degrees. If it is more than this, or if the head is excessively long it may prove a loose fit. Particularly useful in such cases are small brass washers placed under the spoke head to take up the slack. It is surprising how much difference they make and they are particularly recommended for touring and tandem wheels.

Spoking Patterns

Radial spoking is the simplest spoking pattern, the spokes radiating out like rays from the sun, none of them crossing any other. Radial spoking is rarely used. It has less 'give', transmitting more road shock. Because the spokes leave the hub flange perpendicularly, instead of across it, there is a greater possibility of spoke pull cracking the hub flange – although specially made and cold-forged hubs resist this. Without the additional bracing of other spokes, radial spokes can work loose more easily. Radial spoking is only recommended for special aerodynamic wheels where the components are specially designed for this; it is not recommended that you build these yourself. Despite these disadvantages radial spoking is sometimes used on time trialling wheels as they offer slightly reduced wind resistance, and for cyclo-cross, as they are less prone to collecting foliage.

Most wheels are built with tangential spoking, where each spoke leaves the hub at an angle. Three-cross spoking is the norm, each spoke crossing over or under three others before it reaches the rim. Compared to radial spoking, the spokes are better aligned for transmitting torque and because they are braced against each other they share the work load more effectively. The longer spokes necessary result in a slightly more comfortable wheel.

As the rim becomes smaller, the hub flange larger, or the number of spokes is reduced, the angle at which the spokes leave the hub and enter the rim becomes more acute. The nipples can then exert excessive pressure against only one side of the rim hole, causing it to crack. The spoke also becomes liable to break at the point where it meets the nipple. In these situations two-cross or one-cross spoking should be used instead. It is not normally a problem unless using a very large flange hub, such as a hub brake.

Buying Wheels

Factory-built wheels are assembled and tensioned by machine. Spoke tension and truth will sometimes only be barely acceptable and spokes may suffer from 'wind-up' (*see* Wheel Building below). Unless remedied by some careful extra truing and tensioning, the wheel may have a relatively short life. Good bike shops will normally do this but do not expect hand-built standards at factory-built prices. With practice, you can remedy this yourself.

The alternative are hand-built wheels, built by an expert, or yourself. A good hand-built wheel will offer the longest life and greatest reliability. Individual components and the spoking pattern can be chosen to meet your needs exactly. The main considerations are detailed below.

Upgrading from 27in to 700c?
700c rims are 4mm smaller in radius than 27in wheels. While you may deliberately choose to upgrade to the now standard 700C size, brake reach and bottom bracket height will be slightly affected, and you will need new tyres. Mudguard clearance will be increased.

Rim Width
Check that the rim's inner width is compatible with the tyre width you intend to use. A change in rim outside width will effect cantilever brake positioning, possibly beyond the limits of your brake adjustment.

Hub Width
The hub width, as measured over the outside edges of the bearing lock-nuts, must match your frame. Most MTBs, hybrids and tourers use 135mm (eight-speed) or 130mm (seven-speed) spacing. Road bikes and some tourers use 130mm (eight- or nine-speed) spacing. Most six- and seven-speed bikes use 130mm or 126 mm spacing. Tandems can be anything up to 160mm.

Cassette/Freewheel Compatibility
See the information in Chapter 6.

Component Quality
An aluminium hub shell is recommended as these support the spokes more fully than steel ones (which you will only find on the cheapest wheels). Bearing quality and sealing generally increases with price. The cheapest rims can be difficult to true. As a failure of a single part of a very cheap wheel can mean its total replacement it makes sense to buy something of reasonable quality.

Spokes
See the main text.

Forty- and forty-eight spoke wheels used for touring and tandems commonly use four-cross spoking. The angle that the spokes make with the rim is much the same as on a typical thirty-two or thirty-six spoke wheel but the spokes are longer, which can increase comfort.

Calculating the Spoke Length

Spokes are measured from the inside of the bend (under the head) to the end of the threads. You will need to take the following into account to determine the correct length:

- Hub flange diameter (measured across the centres of the spoke holes)
- Rim size and type – some rims have a deeper well than others
- The number of spokes and the number of times they cross each other in the intended spoking pattern – three-cross, four-cross and so on
- It is also helpful to use spokes 1 or 2mm shorter on the drive side of the rear hub

Your local friendly bike shop will probably be happy to calculate the correct spoke length for you if you are buying the parts from them. Any good shop will have special tables to do this. You can also measure a spoke from another identical wheel, or use the spoke calculator on the Internet, kindly provided by Roger Musson at www.netcomuk.co.uk/~hw/wheels/

WHEEL BUILDING

Summary – Wheel Building and Repairs

Wheel building 🔧🔧🔧🔧🔧 Allow a day for your first wheel

When?
- To replace a damaged or worn rim
- To build a quality wheel from selected components
- To true a wheel or replace spokes

Special Tools
Wheel truing jig and dishing stick or substitutes (*see* main text below)

Preparation/Notes
- The instructions are for three-cross wheels
- You will need a hub and rim with the same number of spoke holes and the correct-length spokes
- Before starting truing, ensure that your hub is smooth running and free from play
- If using an old hub, remove the cassette or freewheel before cutting out the old spokes

Wheel building is a challenge, but the extra feeling of satisfaction it can give to transform loose components into a solid, dependable wheel makes it an exercise many wish to try. This skill will of course make you more independent, especially useful on tour, or if you depend upon a single bike. If you are diffident, you should be able to build a wheel at least as good as a factory-assembled one straight off. With a little practice, you will soon be able to build a far superior wheel.

The exercise of wheel building has a therapeutic feel, needing care and attention to detail to ensure the correct lacing of the spokes and then a deft touch to bring the wheel gradually up to tension and perfectly centre and true it. Patience is far more important than special tools or mysterious skills.

If you do not have a jig, use an old pair of forks in a vice; spring them apart for rear wheels. Alternatively use your bike frame, with cocktail sticks tacked onto the forks as pointers to gauge wheel wobble. A dishing stick (*see* page 173) is the most useful of the more expensive tools and will ensure that you get the rim perfectly centred over the hub. If you do not have one you can simply measure the distance between the rim and the frame on each side and ensure it is equal on both sides.

If you are reusing an old hub, you should first check that the hub's spoke holes are not deformed or cracked, a possibility if the existing rim is buckled, and overhaul it. If the existing spokes are no good, you can cut them out, but remember to remove the cassette or freewheel first, as this is almost impossible to do afterwards.

You will need to follow this method exactly in the lacing stage. Read it through fully before you start because mistakes will be very time-consuming to correct later. Make yourself comfortable; siting on a low stool with the components on the floor can be the most comfortable way to work. Throughout the lacing attach each nipple by an equal three turns.

Lacing

Lubricate the spoke threads and rim hole sockets with a thick oil. If using shorter spokes for the drive side, keep them in two labelled containers to avoid confusion and remember to use each on the correct side.

Holding the rim in front of you, find the valve hole and look into its well. Noting that the spoke's holes alternate left, right, left, and so on, your first spoke will be connected to the first right-side hole above the valve hole. Depending upon

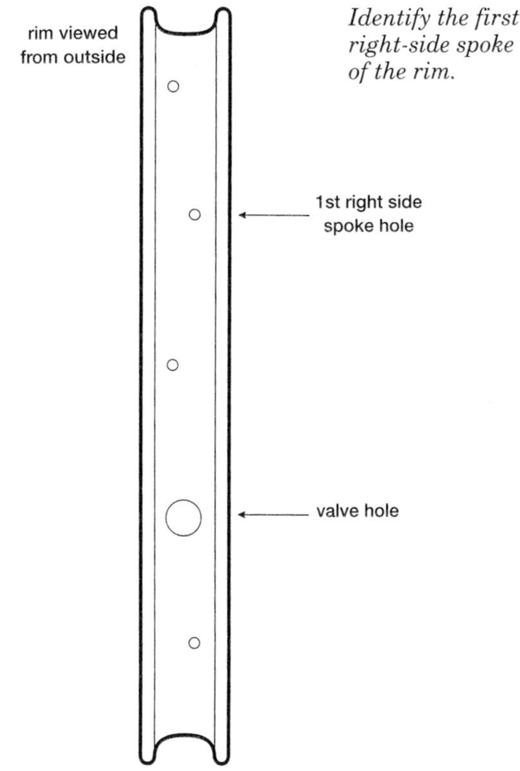

Identify the first right-side spoke of the rim.

your rim, that is next but one to it (the more common type) or the next one to it.

Throughout the lacing you will be fitting 'pulling' and 'trailing' spokes. Pulling spokes have their head on the inside of the flange and point backwards. Trailing spokes have their head on the outside and point forwards.

Fitting the First Two Pulling Spokes

Insert a pulling spoke through a hole on the drive-side flange (either side for front hubs). If the holes are alternately countersunk, the countersinking is designed to accommodate the bend, not the head of the spoke – otherwise use any hole. Connect this spoke to the first right-side rim hole. Mark this spoke with tape.

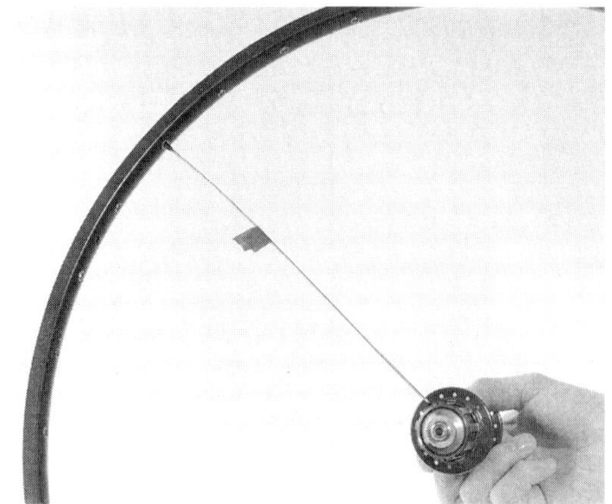

The first spoke fitted.

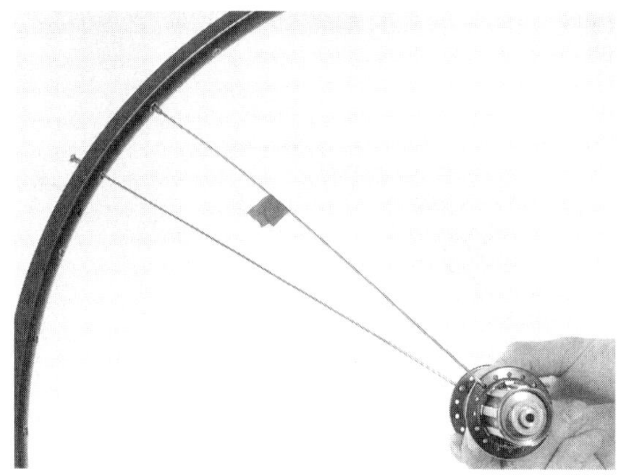

The first left-side pulling spoke is now fitted.

From immediately above the spoke inserted, sight across the hub to the opposite flange. You will see that there is not a spoke hole immediately opposite, but two adjacent to it – one a little to the left and one a little to the right – so mark a dot between the two.

If you have an empty hole between the rim valve hole and the first spoke insert a pulling spoke immediately left of the dot and connect it to this hole. If the spoke hole by the valve hole is taken by

Sight across the hub and mark a dot between the two spoke holes opposite the first spoke.

the first spoke, insert a pulling spoke immediately right of the dot and connect it to the rim spoke hole immediately clockwise of the first spoke.

Fitting the Trailing Spokes

Insert a trailing spoke immediately to the left of the first pulling spoke (marked), its head on the outside of the flange.

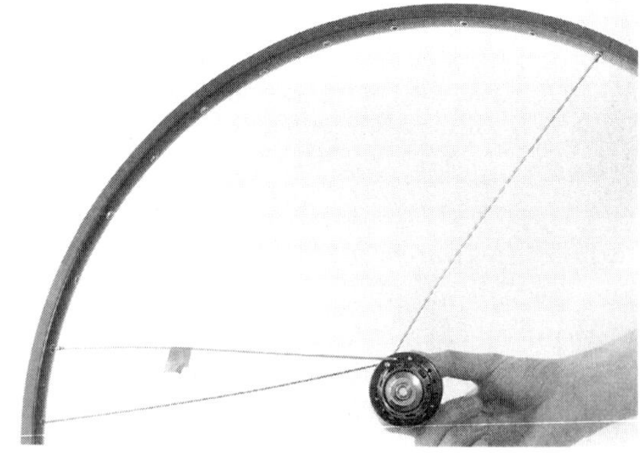

The first cassette-side trailing spoke being fitted.

Remembering that trailing spokes radiate forwards, pass this spoke under the other and count ten rim spoke holes clockwise from it and attach here.

Insert a trailing spoke from the hub hole immediately right of the marked spoke and fit it four rim holes right of the trailing spoke already fitted. You can now go round fitting the remaining trailing spokes to every other flange hole, and every fourth rim hole. Work around the first pulling spoke so that it radiates over two trailing spokes and goes under the third. Fit the trailing spokes to the other side in the same manner.

Fitting the Remaining Pulling Spokes

Fit a pulling spoke to the right of the marked spoke – from the empty hole next but one at the hub to the fourth hole

(Right) *The last cassette-side trailing spoke being fitted.*

(Below) *Pull the trailing spokes in with your hand to help them seat against the flange.*

(Below right) *Remember to lace the spokes as shown.*

If you have trouble lacing the spokes do not be afraid to bow them, but do not bend them sharply or you will kink them permanently.

Use a soft-faced hammer to flatten the pulling spokes.

to the right at the rim. Continue fitting the remaining pulling spokes to every fourth rim hole in turn. As these spokes radiate towards the rim, pass them over the first two trailing spokes and under the third to lace them. Repeat for the other side.

Before continuing, check that all the right-side spokes are connected to the right side of the rim, that the valve hole lies between two nearly parallel spokes (this gives maximum accessibility and is an indication that you followed the instructions correctly!), and that all the spokes are correctly laced with the pulling spokes crossing over the first two trailing spokes and going under the third. The pattern should appear symmetrical in every aspect.

Taking Up the Slack

Take up the tension in the loose spokes. Start at the valve hole (this is your reference point) and give each spoke an equal couple of turns. Go round until the spokes lose their slackness, but finish back at the valve hole. Repeat if necessary, but note that when plucked the spokes should give no more than a very dull twang at this stage. The pulling spokes may benefit at this stage by being gently flattened against the hub flanges – use a nylon- or leather-faced hammer. You are now ready to tension and true the wheel.

Wheel Truing and Tensioning

Being able to tension and true a wheel correctly is about developing a feel for the job and being in tune with what is happening as you tighten and loosen the spokes. Spokes act directly on the rim, affecting its concentricity by drawing it in or releasing it out, or on its lateral truth by pulling and releasing it to one side or the other. Spokes must be worked on equally to keep the wheel concentric and true – except when correcting it.

Perfectly built wheels should show no hint of concentric or lateral movement when spun. This means your wheel will be at equilibrium. Cheaper rims are more difficult to true, because they are not perfectly round or have poor joins – resulting in unequal spoke tensioning to true them, or equal spoke tensions but a small degree of untruth; you may need to settle for a compromise between the two.

Put your wheel in the jig, frame or forks. It will help to have good lighting and a white background to view the deflection. Spokes have normal clockwise threads, but if you are using a wheel-truing jig you will be looking at the nipples from underneath, so turn them anticlockwise to tighten them. If you are unsure whether to tighten or loosen a spoke to obtain the result you want, squeeze it against another on the same side (effectively tightening it) and note the rim deflection. You will need to alternate between the following processes to perfect your wheel; use the Wheel Tensioning and Truing panel on page 175 to guide you.

Correcting Lateral Truth

Set your jig's reference points near the rim sides and spin or slowly rotate the wheel to gauge the deflection. Loosen spokes on the same side as the pointer a half-turn at a time to move the rim away from it. As you become more confident you may turn them more than this if

A wheel-truing jig set up for correcting lateral truth.

(Right) *Adjust the spokes as indicated to correct lateral truth.*

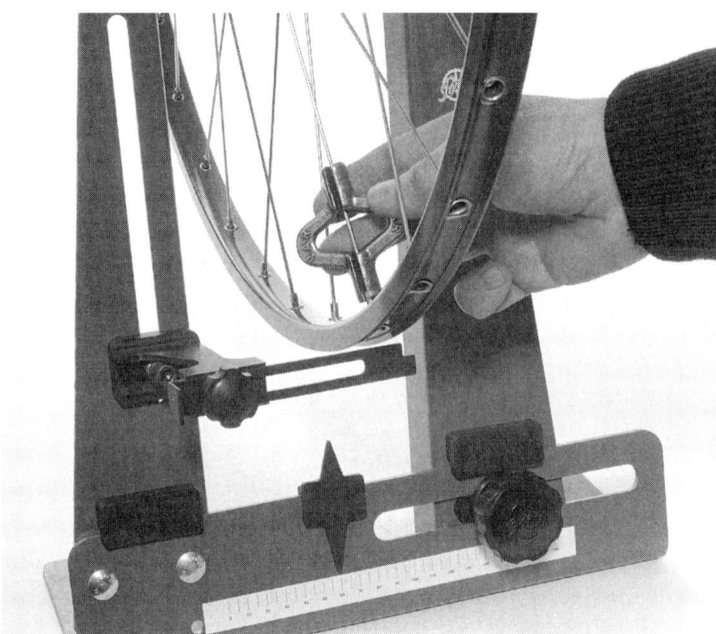

The wheel-truing jig set up for concentric truth.

(Right) *Loosening spokes corrects an inward dip of the rim.*

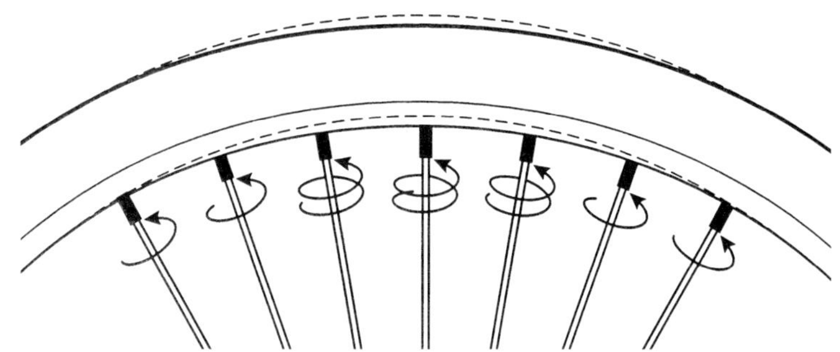

necessary. Tighten the spokes by the other pointer in equal amounts to retain the concentricity, dishing, and tension. As you move away from the worst part of the deflection, reduce the amount you turn the nipples.

Correcting Concentricity

Spin the wheel and use the jig's indicators to note the rim's inward and outward movement. Is there more inward, than outward movement? Work first on that which is least. If the rim moves outwards, pull it in by tightening those spokes directly below the deflection. If the rim moves inwards let it out by loosening the spokes. Make half-turns of the nipples, repeating if necessary and using smaller turns nearer the edges of the deflection. Concentrate more on high or low spots to increase or decrease the overall spoke tension. If the rim is out laterally and concentrically in the same place, try adjusting for the lateral truth on one side of the rim only to correct both faults at once.

Dishing

Rear wheels with a cassette or multiple cog freewheel require the hub flanges to be asymmetric to the axle lock-nuts. To position the rim central over the lock-nuts and central in the bike's frame, it is necessary to tighten all the spokes on the right side of the wheel more than the left. This is known as 'dishing' the wheel. A special tool called a dishing stick measures the distance of the rim relative to the hub's lock-nuts, showing whether it is centralized over them.

The unevenness in spoke tension created between the left and right sides does weaken the wheel somewhat. This is more serious the greater the dish, so for ultimate strength and reliability it is helpful to reduce the dish if possible. Freewheel hubs have various axle spacers, so you may be able to move some of them from the right side to the left, reducing the amount of dish needed. If you do this, check that there is ample chain clearance from the frame when the chain is on the smallest sprocket, and when shifting between sprockets. Also keep the total axle spacing correct for your frame's dropout width. You will then need to check whether the wheel has to be redished.

To check the dish, put the dishing tool over the wheel axle. Loosen the tool's adjusting nut and ensure that both arms rest on the rim, not the spokes, the central pointer/plunger resting on the hub lock-nut. Tighten the adjusting nut to keep it in place. Replace the dishing tool (without adjusting it) on the other side of the axle. If the tool rests exactly as you first set it the wheel is correctly dished. If the arms hover over the rim the spokes need to be adjusted to bring the rim towards the tool. If there is a gap between the pointer and the lock-nut the spokes must be adjusted to bring the rim away from the tool.

A dished wheel; the spokes are tighter on the right to centralize the rim over the axle lock-nuts.

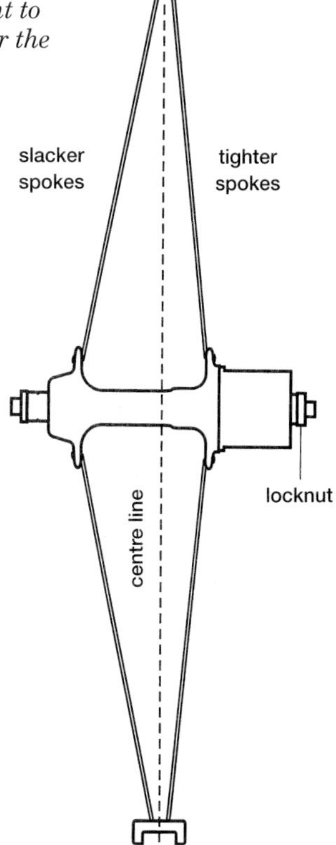

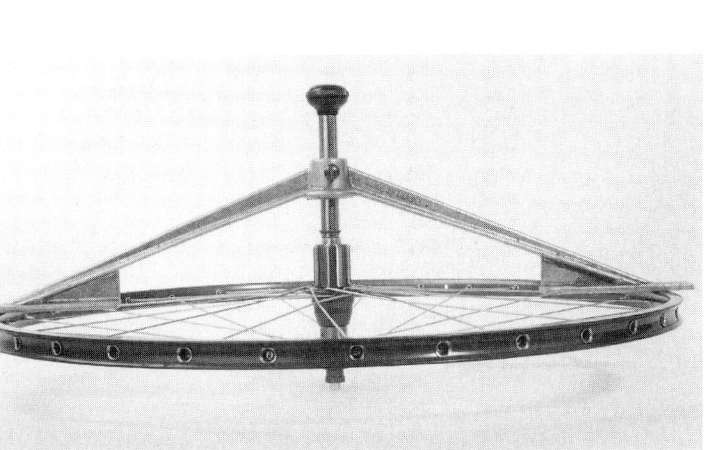

Set the dishing stick as indicated, then test the other side of the wheel.

Correct the dish by adjusting all the spokes on one side of the rim, starting at the valve hole so that you know when you have completed a full circle – the adjustment to each spoke must be identical to avoid the wheel going out of true. It is best to start with no more than full turns until you gauge the effect of the adjustment; check the dishing after each full circle. You can work by tightening or loosening the spokes. Tightening will also increase wheel tension, so if the nipples become difficult to turn backtrack, loosening them off to the valve hole, then work by loosening those on the opposite side to achieve the same effect. If you over-dish, correct it by loosening the drive-side spokes.

Tensioning the Wheel

The wheel has the correct tension when plucked spokes have a bright ring to them, yet when squeezed, still have a touch of give. This is especially so with double-butted spokes. If you can, compare your wheel to a well-built specimen with the same type of spokes, spoking pattern and rim size. Remember that rear-wheel dish means that the drive-side spokes are always tighter than the left-side ones. The left-side spokes should still ring when you pluck them.

Releasing Spoke Wind-up and Stress Relieving

As you tighten the spoke nipples they will wind up and twist the spoke. With the hub resting against the floor, push down on either side of the rim, give the wheel an eighth of a turn and repeat, going right the way round the wheel. Keep going until all the tinkling sounds have gone. Take care when pressing down as it is possible to collapse the wheel if you press too hard. Now repeat from the other side.

The spokes must now be made to bed correctly and any residual stresses in the metal caused by twisting relieved. Take the nearly parallel pairs of spokes on each side of the rim in turn and squeeze them together – do this sufficiently so that you are almost doubling the tension on these spokes. Guard your eyes in case a rogue nipple flies off. This process usually results in the wheel losing some truth, but if you do not do it now, the first five minutes of use will do it anyway.

Push the rim against floor to relieve spoke wind-up.

Squeeze parallel groups of spokes together to help bed them in.

Wheel Truing Problems

Work with a good-quality spoke key that is a good fit. If it slips, it will round the corners of the nipples off. If this happens replace the nipple, or use a flat file to make two new flats on the top part of the nipple.When working on an old wheel, if the nipple turns the spoke with it as you turn it, go carefully or you may break it. Apply a little penetrant to it and try again. The nipple may loosen up suddenly or with a creaking sound, but if not, the spoke will twist until it breaks and will need to be replaced. Work carefully so that the broken end does not fly into your eyes.

There may be some wobble that just will not come out, no matter how much you adjust the spokes – this is usually down to a poor rim, or one that has been damaged. If, when trying to correct this, you find that some spokes have a dull

Wheel Tensioning and Truing – Step by Step

Use the techniques described in the main text to tension and true your wheel. Use these steps to work in the most efficient manner. If truing an existing wheel start at step 4.

1. Correct lateral truth to about 1 or 2mm and concentricity to about 0.5–1mm or so.
2. Check and correct dishing to the nearest 1mm or so.
3. Starting at the valve hole (as a reference point) tighten each nipple an equal one turn and repeat as necessary to make the nipples taut, saving the final tensioning until later.
4. True the wheel as good as you can get it concentrically and to the nearest 1 or 2mm laterally.
5. Stress relieve the wheel and repeat step 4.
6. Bring the wheel up to its final tension.
7. Correct the dishing to within 0.5mm (or perfect it if you have the patience).
8. Repeatedly perfect the lateral and concentric truth, and stress relieve the wheel until its truth remains perfect. Do this by setting the wheel jig indicators so that they barely skim the rim and look very closely at the area you are working on. The final adjustment will be on isolated spokes and as little as an eighth of a turn.
9. If the threaded part of a spoke protrudes above the nipple (or above the internal bracing) file it smooth to avoid it causing a puncture.

twang when plucked or that some are so tight that the nipple starts deforming, you may have to live with the defect if small, or replace the rim.

SPOKE REPLACEMENT

For rear wheels it is almost always necessary to remove the cassette or freewheel in order to feed the spoke through. Remove the broken spoke (cutting it short may help) and measure it or another one from the same side of the wheel. Obtain a replacement of the same type and a couple of spares. Oil the new spoke threads. Before feeding it through note the direction and lacing of the next but one spoke to the one you are replacing on the same side of the hub. Also note whether the head is on the outside or inside, and copy this. Fit the nipple and tighten it until it just brings the spoke to the same tension as the spokes neighbouring it on the same side. This will normally bring the wheel back almost true; to finish truing follow the instructions given for wheel building.

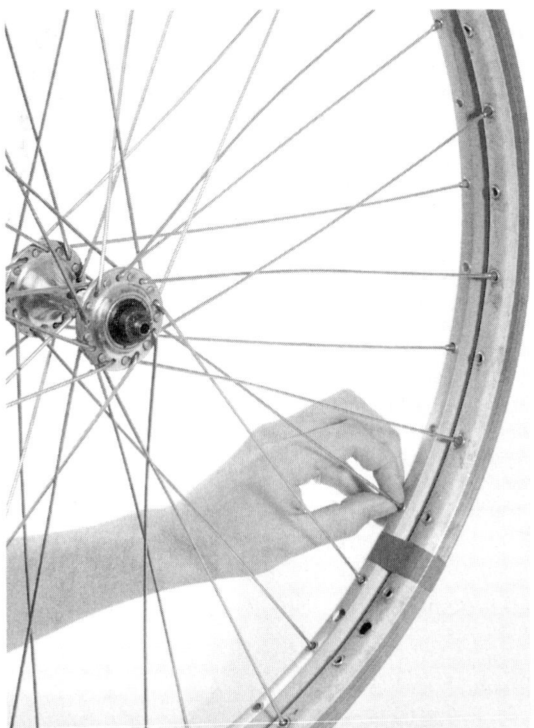

Spokes can be transferred across from an old to a new rim.

EASY RIM REPLACEMENT

If you are replacing a rim with an identical one (or one that requires the same number of spokes and spoke length) the existing spokes can be transferred directly across to it, without special attention to the lacing. If the spokes are corroded, the nipples do not turn easily, or you have had trouble with spoke breakages you should rebuild the wheel with new spokes in the conventional manner.

Go round the old wheel, loosening off all the spokes on the left side by two or three turns and then do the same on the right side. Continue to loosen them all until they are held on by just a few turns. Take the new rim and tie or tape it on to the old one, lining up the valve holes and ensuring that the rim's spoke holes line up, left to left and right to right. If you are using a rim where you cannot do this then stagger the valve holes. The valve will still be in a relatively accessible place.

Transfer all the right-side spokes over to the new rim, attaching them by three turns each. Oil the threads as you go. Now go round and attach all the left-side spokes. When complete, detach the old rim, and take up the slack, tension, and true as for any other wheel build.

10 Accessories

Aside from absolute racing you will need to fit at least a few items to your bike, for touring, expedition or town use – maybe quite a number of different items. As the accessories are almost always manufactured and marketed by completely different companies, compatibility with the bike and with other accessories (for example, lights and pannier racks) can leave a lot to be desired. In short, fitting accessories to your bike may require some Heath Robinson ingenuity.

ATTACHMENT HARDWARE

Stainless steel allen key bolts are the best. For the dropout eyes you will need 5mm bolts 12mm long, longer if they also need to go through a rack. If the bolts are a good fit, you should not need nuts. If they are a loose fit, use Nylock-nuts or Loctite Thread Locker. It is best to use brass washers under the bolt head. If your frame is missing any of the required mountings for panniers and racks 'P' clips can be used; various diameters are available. Check that when tightened they will not be loose on the stay. If the clips are slightly loose or are not plastic coated, wrap some insulation tape around the stay first. If you are fitting mudguards to a bike without calliper brakes you will also need a 6mm 40mm long bolt to go through the fork crown and a 25mm one for the brake bridge. The curved alloy mounting pieces sold for mounting calliper brakes make ideal 'packing', giving the bolt something to bite on.

MUDGUARDS

Mudguards rarely present fitting problems on a bike that is designed to take them with attachment eyes. ESGE are known for making the best mudguards from almost unbreakable cromoplastic. Special fittings are available to allow the mudguard to snap out of its fixings; this is for safety, in case a stick or suchlike jams between the mudguard and tyre but is also useful if you frequently remove and refit the guards. For racing bikes aluminium Fred Salmon guards take the barest minimum of space and fit many frames where others do not.

For most mudguards there must be at least 7mm clearance between the rear tyre and chain- and seatstays and 5mm between the front tyre and underside of the fork crown. Clearances can be increased by using a skinnier tyre, for example, on a touring bike a 28mm instead of 32mm. If you have horizontal rear dropouts it is possible to slide the wheel back a bit to increase the chainstay clearance.

Fitting Mudguards

Remove the bike's wheels. Loosely assemble the guard, putting each of its eye bolts in place with the stays; slide these through about 30mm and nip them in place. Some types have the eye bolts facing inwards, but ESGE ones face outwards. Those facing outwards will give greater tyre clearance.

Attach the rear guard to the chainstay bridge by the clip provided, ensuring that it is securely attached to the guard. Some frames have a backwards-facing hole here; if yours does, remove the clip and make a hole in the guard, and use a bolt in preference – unless you intend to remove the guard frequently.

Unless you have cantilever brakes, remove the brake attachment nut and put the guard's bridge clip over the bolt. Use a washer and then reinstate the nut, but do not fully tighten at this stage. If your frame has recessed brake bolts, put the bridge between the calliper and the frame. Put a washer large enough to cover the eye of the stay under each bolt head and pass the bolt through the stay and tighten it firmly into the dropout eye. Replace the wheels. Check that the bolt by the cassette will not interfere with the chain. Change up and down the gears a few times to check this. If a bolt does protrude too far, use a hacksaw or file to shorten it. The bridge clips are slotted to allow the guard's height over the tyre to be adjusted. Tighten the brake bolt to grip the bridge giving at least 5mm tyre clearance, greater for touring and mountain bikes. You may need to bend the front bridge out a bit to stop it catching the headset.

Slide the guard in or out on the stays to line it up with the centre line of the tyre. It should clear the tyre by about 5mm for road use and by as much as possible for off-road use. The rear guard can be slid through its bridge to help. Once set, nip the bridge tight with a pair of pliers, so preventing the guard moving further or rattling.

Adjust the stay bolts to centre the mudguard over the tyre, set the clearance and give a neat appearance as it follows the tyre.

Once the mudguard is positioned, secure its bridge clip.

Finally, use a hacksaw to cut the stays to length, allowing 5 to 10mm for further adjustment. Use Superglue to fix on the plastic end caps. Double-check that the brakes are centred and reinstate their quick-releases. If the front guard rubs on the top of the tyre, pulling on it while pressing behind its bridge will bring it up a little.

BUYING PANNIER RACKS

Rear

Almost all rear pannier racks are designed to fit both 26in MTBs and 700C tourers, hybrids, and road bikes. Exact rack leg length varies, but smaller frames need longer rack attachment arms to fit/level. The following table gives a guide to the best fit.

Rack leg length	*Frame size/tyres*
34 cm	26 MTB thinner/slicker tyres
35 cm	26 MTB fatter/knobblier tyres/700C 20-32mm tyres
36 cm	700C 32mm plus/cross type tyres

Four-point Fixing Racks

These have two legs and two more attachment arms going to the seatstays. Most modern touring and less specialist MTBs have brazed-on threaded eyes for firm secure arm attachment. Otherwise 'P' clips are used around the stays. The arms are usually adjustable but often need some careful bending to line up with the frame.

Three-point Fixing Racks

These have a central arm attaching to the seatstay bridge. These are not normally as rigid as four-point racks, but make fitting to frames easier without braze-ons. Problems can be encountered with cable yoke interference when fitting to frames with cantilever brakes – avoiding the interference may not be possible, and if the cable is changed the feel of the brake may alter (*see* Chapter 8, Straddle Wires).

Light Fitting

Your original light fixing points will probably be obscured and in this case you will need to mount the lights on the rack. If your rack does not have suitable mounting points Roberts Products make neat add-on fixings for most lights. ESGE make a simple, reliable, multi-positioning dynamo light fixing for 8mm rack diameters.

Front Low-rider Racks

Not all low-rider racks will fit all brazed-on fittings, so it is best to check the mounting points line up before buying. If you do not have these fittings on your frame, use a clip-mounting type. If you have suspension forks you will not be able to fit a rack. Many MTB front forks use quite large-section circular tubing, and the eyes of these are often too far in to attach a rack satisfactorily.

FITTING A PANNIER RACK

Fitting a Rear Rack

Attach the rack at the bottom first by bolts with spring washers, but do not tighten fully at this stage. If you are mounting mudguards as well, try to fit the stays on the outside of the rack's legs. This will give the rack more support. If your frame has a pair of eyes on each side you can use either the fore or aft ones, whichever allows the rack to line up best. However, if you are fitting mudguards as well, these are better fitted to those furthest back. Check that the right-side bolt will not interfere with the cassette or chain.

If fitting a three-point rack, undo the brake attachment nut and fit the tongue

ESGE (left) *and Roberts* (right) *light fixings designed to attach to rear racks.*

A ball-ended multi-position allen key makes fitting a rear rack far easier.

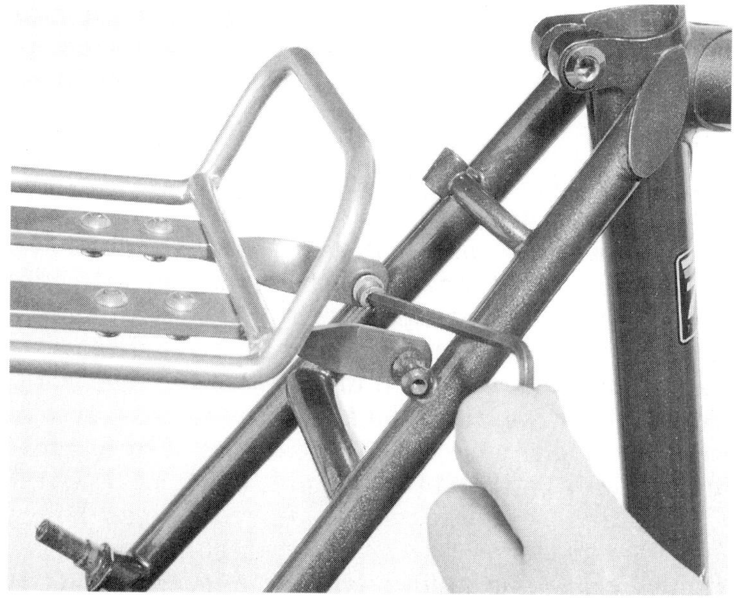

of it over the bolt, a washer and then the nut. If you do not have calliper brakes use a bolt and alloy brake-mounting cups. If fitting a four-point rack, line up the two arms with the brazed-on mounts if you have them, either the inside or the outside ones – whichever involves the least bending. If adjustable, level the rack and then fully tighten the adjusting bolts. If you have difficulty attaching the last bolt because of alignment problems, loosen the other bolts, start the troublesome one, then tighten them.

Fully tighten all the bolts. When tightening the brake nut make sure the brake remains centred to the rim.

Fitting a Low-rider Rack

If you have two pairs of 'eyes', most but not all low-riders attach to the bottom pair – check the rack's instructions. Attach the rack loosely to the dropouts, using spring washers under the heads and nuts on the other side if you can. You normally need to use the special spacing pieces supplied (or plain washers) to position the arms out past the fork blade.

Line up the fork blade attachment, either to the brazed-on fitting or to the clips supplied. Attach and level the rack. Tighten all the bolts.

Positioning Panniers

Most panniers have adjustable hooks. Align them so that they will not slide on the rack and clear your ankles and cantilever brakes if you have a wide-profile model. Low-rider bags should be a adjusted so that two-thirds of the bag is behind the wheel axle; this improves stability.

LIGHTS

Front lights are normally best mounted on the bars, so that they are high enough to be seen, produce a better beam on the road (the shadows obscuring detail are deeper the lower the light) and you can adjust the beam as necessary as you ride.

The bar position may not be so suitable if you have a bar bag, or ride with a cape. Be very wary of mounting a light on the forks and avoid anything that clamps around the fork blade at all costs; the vibration and the light's weight will gradually cause it to slide downwards. It can then very easily slip into the wheel and send you over the handlebars. Some older bikes have a brazed-on special boss for a front light bracket and light, and these are quite safe to use. An alternative is a reflector bracket mounted to the fork crown. The end of this may need to be twisted 90 degrees to bolt a light to it.

Always mount lights with star washers and Nylock-nuts; this ensures that the light cannot slip with vibration and in the case of dynamo lights ensures a good electrical conduct.

Many LED lights and reflectors and their mountings are now designed around a common fixing – two 6mm holes 12.5mm apart. These mountings are also found on some rear racks.

DYNAMOS

Dynamos have a reputation for being unreliable and causing excessive noise and drag. These pitfalls can usually be avoided by buying a quality dynamo (Nordlicht, AXA and Union are recommended) and setting the system up correctly. 'Bottle' designs run on the tyre side wall; ideally there should be a ribbed track for this on the tyre. Bottom bracket-mounting models run on the tyre tread; these are prone to clogging with road muck and slipping in wet weather – just when you need it the most!

Whatever type of dynamo you buy, it will normally come with front and rear lamps. You may, however, be able to choose options such as a halogen front lamp (which has two to three times the brightness of a standard bulb) or a mudguard-fitting rear lamp (useful on a bike with racks and panniers, keeping the light in a conspicuous position).

The set will come with single core wire, the circuit being completed back to the dynamo through the frame and the bike's metal parts. This is often referred to as the 'earth'. This makes wiring neat and less conspicuous, but can be prone to problems. It means that all the parts of the system, including racks and brackets that have lamps attached to them, must make electrical contact with the frame. Plastic coatings, paint and rust must be cleaned off at points were these components meet. For the ultimate in reliability, a second wire should be run back from the lamp's mountings to the dynamo mount.

Fitting a Dynamo

Most bottle models are designed to go on the right seatstay, facing to the rear. Loosely assemble the mounting, saving the small piercing screw for later and holding the dynamo roughly in position. Check that when the dynamo is on, its spring is working against the tyre and not away from it; if necessary move it to the other side of the bike or seatstay. Wherever you put it, check that it will not be clipped by your heel.

Some designs act sideways on the rim instead of vertically. If these are set as intended the tyre has the effect of pulling

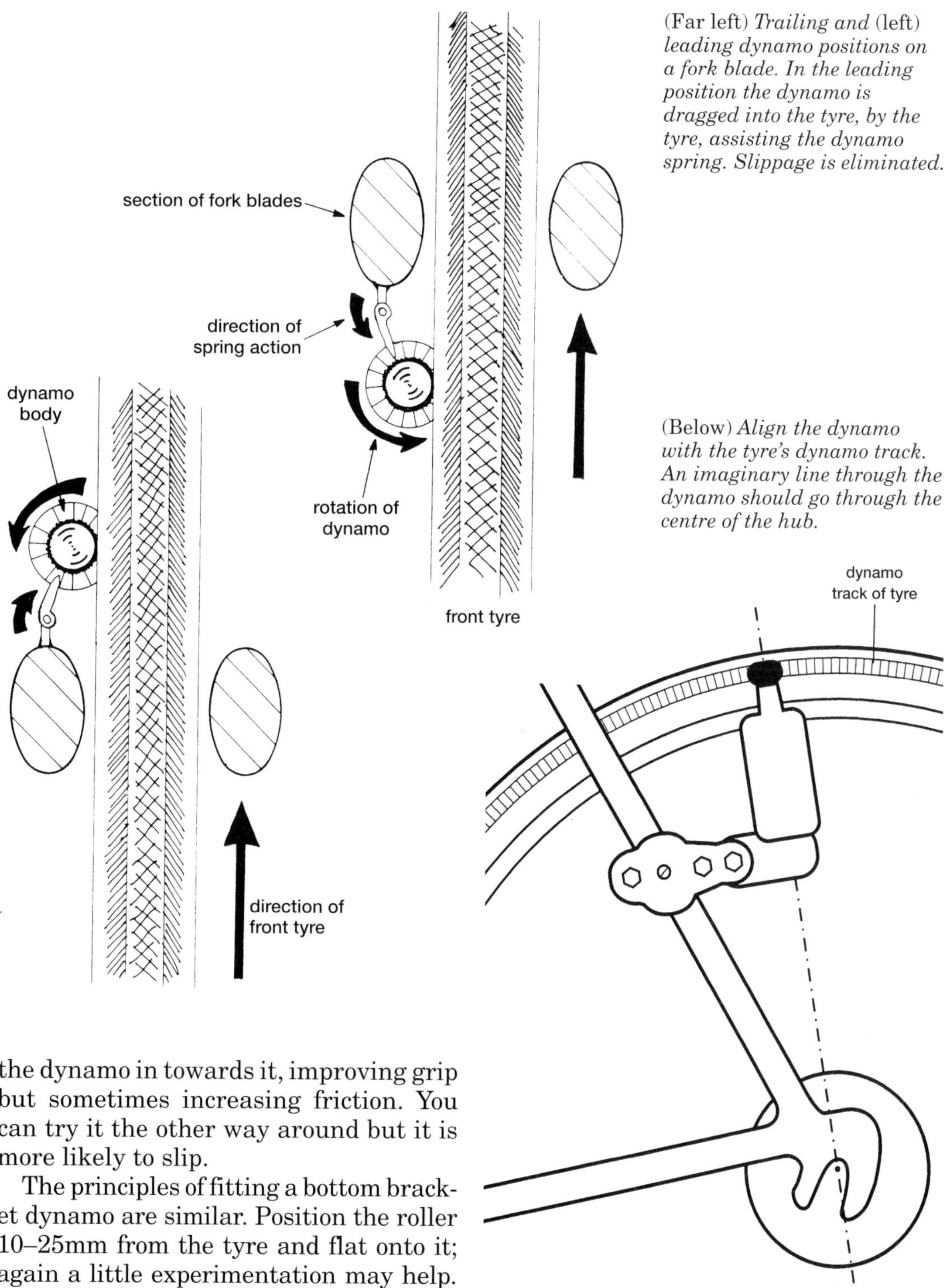

(Far left) *Trailing and* (left) *leading dynamo positions on a fork blade. In the leading position the dynamo is dragged into the tyre, by the tyre, assisting the dynamo spring. Slippage is eliminated.*

(Below) *Align the dynamo with the tyre's dynamo track. An imaginary line through the dynamo should go through the centre of the hub.*

the dynamo in towards it, improving grip but sometimes increasing friction. You can try it the other way around but it is more likely to slip.

The principles of fitting a bottom bracket dynamo are similar. Position the roller 10–25mm from the tyre and flat onto it; again a little experimentation may help.

Align the dynamo so that an imaginary line will go through the axis of the dynamo and continue through the centre of the wheel axle. The height should be positioned so that the pulley wheel runs on the upper half of the tyre's dynamo track (if it has one) or about two-thirds of the way up the tyre wall, and is about 1cm away from the tyre in the off position. You may need to move the mudguard, or file a little from it.

Tighten down the clamp bolts firmly and the dynamo fixing bolt, making sure that everything is still positioned correctly. Put the dynamo 'on' and spin the wheel to ensure that the dynamo runs freely. Sometimes writing on the tyre side wall may give it an irregular sound. If the tyre has writing on one side only, you might find it useful to reverse the tyre. Once you are satisfied that the position is correct, gently screw in the piercing screw that ensures the dynamo makes a good earth with the frame.

Attaching the Front Lamp

Run the wire by a short but neat route back to the dynamo, ensuring that there is sufficient to allow the bars to turn without snagging it, and secure it with zip cable ties (available from any motoring or electrician's shop). Form loose wire into a neat spiral by tightly wrapping it around a spoke.

Attaching the Rear Lamp

If you do not have a rack, the lamp can go directly on its place on the dynamo mounting bracket (bottle dynamos) if on the right side. If it is not, it can be fiddly to find a suitable place. If you do not have a rack, a bracket from the brake bridge is probably most convenient. If you have a rack, there may be a tang on it for the lamp to go onto directly. If the rack is alloy, you can get a small bracket from ESGE to fit it. You may need to change the wire for a longer piece. Open up the light and unscrew the bulb – you will see a channel down the side of the bulb holder to take the wire. Insert the wire and screw the bulb in. Again neatly route the wire back to the dynamo and fasten.

Replacing Dynamo Bulbs

For the front lamp choose 0.5 amp (2.4 watt) 6 volt bulbs. For the rear lamp choose 0.1 amp (0.6 watt) 6 volt bulbs. (A 0.25 amp (1.2 watt) 6 volt bulb can solve bulb-blowing problems.)

When changing a halogen bulb, do not touch it with your bare fingers as your natural oils can seriously shorten its life. When replacing bulbs, it is best to replace them in pairs, as once one bulb blows, the dynamo throws all its current to the other, overloading and weakening it. You then start a cycle of replacing one bulb after the other. If you always blow bulbs, fit a voltage regulator (available from Reflectalight).

Glossary

Alloy A mixture of a pure metal with small amounts of others such as aluminium with zinc, copper and magnesium. Cyclists often use 'alloy' to mean aluminium alloy, though steel alloys are also used – typically for the frameset.
Aheadset The brand name used by Dia-Compe for their threadless headset system and associated handlebar stems, now copied by others but still generally referred to as Aheadsets.
Anodize Applying a protective or decorative coating to aluminium alloy components by electrolysis.
ATB All-terrain bicycle (mountain bike), a term less frequently used than mountain bike.
Axle The central element or turning point of a bearing system.

Ball-bearings Loose steel balls used to reduce friction. The term 'steel balls' often refers low-grade ball-bearings.
Bead The wire or Kevlar-reinforced outside edges of a tyre, designed to keep it firmly seated against the rim.
Braze-ons Small fittings that are normally brazed to the frame for the attachment of accessories.
Brazing A process using molten bronze to join steel tubes or components.
Bridge Clip The sliding clip that attaches the rear mudguard to the seat stay bridge/calliper brake bolt.
B-Tension Bolt The bolt that sets the distance between the rear derailleur and the rear cogs.
Bushing A simple arrangement allowing free movement without friction or wobble.

Calliper Brake A term normally used for a single brake unit with arms reaching to each side of the wheel rim.
Cantilever Brake A brake utilizing separate arms on each side of the wheel.
Cassette Usually used to mean a set of rear cogs designed to fit a freehub.
Chainring/Chain Wheel The one, two or three sprockets (cogs) bolted to the right crank.
Chainset The right crank and its one, two, or three chainrings.
Chainstay The frame tubes that go from the rear wheel dropouts to the bottom bracket shell.
Circlip A circular sprung clip.
Cog A general term for a toothed ring, usually used to refer to those on the rear wheel.
Cold Forging A manufacturing process used to increase strength and reliability of a metal component by aligning its microscopic grain to most advantage.
Cold Welding *See* Galling.
Cotter Pin Wedge-shaped pin used to attach the crank to its axle.
Cotterless Crank The modern type of crank, attached without the cotter pins used by older designs.

Derailleur The front derailleur is the mechanism that shifts the chain between the chainrings. The rear derailleur shifts the chain between the rear cogs and tensions the chain.

Dish(ing) Centralizing the rim over the hub.

Dropout The fixing of the frame designed to accept the wheel axle.

Dust Cap A protective cap used to keep to keep dirt out of a bearing, thread or valve.

Ergopower Campagnolo and Sachs term for their combined brake and gear controls.

Expander bolt The internal bolt inside conventional handlebar stems that draws up a wedge, so gripping the stem in the fork column.

Facing The squaring-off of the outside edges of the head tube and bottom bracket shell to ensure the correct fit of the components.

Freehub A rear hub that also contains the freewheel mechanism.

Freewheel A rear cog or set of cogs combined with a ratchet mechanism that locks and turns the wheel in forward rotation, but releases and freewheels with backwards rotation. Most modern hubs (freehubs) have a built-in freewheel and separate cogs.

Friction Adhesion, traction or rubbing.

Front Mech Slang for the front derailleur.

Galling A welding effect caused by friction.

Gauge An old British standard used to measure the thickness of thin objects.

Gear Ratio A number obtained mathematically to compare the work or distance travelled forwards for a given size of rear cog, chainring and wheel size.

Groupset A matching set of mainly gearing, braking and bearing components from a given manufacturer, of comparable quality, and designed to work efficiently together.

Halogen Often used to mean a light bulb containing a halogen gas, which increases its brightness and efficiency.

Headset The bearing components that connect the fork to the frame.

Low-rider A low-mounting pannier rack designed to attach to the front forks.

Metal Fatigue Weakness leading to eventual breakage of metal parts caused by repeated flexing or bending.

MTB The common abbreviation for a mountain bike.

Neoprene A rubber-like compound often used for sealing rings.

Nipple The long threaded nut used to connect a spoke to the rim and tension it. Also the fixed end of a cable that fits into a lever or fitting.

Nylock-nut A nut with a built in nylon ring that improves its grip on a bolt.

Pre-load A force used to reduce free play (wobble) or movement.

Quick-release A lever, usually working on the cam principle, to attach wheels and seat posts and some brake fittings.

Reaming Increasing and levelling the bore of a tube or cylindrical component such as the head tube or seat tube.

Rear Mech Slang for rear derailleur.

Roller Bearing (needle roller bearing) Usually a form of cup and cone bearing using thin narrow rollers instead of ball bearings. Commonly used for high-quality headsets.

Seatstay The frame tubes that go from the rear wheel dropouts to the top of the seat tube.
Shim A thin washer, often used to take up free space.
SPD Shimano Pedalling Dynamics; Shimano's term for their clipless pedal system.
Spider The arms that connect the crank to the chainrings. This is usually an integral part of the crank.
Spindle An axle that spins, such as that used for the bottom bracket. For simplicity I have only used the term axle throughout the book.
Sprocket A general term for a toothed ring.
Stack Height The fitting space required by a headset; a determining factor of the fork column length required.
Stanchions The upper legs of suspension forks.
STI Shimano Total Integration; Shimano's term for their combined brake and gear controls.

Tang A protrusion that locates in a recess or groove. A tanged washer resists rotation, making it easier to adjust bearings.
Thread The spiral grooves of a bolt or nut.
Torque A twisting force.
TPI Threads per inch, or teeth per inch in the case of a saw.

'V' brake A modern form of cantilever brake where the cable pulls from the side instead of the centre.

Manufacturers, Suppliers and Further Information

Items or brands that are mentioned in this book and not listed below are readily available from most good cycle shops. Many of these companies will supply by mail order or recommend your nearest dealer.

Argos Racing Cycles
Unit 12, Riverside Business Park
St Anne's Road
Bristol
BS4 4ED
Tel: 0117 972 4730
Frame builder, repairer and respray specialist

Aylesbury College
Hampden Hall
Wendover Road
Stoke Mandeville
Buckinghamshire
HP22 5TB
Tel: 01296 434111
Cycle maintenance and repair courses, City and Guilds qualification

Bicycling Books
309–311 Horn Lane
London
W3 OBU
Tel: 0181 993 3484
The UK's most extensive range of cycling books

Cyclist's Source Book
Mark Allen Publishing Ltd
Croxted Mews
286a–288 Croxted Road
London
SE24 8BY
Tel: 0181 671 7521
Complete UK directory of cycling organizations, companies and products

Cyclo Limited
Crown Works
Baltimore Road
Perry Barr
Birmingham
B42 1DP
Tel: 0121 356 7411
Manufacturer of a wide range of bicycle tools

Highpath
Cornant
Cribyn
Lampeter
Dyfed
SA48 7QW
Tel: 01570 470035
Manufacturers and suppliers of many hard-to-find cycle transmission components

Ison Distribution
The Maltings Warehouse
Prospect Row
Cambridge

Cambridgeshire
CB1 1DU
Tel: 01223 213800
Suppliers of a vast range of bicycle tools, workshop equipment, injection maintenance kits and some hard-to-find spare parts

Kestrel Engineering
Unit 10, Dartmouth Buildings
Fort Fareham
Hampshire
PO14 1AH
Tel: 01329 233443
Manufacturers of workstands and workshop equipment

Longstaff Cycles and Allied Engineers
Albert Street
Chesterton
Newcastle-under-Lyme
Staffordshire
ST5 7JF
Tel: 01782 561966
Frame builders and repairers; tandem and touring bike spares stockist

Loose Screws
12225 Highway 66
Ashland
OR 97520
USA
Tel: (001) 541 488 4800
Worldwide mail order available of an extensive range of spare parts, including obsolete equipment

Nimrod Products
Leek Road
Rushton Spencer
Macclesfield
Cheshire
SK11 ORN
Tel: 01260 226696
Racks, accessories and their fittings and fixings, lubricants

Madison Cycles PLC
Buckingham House East
Buckingham Parade
The Broadway
Stanmore
Middlesex
HA7 4EA
Tel: 0181 954 7798
Suppliers of Park tools, Finish Line lubricants and Shimano parts and spares

Mercian Cycles Ltd
7 Shardlow Road
Alvaston
Derby
Derbyshire
DE24 OJB
Official Campagnolo spares and service centre, frame builders and repairers; tandem and touring bike spares stockist

Reflectalite Ltd
24 Orchard Road
Brentford
London
TW8 0QX
Tel: 0181 560 2432
An extensive range of bulbs and batteries for lights and computers, and dynamo regulators

Roberts Products Ltd
90 Tottenham Lane
Crouch End
London
N8 7EE
Tel: 0181 348 7621
Light brackets for all situations

Saint John Street Cycles
91–93 St John Street
Bridgewater
Somerset
TA6 5HX
Tel: 01278 441502
Components, spares and hard-to-find items

Derek Shackles
Roman Road Cycles
Ddôl Las
Ffarmers
Llanwrda
Dyfed
SA19 8JP
Sachs hub gear spares and repairs

Sturmey Archer Ltd
Triumph Road
Nottingham
Nottinghamshire
NG7 2GL
Tel: 0115 942 0800
Hub gear technical information

Index